Pluralism and Corporatism

Pluralism and Corporatism

The political evolution of modern democracies

Reginald J. Harrison

Department of Politics, University of Lancaster

London
GEORGE ALLEN & UNWIN
Boston   Sydney

First published in 1980

GEORGE ALLEN & UNWIN LTD
40 Museum Street, London WC1A 1LU

© George Allen & Unwin (Publishers) Ltd, 1980

British Library Cataloguing in Publication Data

Harrison, Reginald James
    Pluralism and corporatism.
    1. Pluralism (Social sciences)
    2. Corporate state   3. Democracy
    I. Title

    321.8   JC330

    ISBN 0-04-321024-4
    ISBN 0-04-321025-2 Pbk

Typeset in 10 on 11 point Plantin by Trade Linotype Ltd., Birmingham.
Printed and bound in Great Britain by
William Clowes (Beccles) Limited, Beccles and London.

Preface

This work was started in a spirit of discontent with the prevailing 'pluralist' model of the advanced, democratic and industrial society. It reviews some of what have seemed to me to be the outstanding implicit and occasionally explicit criticisms of the model in the recent literature of the social sciences. The review does not pretend to be comprehensive – it selects what is most effectively and objectively critical. Furthermore, in drawing the empirical support for the critique from various countries the first priority has not been to achieve the country-to-country balance of a straightforward text in comparative politics, but to dwell on the most appropriate illustrations of a theme. For a positive theme does, indeed, emerge from the critique – an alternative conception of the advanced democratic society for which the label 'corporatist' seems temporarily appropriate, particularly as it has been increasingly used, during the period of writing, by a number of other critics of the pluralist model.

Without wishing to associate them in any way with the failings, or for that matter the merits, of the book, I would like to express my thanks to colleagues at Lancaster who have read parts of the work and commented on them; to Vincent Wright and Gordon Smith who were encouraging about a preliminary paper I read to an LSE seminar, and finally to my colleagues of the Workshop on Corporatism at Grenoble, in April 1978.

Contents

I

Introduction

Political change is one of the most elusive of the phenomena which challenge the contemporary social scientist. It is, therefore, a somewhat tentative contention of this work that elements of 'corporatism' can be discerned in the political evolution of advanced industrial democratic societies. That is to say, there are tendencies towards the fragmentation of government responsibility and its joint assumption by governmental and organised group bureaucracies making an often dubious claim to exclusive representation of class and other interests in the various functional sectors.

However, in such societies, the complexity of change, its variety, its pace, and the difficulty of producing tangible, measurable evidence of many of its aspects have taxed the analytical ingenuity of scholars. The difficulties emerge as soon as any attempt is made to answer the immediate questions posed by the proposal to examine such societies. What are the advanced industrial societies? Why study them? How shall they be studied?

Some of the possible, varying answers to the first of these three questions are indicated by the significantly different descriptive labels which have been attached to them by recent writers: the technetronic society (Zbigniew Brzezinski), the post-industrial society (David Bell and Christopher Lasch), post-capitalist society (Ralph Dahrendorf), the new industrial state, or the affluent society (J. K. Galbraith), corporate society (Robin Marris, Nigel Harris), industrial technological society (Ghita Ionescu), the post-welfare state (Hancock and Sjoberg). These all indicate a somewhat different perspective and emphasis on the same actual phenomena: the leading states of Western Europe, Japan and the United States.

Succinctly, and with more concern for measurability than obvious political significance, advanced industrial societies might be identified as those which, today, like Britain, have an overwhelmingly urban industrial population. They are countries in which agriculture accounts for 10 per cent or less of the gross domestic product. They are, also, countries in which the value of the product of manufacturing industry plus service industries does not fall below 55 per cent of the value of the gross domestic product. Another marked measurable characteristic of such societies is that they do show a high degree of export diversification.

Taken together, these can serve as concrete defining characteristics. They successfully exclude countries which are outside the general, impressionistic conception of the advanced industrial society of which Britain, from the present author's standpoint, is the key example.

The identification is expressed entirely in economic terms, but these, in 1978, exclude the countries of Eastern Europe and the Third World and serve to identify a group of countries governed, at least prima facie, by elected representatives.

All the states 'caught' by these terms are developments of the modern 'democratic' nation-state, a conception which itself requires elaboration. It includes the states in which, to follow a model suggested by Huntington, authority has been rationalised, there has developed functional differentiation and administrative specialisation, and there is widespread participation by the citizenry.[1]

Rationalisation means, first, the assertion of the authority of the national state against transnational influences like religion and the authority of the church, or against prevailing concepts like natural law (which also pretends to a universal application) which limit the scope of kings and other kinds of national leaders. It means also the assertion of central authority against local and regional powers and loyalties.

Then, the modern nation-state is characteristically one in which there is differentiation of government functions and increasing specialisation in carrying them out. There is at least a partial separation of administration from policy making, and from the administration of justice – all of which in primitive societies may well be found in the single person of a chief or king. Beyond this basic separation, areas of peculiar administrative competence emerge – financial, military, economic – and are found as semi-autonomous, specialised departments of the bureaucracy.

As a corollary of this specialisation (and another basic attribute of the modern state), office and power is, increasingly, distributed on the basis of achievement or merit, rather than ascription (i.e. family or status).

Finally, there is, in the modern state, increasing participation in politics by social groups throughout society, and the development of structures (like parties and pressure groups or vocational cadres) which organise this.

This abstract, or stereotype of the modern nation-state provides one way of distinguishing between the industrial societies of Europe and the so-called 'developing' countries. The developing countries have not fully achieved rationalisation of authority. Religion has a significant influence at both the grass-roots level of individual initiative, and in national policy formation. In many developing countries too, the authority of locally based traditional or military leaders may well compete with that of the central authority. Central administration is riddled with patronage. The army, theoretically a professional specialist body, often plays a highly political role. Large sections of the populations have no involvement in, understanding of, or even awareness of the central political activity and the modernising goals of the elite.

The modern state with its very different character must be seen, however, not as an ultimate or even necessary stage of development to which developing societies must come, but, in the context of *environmental adaptation*, as a *temporary* phenomenon. The argument is summed up well by Michel Crozier. We have, he says, 'to avoid the temptation to describe and celebrate the temporary equilibrium, the harmony of the moment, as the sole possible system'.[2] He argues an observable process of continuing adaptation to the environment. His thesis is that human groups and societies are able to set new objectives for themselves by continuous organisational innovation, adapted successfully to a changing human and physical environment. Maladaptive innovations perish.

The modern state may be seen as the most recent of many stages of successful adaptation to a particular environment. In this light, the river kingdoms of China, the Greek city states, empires, confederations like the US confederacy and the British commonwealth, all in their time survived temporarily because they were adapted to an environment and obtained its sanction. The Chinese war-lord who could subjugate an area big enough for adequate river control laid the basis for a new, larger dominant form – the river kingdom. The Greek city defended an agricultural hinterland in conditions of poor communication. The Romans by political and military organisational innovation were able to create and maintain an empire. The British commonwealth, when it emerged, was a highly original response to a relative decline in British power in comparison with other actors in international politics, and to a prevailing ideology – liberalism, with its powerful justification of self-determination. These two factors between them made it physically difficult and domestically unpopular to maintain an empire by direct rule. The commonwealth system institutionalised a pattern of international functional co-operation of considerable utility to all its members. It gave some satisfaction to what are now called the 'patrial' links and sentiments across the commonwealth. It institutionalised consultation and the handling of the mutually profitable interdependence created by trade and investment. But the commonwealth itself declined as other patterns of co-operation and interdependence developed internationally, and also as, after the Second World War, it became bigger than the original patrial grouping – the first independent states in the association.

The modern state can itself be seen in this context of environmental adaptation: it was an adaptation to industrial and commercial opportunities. First, centralised administration – the establishment of the king's peace in Britain – provided the conditions in which commerce and industry could flourish. Louis XIV, with his ambitious schemes for industrialisation and commercial development in France, assisted by the great forerunner of modern planners, Colbert, established the same centralised power in France. Bismarck made possible a central administration and, thereby, a nationwide economy for Germany, Napoleon III for Italy, Commodore Perry and the Meiji restoration which followed, for Japan. The centralisation and specialisation of the *courts* and their divorce from politics had the same effect – the increasing predictability and, therefore, security afforded by the law. In this security there was less of a premium on regional self-sufficiency, an easy reliance on trade over safe routes, and an obvious incentive to investment rather than hoarding.

Law making by a representative specialist body, not subject to check by the courts in the name of divine law or natural law, helped to ensure that new social and economic forces were not unduly frustrated. Thus, in England, the paternalism of the Elizabethan era gave way readily to enclosures and the needs of the factory system, with the blessing of the accommodating parliaments of the time – representative mainly of those who stood to gain by the changes.

Extensions of the franchise and increasingly widespread political participation liberated newly effective sources of economic initiative. It also completed the process of smashing one important part of the anachronistic survivals of the old order – the vestigial economic privileges, under the law, of religion, the aristocracy and the local squirearchy in these states. The privileges survived to some extent but they did not depend on legal monopolies or exclusive political power. They could be breached by newcomers and modified according to the needs of the time.

Considerable importance attaches to the timing of these changes, and the manner in which they were brought about historically in the modern states. This appears to affect their present policies and administration.[3] In Britain, the centralising activity and the extension of participation were early developments, and they were limited at first in scope. Initially participation, through parliament, set limits to the centralisation process. Parliaments were ready to have the Crown provide order and security, but not to intervene paternalistically in economic promotions in which many of their members had interests. The eventual industrial leadership of Britain may well be ascribed to the grass-roots economic vitality which evolved in the absence of interference. An elaborate bureaucratic machinery was an unnecessary adjunct and, therefore, emerged very late, after the industrial revolution had been accomplished. France, on the other hand, was deliberately centralised to promote an economic revolution under the direction of the monarchy of Louis XIV. A highly centralised administrative machinery was built up for the purpose and has survived. These developments helped to establish the French lead in industrialisation and commerce until the later eighteenth century, when the individual-istic economy of Britain proved much more innovative and adaptable just at the point when French economic life began to stagnate.

In Germany the modern state was largely a creation of Prussia under the management of Bismarck. Centralisation and bureau-cratisation were rapidly achieved. Its industrial revolution followed in the 1890s, fostered by the states and the banks, and regulated by a highly efficient, but very authoritarian central administration. Author-itarianism remained a problematic feature of German government, well into the modern phase. Britain, it may be argued, is, consequently, the least planned and least amenable to planning among these three states.

We have stressed that the characteristics of modernity, abstracted in the Huntington model, do not have any kind of permanent value in operation. Rationalisation, differentiation and specialisation may have been necessary in the militarily insecure, privilege-ridden, Catho-lic European situation, but in a different environment they may be irrelevant. Huntington, for example, has argued that 'the American experience . . . demonstrates [that] a Tudor polity is quite compatible with a modern society'.[4] America, for her industrial revolution, had no need to disestablish a church, rid itself of class privilege, or develop a large professional army and centralised administration. It could afford inactive government with a large degree of local autonomy in the Tudor style. And yet, the United States has become the most technologically advanced state in the contemporary world.

It is of course true that the powers of American central government have increased, that the United States now has a large professional army and a specialised merit civil service, but the individual states have not lost their identity in the process, and the top ranks of the civil service remain political. The President, like a Tudor king, has legislative *and* executive power, appoints the judges and represents the whole people against other forms of power in the realm. And the judges draw occasionally on the superior authority of the constitution and natural law in challenging secular authority.

There is therefore nothing sacrosanct in our present model of the modern state. If the sanction of the environment is withdrawn and it fails to adapt to the change, there is every chance that it will decline.

Applied to the advanced industrial societies in which we are interested, the model prompts questions about how far apparent failures of government and constitutional collapse in the recent past of the industrial era have been the result of atavisms, survivals of pre-modern elements in government and society (a failure to approximate to the model), or on the other hand are the result of a failure to adapt to environmental challenge. Transcendental anachronisms like religious claims to authority, organisational ones in administration (like the failure to divorce the army from policy making in prewar Germany), or structural barriers to meaningful participation (like the French electoral system) are possible examples. There is some question also whether the postwar governments of Western Europe are demonstrably better adapted, by reference to the model, than the prewar varieties. Alternatively, and perforce, we may ask whether the environment has changed in ways that make the model, for them too, obsolete.

We shall contend that there has indeed been a developing and a contemporary environmental challenge to the viability of the modern state.[5] It can be initially summarised in a way which helps to identify somewhat further the advanced industrial society, showing, first, that there are factors affecting the burden on the nation-state, and second, factors affecting its capacity.

THE BURDEN

Technological change and its economic structural implications have been the underlying factors determining the burden of state activity. There has been an important transition from a negative to a positive role for the state. In the first phase of industrialisation the role of the state was to clear away the impediments which existed to competitive economic development. There were extraordinarily wide patents. There were monopolies which had been granted to individuals and to great trading enterprises. There were penalties against vagrancy which worked against labour mobility, as did the apprenticeship rules. Such laws were swept away or fell into disuse or were perverted in the eighteenth century. The doctrine of minimal interference, or *laissez-faire* prevailed. The Elizabethan Poor Law which had provided for apprentice places for poor children was adapted to the new needs of the factory system, gangs of paupers and pauper children being leased out to the factories virtually as slave labour.

This negative role gave way in the nineteenth century to positive involvement in economic activity as consequential structural and social problems arose. The state shouldered the burden of maintaining competitive conditions against monopolistic practices, or protecting workers against dangerous and unhealthy factory conditions, of providing education, regulating trade union organisation and industrial violence. By the twentieth century, it was trying to do something about the vagaries of the business cycle.

It follows that the functional scope of activities of the modern state has continually increased. This can be charted indirectly by looking at the increase in the number of departments of state and the growth in the size of civil services. Even though some European states took a more decisive role than Britain in promoting industrialisation, and therefore had a much larger civil service, one can see the common growth in functional range reflected in the comparative figures (see Table 1.1).[6]

Table 1.1

	France		Great Britain	
	Numbers	*% of Population*	*Numbers*	*% of Population*
1871	200,000	0·6	53,000	0·2
1914	469,000	1·2	281,000	0·7
1950	1,095,000	2·6	684,000	1·4

Another factor which has determined the burden on the modern state is urbanisation – the growth of a city-centred environment. There was a pattern of substantive integration around cities during the nineteenth century. Great cities like Manchester, Birmingham, Leeds, Lyons, Marseilles, or groups of cities, became regional nuclei without becoming centres of political power for their regions. They exerted economic, social and cultural attraction on villages and smaller towns, the closest of which were swallowed up physically in suburban sprawl though they often retained their political identity. But these units of local government were increasingly incompetent to meet the demands in the locality for services and facilities and meaningful participation. Their great number and variety, their inadequate financial means and the poor quality of their staff led to a loss of interest and faith in local government and a gradual, often reluctant, but necessary assumption of their functions by central government. This additional burden is complicated in many cases by the continued involvement of local government in some aspect of the activity. The function is shared and it becomes more complicated to administer. Urban growth is accompanied by problems which still further increase the difficulty of government. A positive correlation appears to exist between urbanisation and crime, particularly violent crime. There is a correlation with other social problems – sanitation, water supplies, mental health, transport.

Two other related factors are the increase in the technological expertise involved in decision making, and the actual pace of technological change with which governments have to cope. On the one hand this has resulted in the evolution of the technocrat, a word embracing all those who contribute a specialised knowledge to decision making. It includes the economists who make detailed analyses of

trends upon which fiscal decisions are partly based, and who forecast
the effects of proposed decisions. It includes the scientists upon whose
advice the feasibility of major projects are based, who are indispens-
able to the defence establishment, to departments of agriculture and
fisheries, to Labour and social security, to communications services –
not merely in their operations but in important policy decisions involving the allocation of very large sums of money. It includes also their
'private' counterparts in industrial and trade union management, and
in commerce, banking, agriculture etc. whose views are canvassed.
It has been suggested that the future of modern society 'depends on
how willingly and effectively the intellectual community in general,
and the educational and scientific estate in particular assume responsibilities for political action and leadership'.[7] Yet this situation, in so
far as it promotes the growth of government-designated, exclusive and
elitist 'corporate' bodies with a formal consultative role, poses problems
for liberal democracies in which the accountability of government to
elected assemblies is a cardinal rule. For where the government and
private experts agree on a solution there is a tendency to presume that
this is not open to question, even where the formal legal decision-
making power has not been delegated but remains a parliamentary
prerogative.

   The other technological factor, the pace of technological change,
exacerbates this problem of coping with new expertise. It also produces a number of others – problems for society with which government must cope. In particular, the unstable relationship between men
and machines is a constant threat to peaceful industrial relations.
Skills continually become obsolescent and new skills are in short
supply. Automation replaces routine, production line labour. Government is strongly impelled to manage the socially and economically
disruptive effects of rapid change. Generally speaking, too, governments have felt it necessary to promote the research and development
that is needed to keep a country in the technological race, and they
have tried to guarantee the sale of the product by their procurement
policies.

   There is, finally, the burden which results from the increased
interdependence of the functions of government, resulting in turn
from the *scale* of economic and technological operations. In government contracting, or financing of research and development, a single
decision can send a ripple through the whole economy. One does not
simply order an aircraft. One makes a whole town dependent on its
production. The production orientation and schedules of a dozen
important industries are determined throughout the country. To build
a motorway is not simply to build a road. It is to create a construc-
tional complex, which takes over huge tracts of land, destroys villages,
ways of life, industries, landscape.

CAPACITY

There is some question whether, in the face of these increased burdens, the capacity of states to meet them has been enlarged. There are evidently a number of positive factors.

The number and the skills of civil servants has increased rapidly in the twentieth century in most industrialised states. Advanced education has been made generally available to talented people, and the bureaucracies have been able to recruit some of its best products. Then, planning techniques have been continually developed. A third positive factor is that the potential for societal control is apparently enhanced by the available devices for mass communication, data collection and processing, and the use of computers. Another potential positive factor is that widespread education, coupled with instant communication possibilities, increases the possibility of decentralised decision making for appropriate functions – in other words, for regional devolution.

Against these must be set a number of negative factors, reducing relative capacity. The other side of the coin of the development of bureaucracy is the problem of achieving bureaucratic–technocratic co-ordination in furthering a coherent policy – bridging the gap between what C. P. Snow has called the 'two cultures', spanning also the disciplines of the experts. If the controlling role of the central government is necessary both to avoid policy chaos and to maintain the notion of responsibility on which meaningful participation depends, then communication between experts and responsible elected leaders has to be achieved. Instead, there has been a tendency to delegate decision-making responsibility to corporatist bodies within functional sectors. The problem has yet to be solved.

Added to it is a second factor reducing the capacity of governments to engage widespread popular participation: this is the remoteness of government. It is a function of its scale of operations and the pyramidal organisation which has been developed to meet it. The pressure in a number of advanced societies for sub-national regions is some evidence of resultant discontents. The assumption of the tasks of local government by central government was not really a satisfactory response to the weakness of the municipalities. Functions were transferred which might well have been assumed by regional authorities with executives and elected assemblies, capable of providing a new locus of participation. Hence the regional movement. In France, de Gaulle saw it as the answer to the alienation which became evident in May 1968. In Britain, regional demands became one of the most severe problems faced by the Labour government after it took office in 1974.

A third negative factor is a corollary of the burden of promoting research and development, and backing the product up with massive procurement policy. None of the European states individually is big enough to back an advanced aircraft, a new kind of nuclear reactor, a communications satellite – without very serious economic difficulties.

Still another factor diminishing the relative capacity of government is the growth of large-scale organisation in the economic sector, whether public or private; the development, in other words, of rival centres of power. In the United States, the technostructure of the large corporation, as Galbraith points out, 'tends to become an extension of those parts of the Federal bureaucracy – notably the Armed Services, NASA, AEC and other agencies concerned with technological development – on which it most depends'.[8] The agency and the corporation become adapted to each other's needs. They become a power complex with immense resources, extremely difficult to bring under the sway of central policy.

The multinational business corporation presents an additional dimension of the same problem. Such companies are controlled by boards drawn from the country or countries of origin. According to the Fortune Directory for 1971 there were 197 companies in manufacturing and mining with yearly sales of over 1 billion dollars, multinational in their operations. Of these, 120 were American owned and 77 were owned outside the US. The pattern of international banking, ranked by assets, is similar. By 1975 some 300 corporations, 200 of them American, owned 75 per cent of all industrial assets in the non-communist world. Slightly less than half the sovereign states in the world had a *lower* gross national product than a billion dollars.

There is no evidence that these great corporations contribute notably to the general welfare in the host countries – in particular in the advanced societies in which they mainly operate, and from which they spring. Even their supposed investment contribution is doubtful. The Gray Report on their activity in Canada says that some three-quarters of all so-called foreign investment in recent years comes from reinvesting profits earned by foreign firms within Canada, or by borrowing on the Canadian market. Much of the investment in Europe by US multinationals has been raised in Europe itself. Their managerial record, research and development, and economies of scale, appear to be no better on average than the purely national firms, if productivity can be taken as an indicator of these qualities. Furthermore, it is the interests of the *parent* company, nationally based, that determine investment policy, currency holding, internal costing and the pattern of diversification of interests. The corporations are not concerned, and are particularly well placed to avoid the concern of governments with problems like structural and regional unemployment, environmental improvement, provision of health services and pensions schemes and other aspects of welfare provision by the state. They prefer to provide their own for their own employees.

Neither states, nor existing intergovernmental institutions can, at present, adequately regulate the multinational corporation.

There is finally the incapacity which is a result of growing international economic interdependence. In the EEC and EFTA countries, considered together, the average percentage increase in the GNP between 1959 and 1967 was less than the growth of imports. World trade increase is concentrated among the advanced industrial societies. Their trade with each other is more than twice that of the rest of the world.[9] It is not at all clear that all this increase in trade is related to improvements in the standard of living. What is clear is that the interdependence which it creates makes for problems beyond the capacity of any single state to resolve. The extent of economic interdependence is so great among the advanced societies that the vagaries of economic policy in any one country affect all the others.

On 15 February 1973, for example, Britain was in the thirteenth day of a monetary crisis. It had brought all currency trading to a standstill except in Switzerland, where there were still some transactions going on. The problem had been that the United States, investing in industry overseas, paying for the Vietnam war, financing an import surplus (especially from Japan), had had a balance of payments deficit for many years. While people were willing to hold US dollars – to use them for international settlements, like gold – there was no problem. From about 1967 confidence in the dollar started to dwindle, and there was an inclination to exchange them for marks and yen, Germany and Japan having a trading surplus. This inclination became a panic on a number of occasions and wrecked the parities agreed on in elaborate international agreements like the Smithsonian agreement of 1971. That agreement cost Germany, which attempted to fulfil it, an enormous amount of money in February 1973. There was a sharp curtailment of international commodity trading. It made the proposed EEC monetary agreement on a narrow currency band (which had not worked properly since it was introduced in spring 1972) look hopeless. It now seems clear that any currency agreement which does not include Japan and the United States is unlikely to be viable; and there is a further doubt whether fixed parities can be held at all.

BASIC QUESTIONS AND PROPOSITIONS

This is the environment that challenges the UK, French Fifth Republic, West Germany, Holland, Japan, the US and all other advanced societies, and the existence of the challenge provides one answer to the question as to why these societies should be studied. For those who actually live in this kind of society this is reason for a particular kind of concern.

The business of the political scientist is like that of the politician in some respects. Both must attempt to understand an enormously complex system of action and interaction, co-operation and conflict, between men and groups. Both must penetrate the mysteries of structures and processes by means of which this activity is subjected to government.

The politician works within the system for specific goals. The political scientist provides a critique of the system, examines alternatives and makes comparisons. The task of both is alike, however, in having no point of completion, since political systems, goals of action, and the environment are continually changing.

The present study is concerned then, inevitably, with a changing form – namely, the advanced industrial pluralist society and its politics. If a parochial rationale for such a study is needed it is that in spite of the individual cultural and political peculiarities of such societies, their similarities, particularly their economic similarities, offer the prospect that we may learn something which enhances our understanding of political behaviour in this our own kind of society. It is not unreasonable to expect linkages between economic and political factors. France, Japan, Germany, Italy, Holland and Britain seem to be countries with very close similarity of economic development. They may be different in other respects but they are similar enough in this to make comparisons quite likely to be fruitful. For individual members of these societies, the inhabitants of Megalopolis, the task of describing the changes and of understanding the conflicts to which they give rise may well seem vital. They see their surviving traditions, religious beliefs, the authority that they have acknowledged, and their social arrangements, apparently crumbling before the on-slaught of restless innovators. The pace is vertiginous. An attempt to achieve an overview of its direction is imperative.

There remains the question as to how a study of this kind should be approached. In this work the emphasis is placed advisedly on 'politics'. By politics we mean to comprehend the major factors which produce and condition conflict and conflict resolution in society. We are asking in effect a number of linked questions.

What are the main conflicts and their sources? What are the main attitudes, values, beliefs and general historical and environmental (internal and external) conditions which produce or affect conflict and affect how it is resolved? How are the conflicts expressed – what are the means by which conflicting pressures are brought to bear on society as a whole? Why does the expression take the form it does? To what extent, and how, are conflicts resolved? Do the existing forms of conflict resolution affect the nature of the resolution – by affecting the value of the different assets of conflicting groups or by apparently affecting the level of governmental capability?

These basic questions can be grouped, simply under four basic headings: What is the political culture? What is the pattern of conflict and of interest definition and expression? What is the pattern of controls? What is the relevance of the external environment?

Any working political system can be summed up as an interplay between these four variables and they provide a basis for a comparative perspective. In this work, therefore, each is considered and their interplay is noted through the examination of a number of contemporary hypotheses about the way these categories are developing or changing in the advanced industrial societies. Two of the categories – the pattern of conflict and interest definition, and the pattern of controls – warrant immediate comment.

There has been a tendency in political studies since the early 1950s to focus attention on the first of these – conflicts and interest definition – the behavioural component. Controls have been treated in some cases as virtually neutral 'process variables'. They are depicted rather like a sausage machine – the behavioural meat is put in at one end and out comes the policy sausage. Even where it is allowed that the process can affect the policy outcome by, metaphorically, mincing finely or coarsely, determining the thickness and length of the sausage and the speed of its output, what is not usually allowed is that the machine can affect the meat *well before the processing starts*.

But there is an affective relationship of this kind between conflicts and controls. In fact, a general proposition that can be made about any political system is that, in conflicts over goals, a society depends on a mix of two factors for its resolution: that is, mechanisms of control, and mechanisms of consensus formation.[10] Up to a point they are alternatives. The more you have of one, the less you need of the other. Consensus-formation mechanisms are those institutions which bring together differing conflicting interests and produce the compromises which define a group interest. 'Consensus' may be nothing more than an agreement in which some interests have been defeated. However, so long as such interests concede defeat because they accept the procedures through which decisions are taken, and so long as they are prepared to abide by agreements made under such procedures, the need for controls is reduced. A massive apparatus of controls, on the other hand, makes consensus formation relatively less important. Policy decisions can be imposed.

There is the basis here for a crude comparative typology of societies: consensual and controlled societies. It is a distinction which has explanatory value. In those societies which rely most heavily on consensus, attempting to secure it before major decisions are taken, policy making is characteristically incremental. The societies increasingly, with the decline of the ideological component in party politics, muddle through as a developing and often shifting consensus allows. Governments adjust in a piecemeal fashion to problems as they arise and after organised pressure groups have been formally consulted. There is some continuity – the continuity of inertia and of the interests of the dominant groups – but decisions are not very easy to relate to any coherent set of long-term overall policy goals.

In the controlled societies – those which rely most on governmental punitive sanctions, leaving consensus formation to follow action, there is more likely to be a coherent set of policy goals – a long-term plan. Both forms have their different social and economic values. Planned societies may achieve greater equality; but controls are a downward specification of values, coercive and alienating. The consensual societies are passive and drifting but they are less likely to make catastrophic mistakes. But because they tend to reflect and perpetuate in their policies the relative strength of existing interests in society, they too can be alienating.

Unfortunately there does not seem to be a halfway house between the two types. Consensual societies cannot impose increased controls without arousing the kind of opposition that can only be dealt with by further controls or by retreat and relaxation. The controlled societies, if they relax or thaw, are likely to be faced with demands for further relaxation, and leaders are exposed to competition from elements opposed to their policies and even to the style of government itself. Their choice is to concede and go on conceding, or to reimpose controls.

A second, relevant, general proposition is that the pattern of consensus formation is, to an extent, dependent on the pattern of controls.

The group interests which are defined and expressed as a consensus, and the structure of group organisation for this purpose will be, in any society, very much a function of the level or levels at which controls come into operation. The specialist consensual mechanisms – pressure groups and parties – will organise to influence or to capture (respectively) control centres at all levels. The extent to which an equitable accommodation of interests, i.e. a community interest, will be achieved is also determined in part by rules which affect the assets of groups. Control through corporatist institutions, it may be argued, makes it less likely of achievement. The next chapter, an examination of the changing environment in which consensus has to be formed and controls exercised – the political culture – will suggest, somewhat paradoxically, that a decline in the political and economic divisions between groups and of the fervour with which competing goals are pursued, may be favourable to the development of corporatism.

NOTES

1 For Max Weber, as Daniel Bell points out, 'rationalisation is an axial principle for understanding the transformation of the western world from a traditional to a modern society': Daniel Bell, *The Coming of Post-Industrial Society* (New York: Basic Books, 1973), p. 480. Functional differentiation, administrative specialisation and participation are categories borrowed from S. P. Huntington, 'Political modernisation: America vs Europe', *World Politics*, vol. XVIII (April 1966), pp. 378–414.

2 Michel Crozier, *The Bureaucratic Phenomenon* (Chicago: University of Chicago Press, Phoenix Books, 1967), p. 295.

3 See Hans Daalder, 'Parties, elites and political developments in Western Europe', in M. Dogan and R. Rose (eds), *European Politics* (Boston: Little, Brown, 1971), pp. 4–11.

4 op. cit.

5 Since the focus of this work, however, is on contemporary responses rather than on the 'challenge' itself, reference may be made to the useful introductory level analysis by Brian Harvey and J. D. Hallett, *Environment and Society* (London: Macmillan, 1977).

6 From F. Ridley and J. Blondel, *Public Administration in France* (London: Routledge & Kegan Paul, 1964), p. 29.

7 J. K. Galbraith, *The New Industrial State* (Harmondsworth: Pelican Books, 1969), p. 381.

8 ibid., p. 380.

9 EFTA, *The Trade Effects of EFTA and the EEC 1959–1967*, June 1972, pp. 24 and 42.

10 For an expansion of this argument see Amitai Etzioni, *The Active Society* (New York: Free Press, 1968).

2
Political Culture

It is the contention of this chapter that the political culture is under-going a significant transformation along similar lines in all the advanced industrial societies. The agencies of socialisation – the school, the church, the family and the local community – have all been affected by the economic impetus which these societies are experiencing, altering their influence and weakening the traditional culture which they have imparted and upheld. This, accompanied by the impact of contemporary economic change on the class structure, has led to modification of political attitudes in the direction of greater uniformity between societies and less sharply marked political division within them. This cultural change has provided a climate favourable to corporatist development.

The notion of political culture is used in political analysis as a shorthand term for the emotional and attitudinal environment within which government operates. Broadly speaking, any attitudes which may be partial determinants of governmental style and substance are part of the political culture, but there are levels of increasing relevance. Political traditions, the accepted version of the society's history, common values, social structure and norms, and commonly recognised symbols, are all factors which may be linked with predispositions in a society towards various kinds of political beliefs. They may affect, for example, the citizen's perception of his political role (including the proper, the desired, and the efficacious limits of participation), his acceptance of the roles of others, especially constitutional roles, concepts of political obligation, and of the proper limits of government action.

These will in turn affect political behaviour: the degree to which people take an active political role, join parties and pressure groups and vote. Their tendency to obey the law or evade it, the methods that they will use in pursuing their political interests, will be other consequences.

For political leaders and office holders it will set limits to the range of their actions, the policies they propose, their readiness to trust each other and to make compromises, and the ways in which they will seek to ensure compliance with their decisions.

Two strongly contrasting examples will help to make the point.

The Russian people have a long tradition of very severe control by government. They were the last Europeans to be emancipated from serfdom. Then, during the Stalinist period they were subjected to a repression in which millions died, old social bonds and values were deliberately and ruthlessly destroyed, whole nations were moved physically thousands of miles, all with an arbitrariness which conceded nothing to Tsarist tyranny. This, in conjunction with an intensive political re-education campaign was designed to effect a totally directed society. The effect of this shared experience of repression and intellectual and social manipulation may be seen in contemporary Soviet politics. The business of politics and policy making is left to a relatively small number of political managers. The role of the citizen is to act as recipient and implementor of political outputs without himself contributing to or participating in their formulation. The Soviet citizen concerns himself with the maximisation of self-interest either through devoted service to the state, with the rewards of elite status, or by avoiding the notice of the state and maintaining a low profile.

The obvious contrast to be drawn is with Western democracies like France, the USA or Britain. In France the revolution established a popular conception of citizenship associated with the ideas of liberty, equality and fraternity. The citizenry is seen as the fountain of authority, carefully represented by the sovereign assembly, the ascendant arm of government, threatened from time to time in French history by executive usurpation of power. The source of the obligation to obey is the compact between citizens, each his own interpreter of the extent of the compact. This conception, on the one hand, produces a very generous view of the functional scope and responsibility of government – it is after all self-government – but on the other hand, a suspicious, even jaundiced view of executive power. The people of the United States, in contrast, whose revolution was not against an internal domination but an external imperial power, are less wary of the executive arm, as opposed to the legislature, but, since their compact was not between citizens but states, they maintained a general tradition of reserve towards the idea of the exercise of federal power. George Bernard Shaw once said that 'The American constitution was a guarantee to the whole American people that it never should be governed at all'. The guarantee has not proved wholly effective, given the present range of powers of the federal government, but the attitude remains significant as a determinant of US political style. Then, the fact that the constitution did not effectively establish immediate equality of citizenship for all Americans has meant that classes and groups have had to struggle for constitutional rights. This, in conjunction with a strong, still recent history of local township and state self-reliance, while federal government was still weak, has helped to evolve an attitude and a tradition favourable to an extensive and intensive degree of involvement in political action, particularly through pressure groups.

British parliamentary sovereignty has no revolutionary or compactual basis. As in the United States, however, citizenship equality was extended gradually as a result either of party strategy or a struggle for enfranchisement by a particular group. All three of these Western democracies, though they differ from each other in their degree of political participation, consequently exhibit a greater determination on the part of individual citizens to participate, to have their views heard, and to control and limit the independent role of political leaders, than is the case in the USSR.

A qualification must evidently be entered in the French case but it serves to illustrate the linkage between political culture and behaviour still further. France has a dual political tradition. The elements which sustained General de Gaulle and maintained his ascendancy for ten long years in French politics, and the kind of appeal which he made to the French people, are not entirely to be found in the General's own personal dynamism and the problems of the moment during his period of office. They are not to be found wholly in the inspiration of the General's personal history, particularly the role he played during the war. They must be seen, also, in the light of the historic political culture.

The perhaps unfortunate truth is that the periods of French greatness have not been the periods when democracy has been in the ascendancy. France was brilliant and powerful under the Bourbon monarchy. In this period, with aristocratic values dominant, the French court was the glory of Europe, the Roi Soleil the brightest star in the firmament. The French have not forgotten this.

The French revolution, on the other hand, was a failure, if success be measured in terms of the apparent happiness and prosperity of the French people and the prestige of France. There was inspiration, of course, for foreign revolutionaries in the overthrow of the monarchy, but until affairs in France were taken over by Napoleon, little that was positive was substituted for what had been destroyed.

The Napoleons gave France its code of law, the stable, centralised administrative machinery, which has often been the only government France really had, and its citizen army; and they gave Paris, the heart of France, much of its present character. Andre Malraux sums up the effects very well at the conclusion of his biography of Napoleon. He says: 'If his tomb in the crypt of Les Invalides remains for the French people a place of pilgrimage, it is not merely because of

Arcola, Austerlitz and Montmirail, but because modern France knows herself to be fashioned at the hands of Napoleon'.

This helps to explain why there has never been a solid consensus on politics in France, that is, a consensus on how France should be governed, let alone on the content of policy. Thiers' phrase, 'The Republic that divides us least', his comment on the Third Republic, sums up the extent of the minimal consensus. The Third Republican constitution of 1875 was in fact established by a bare majority. It owed its existence to the fact that the monarchists, who were dominant in the Assembly, could not agree on a king. There is, therefore, a sense in which all the governments of France since the revolution have been working hypotheses, not products of a consensus in evolution. A numerous, active, dissident, disaffected group, varying in character, has always existed, wanting to do away with the existing constitution.

This explains the frequent spurious solution of conflict by resolution on a man. General de Gaulle was cast in an old mould: the mould of Napoleon Bonaparte, Louis Napoleon, Marshal MacMahon and, in a more limited way, Pétain.

However, the imperial tradition, like the republican, is tainted with failure. The Napoleons gave France its moments of glory but also its most humiliating defeats. In particular, the defeat of the empire by Bismarck, the defeat of the army regarded as the flower of France, made an important contribution to French political attitudes. Faith in the man on horseback is an uncertain faith, tinged with distrust.

Again and again, this uncertainty and other divisive cultural factors like religion, class, Jacobinism and right-wing extremism have helped to produce paralysis of government in France (or 'immobilisme') and the capacity for action has had to be restored by resolution on a man. The man does not really resolve the conflict. He ignores it or suppresses it when it impedes action.

There are some signs today that these basic divisions and the institutional arrangements which reflect them are being modified. The constitutional gap between republicanism and authoritarianism appears to have narrowed. It seems as though Presidential government in the Fifth Republic provides some satisfaction to both of these traditions – an acceptable synthesis.

A further observation is that the French political culture is being modified in much the same way as that of other Western European democracies, fortunately along lines favourable to the establishment of the new constitution. Thus, the erstwhile divisive religious issue is of declining importance in the more materialistic France of today, as it is in the rest of Europe. Class tensions and their extreme political expression have been similarly and generally reduced.

Although the overwhelming majority of Frenchmen – 84 per cent –

still declare themselves to be Catholics, religious practice in France
has declined steadily. According to a poll carried out by the SOFRES
for the first television channel in 1975, of 100 people polled, 16
declared that they went to church every Sunday or Saturday, as
against 21 per cent in 1971, when the poll was last taken. Of the
Catholics, 51 per cent said that they only set foot in church for
weddings, christenings and funerals. Religion is still an important
variable in voting behaviour and party affiliation but it is a 'passive'
factor, not a serious policy issue between the parties or within them.

An important modification in the class structure is rapidly taking
place. This is the disappearance of the peasant and the petty bour-
geoisie. The rural population is in decline, its young workers attracted
by urban employment opportunities and life styles. Small family
businesses succumb to the same attraction and to the competition of
large enterprises. The process is far from complete, but it is becoming
less and less likely that a surge of petty bourgeois sentiment like that
behind Poujadism in 1956 will ever occur again, and less and less
will the existence of this class obscure the lines of party division
between left and right.

Finally, the appeal of political extremism seems to be changing.
On the left, the Communist Party has come to terms with the Fifth
Republic and become a party of discriminating opposition to the
government, willing to take a governmental role itself in a rather
tense coalition with the Socialists. It behaves as though it has seen the
writing on the wall for Jacobinism in the affluent society. On the other
side of the spectrum there are very few indications of vitality on the
extreme right. One view, and partial explanation, is that authoritarianism has been an element of the political culture sustained by some
of the most important agencies of political socialisation: the educational system, the church and the family. In this the French experience
is by no means exceptional in Western Europe and serves to illustrate
the more general phenomenon.

In both the first two of these institutions the maturing citizen
is habituated to an authoritarian structure and to accepting non-
arguable 'truths', 'facts', 'values'. The family, particularly in the still
important rural milieu, is 'extended' and, again, authoritarian. Outward conformity to a code of behaviour is more important than consensus on values so that discipline is, in a sense, the price paid for a
considerable degree of 'inward' freedom. One often cited piece of
politically relevant evidence of this pattern is the fact that only a
small percentage of children in France know their parents' political
affiliation.[1] An outward conformity to law and respect for authority,
combined with a determined personal evasion of it (particularly notice-
able in tax collection), seems a plausible behavioural product of this
family socialisation process.

The drift away from the church, recent educational reforms in the direction of a more technology-oriented, participatory, questioning, and less authoritarian pattern of teaching have tended to reinforce the effects of changes in family structure and influence, away from authoritarian paternalism.

Recent migration from the rural areas and a generally increased population mobility serve to fragment the extended family and alter its socialising role. The nuclear family is, generally speaking, more intimate and demanding than the extended family. It relies much more upon consent than impersonal authoritarian prescription. It requires a subscription to values, not merely behavioural conformity (and is correspondingly less tolerant of 'inward' freedom).

The changes which appear to be taking place in France are paralleled by changes in other advanced societies. All have become more heavily urbanised. The most important agencies of political socialisation, the education system, churches and the family have all been affected by similar economic impulses. The curriculum of education has responded to demands for new skills in science, technology, social science and business, challenging established educational values, methods and hierarchies. An environment of continued public debate and criticism of all values, brought home through the mass media, has altered the environment in which churches have to operate.

To some degree these changes conform to, and so help to support, the thesis that the advance of the industrial societies towards affluence has bred a new, quieter politics of consensus, a favourable setting for the development of corporatism. It is allegedly a consensus on goals, without severe divisions in society, and without ideology. This thesis must be considered.

DEVELOPING CONSENSUS AND THE END OF IDEOLOGY

The End of Ideology is the title of a book by Daniel Bell, published in 1960. It was also the title of an essay by Shils in *Encounter* in 1955. Raymond Aron's essay, 'Fin de l'âge idéologique', also appeared in 1955. Aron's essay was probably the most influential, but, in any case, there was a spate of work between 1955 and 1960 expounding some version of the basic thesis that the nature of political debate in advanced Western European society was changing. In particular, its ideological content was diminishing.

The term 'ideology' has been very widely interpreted in discussion of this thesis. For instance, one kind of critical appraisal is that ideology has not disappeared as a factor in politics at all. There is, rather, one unifying ideology in Western societies, that of liberalism, or welfare capitalism, which so strongly prevails that other ideologies can be dismissed as insignificant. This is an exercise in missing the point of an argument by defining one of its terms in a perverse way. If ideology is, as James Christoph has defined it, 'a more or less institutionalised set of beliefs about man and society',[2] then there is a prevailing ideology. But this is not the kind of ideology that Aron or Shils or Bell were quite clearly talking about, nor is it the common usage. The popular conception is fairly well summed up in the Oxford dictionary as 'science of ideas' and [also] 'visionary speculation'. The second clearly sums up the popular judgement on the possibility of the first.

Daniel Bell defines a total ideology as 'an all inclusive system of comprehensive reality; it . . . seeks to transform the whole of a way of life . . . Commitment to ideology . . . is *not* necessarily the reflection of interests'. And he explains the psychological need for a 'cause' and the satisfaction that people may derive from deep moral feelings. 'Ideology, in this sense, is a secular religion.'[3] Elsewhere Bell reiterates the action orientation of ideology. It is 'the conversion of ideas into social levers'. Shils, too, stresses the challenging aspect of ideology. He says it is deviant to futuristic, demanding commitment. This, then, is the political force which, it is alleged, is on the decline.

Historically ideology, in the sense we are concerned with – something which wins mass support for the transformation of the political system – is a relatively modern phenomenon. It can be associated with the enlightenment of the eighteenth century though the term was not used until the nineteenth century. The enlightenment atmosphere suggested the possibility of a science of society, comparable with the natural sciences. This is one of the ways of distinguishing ideology from religion. Religion provides a primarily supernatural explanation of the inexplicable; at the same time it may lend sanction to the mores of a society or provide a fundamental challenge to them. But even when a challenge, it is fundamentally different from ideological challenge in its inspiration – divine rather than scientific.

The first politico-philosophical product of the enlightenment to capture popular attention in Britain was scientific hedonism or utilitarianism. On the Continent it was the philosophy of Rousseau. Both were quasi-scientific in their approach to the study of man. Both had profound political reformist implications and effects. Both were used as instruments to challenge a ruling class.

With the industrial revolution, further social–scientific explanations were stimulated. Marxist explanation called for an eventual revolution to establish the dictatorship of the proletariat. Herbert Spencer's social Darwinism was also a challenge to the existing order of legally based privilege, calling as it did for a ruthless *laissez-faire* as the environment for the social survival of the fittest.

National socialism and fascism were malevolent syntheses of these three ideas, incorporating Rousseau's notion of the general will (realised through the leader), socialism (state directed), and the survival of the fittest (the master race), as well as many other currents of thought.

These eruptions of the thirties differed in a number of ways from the Marxist and Spencerian ideologies. First, they were national in their orientation. Second, they were much less self-consciously scientific, fascism, in particular, embracing faith in God, syndicalism and a strong anti-intellectual element. Third, though they offered a more or less internally coherent set of ideas, challenging the basis of existing society, the purely ideological commitment was deliberately augmented by the considerable emphasis on individual leaders in the movements which espoused them. Marxism in Russia was perverted in the same direction in the thirties, with Stalin's personal dominance.

Nazism and fascism were, in any case, temporary phenomena in Western Europe as reforming ideologies. Marxism or socialism, however, became the creeds of major political parties struggling to transform society. Debate between them and the various conservative parties was about ends and values, not merely about the means to achieve agreed ends. Virtually every country in Western Europe, and most of Eastern Europe before the war, has had a Socialist party, strongly influenced by Marxism, but in any case professing a set of ideals for the evolutionary or revolutionary reform of the existing society to achieve a different set of values which would profoundly alter the capitalist system. The voter was confronted, from the late nineteenth century to the late 1940s, with alternative models of the good society; equality and community versus individual freedom and diversity.

The argument of Bell and others, simply, is that these alternative models are no longer proffered. The political debate has become a debate over *means* rather than ends. The basic values of a modified capitalism are accepted by both left and right. 'We are all socialists now.' Equally, we are all capitalists. Denis Healey, who aroused some suspicions on this score with a promise to 'soak the rich' in 1974, quickly reassured the British voter, a few days later, that he was not out to destroy private business.[4] Social ownership of the means of production and distribution had become an irritating bogey.

The same things that have happened to the Conservative and Labour parties in Britain have happened also on the Continent.

The German Social Democrats (SPD) celebrated their centenary in 1963. Their programme was originally one of strict Marxist orthodoxy, drafted largely by the strict Marxist, Kautsky. Early members were Liebknecht and Bebel, associates of Marx. Marxist orthodoxy, with a reformist graft in the Heidelberg Programme of 1925, was retained as the official line up to the postwar period. Then, in 1949 a new programme began the playing down of the Marxist element, concentrating on practical reforms – not exclusively socialist – and on foreign policy and defence questions. The Bad Godesberg Congress of 1959 was explicitly revisionist since it proclaimed the party's attachment to Christianity, the profit motive and a moderate social reform programme. The SPD in office under Brandt made no attempt to disturb the workings of economic capitalism, nor has it under Herr Schmidt. They have substantially confirmed Lenin's verdict. He said that when the Germans decide to start a revolution, and want to capture a railway station, they will first buy platform tickets. The novelist Gunter Grass, who has written what is, in part, an allegorical history of the SPD, calls it, aptly, *The Diary of a Snail*.

In France, the Socialist Party – until 1969 the SFIO: Section Française de l'Internationale Ouvrière – founded by two earlier Socialist parties in 1904–5, has been, as its name implies, a section of the International Socialist Movement. As late as 1946 in its declaration of principle, in force until the late sixties in theory, it declared its aim 'to make the freedom of the individual dependent on the abolition of the system of capitalist property . . . The Socialist Party is essentially a revolutionary party.' In practice, however, the Socialists drifted to the right during the life of the Fourth Republic, forced continually to defend the parliamentary system against Communist and Gaullist attack. Then, it was split and very much weakened in 1958 over whether to accept de Gaulle, the majority deciding to do so. Throughout the Fifth Republic it has gained strength spasmodically, assimilated to, and dominating, the Alliance of the Left, moving towards the centre in policies but, at the same time, picking up the Communists on the left because they too have moderated their aims and their ideological rigidity. Diversity was institutionalised in the Epinay Congress of 1971, with representation of different minority views on governing bodies of the party being guaranteed in its new constitution. The programme of the Alliance, formulated in 1972, provided for only *limited* nationalisation, *marginal* social reforms, and a European and Atlanticist foreign policy.

In Italy the Socialists created the first modern political party, coming together in the 1890s. They played only a small part in parliament at first, partly because of the limited suffrage, partly because as Marxists they eschewed participation in bourgeois government. Some entered parliament in the interwar years, and this provoked the split which produced the Communist Party in 1921. The Communists, however, from 1945 on, under Togliatti, have had a policy of collaboration with other left parties in national and local government and have been committed to a democratic socialist state. This was a very early, nationalist departure from ideological purity. The party talked of an Italian way of socialism. The Socialists from

1945 to 1956 in Italy were a Communist party under a different name. Their organisational structure was the same. Their ideological commitment followed the PCI. Since 1956 it has been a major task to follow faithfully the bewildering splits and reunifications the party has gone through, most of them turning on whether to collaborate with bourgeois parties in government or with the Communists. The party has remained Marxist for the most part, but with kaleidoscopic variety of tendencies and factions. This makes it harder to assess the importance of ideology. It probably is stronger in Italian politics than elsewhere in Europe but it is difficult to isolate it as a factor and it has no notable influence on governments. Italian government has been very unstable and weak for the past twenty years. The Socialists have played their part in coalition. But with a complex multi-party system, in which the major forces are the Catholic Party or Christian Democrats, followed by the Communists, Italy preserves all kinds of pre-modern orientations. A very complex, fractured ideological debate is one of them but it does not seem to be a major factor in generating a commitment to politics. Referring to the Socialists principally, one writer says that 'the principal reason for membership still appears to be family tradition, son following father, and the chief motive for going along to the party section is recreation; members go to play cards or watch television and seldom discuss politics'.[5] The referendum on 14 May 1974, on the divorce law, suggests that this ideological voter apathy on the left may be matched by a degree of religious emancipation on the right. This is a stage that other countries have experienced in their apparent decline of ideology.

In Holland, a system of proportional representation has helped to preserve a complex factionalism, so that apparent ideological and even religious differences are preserved there also. Though Cabinets are difficult to form (because that is when these differences become preoccupations), they have however had little effect on government policy. There is an easy pragmatic consensus in practice. Furthermore, the alliance of religious parties and liberals on which most governments have been based has been progressively weakened by the decline in the aggregate vote of the religious parties. Religion is a declining feature in Dutch politics. The major party on the left is the Labour Party. Its former ideological component has largely evaporated, and it has easily participated in coalitions. It has been, since May 1973, a very moderate party in government.

The consequence of the general doctrinal decline in Europe may, therefore, be summarised:

(1) The competition between parties has become, in intention at least, one of furthering different and competing economic sectors of the population in the allocation of resources. Consequently,

victory at the polls, though still of prime importance, is slightly less important. Displacement of the existing government is partially subordinated to improving the bargaining position of the party clientele. Even in opposition, influencing government is easy. Consultation with interest groups has been institutionalised in bodies to whom policy responsibility has been partially shifted.

(2) Party competition is also a competition stated in terms of the competence of the alternative administrations – their records in dealing with prices, exchange stability, housing etc. – and much less in terms of basic differences in values and programmes.

(3) A third consequence is that no party has an interest in clarifying the political goals of the society, and is embarrassed by internal attempts to do so. Party image is at least as important, if not more important than party programme, and more or less ambiguous slogans and symbols are manipulated by both parties.

These then are some of the empirical grounds of the end of ideology argument. A controversial part of the thesis, however, is the attempted explanation. First, it should be noted that the alleged decline of ideology has taken place in an international environment in which a Russian national ideology, making use of its internationalist origins, became the basis for a vast extension of Russian power and influence. This, in the Western democracies has helped produce a reaction against communism in domestic politics and a consensus. The consensus is on an alternative existing economic and social system sufficiently powerful in its actual operation to inspire loyalty and sacrifice against what is perceived as the enemy. It can also be argued that as the ideological content has diminished in US–USSR relations from the early sixties the consensus in Western societies has suffered. What some have seen as a reideologisation has been apparent – the challenge of the so-called New Left. With an avowed policy of *détente* between the United States and the USSR, this reideologisation challenge has become stronger. It poses a threat to the stability of Labour and Socialist parties of the orthodox cast.

A second explanation of the end of ideology is Aron's argument in 'Fin de l'âge idéologique' that socialism widened its appeal originally because people saw it as a rationalisation or extension of the fight for democracy – social and economic freedom added to political freedom providing equality of opportunity. As economic goals of left-wing parties were progressively achieved without any sign that the high levels of consumption by the rich and privileged had to be sacrificed; and with the productivity of labour actually increasing rather than diminishing, much of the opposition to reformist policies collapsed. The fervour of ideological commitment collapsed with it. The political system became a symbiotic relationship between a modified left and a modified right. The parties retained and actually increased their class support, but not their political militancy. Affluence itself, it may be argued, decreased the urgency of the ideological appeal on the left. Needs were, absolutely, diminished and, more important (because the concept of need constantly expands), the difference in style of life, though not disparities of income and wealth, became less marked – a factor contributing to a reduction in class tension until more refined perceptions of remaining differences could develop, and providing a receptive environment for class co-operation within functional sectors.

Another argument is that modern society has produced increasingly sophisticated science, and the acceptance of scientific thought has gradually produced a diminution in the mythical, mystical elements in social attitudes: the magic of birth and blood and the aristocratic conception of its superiority, the religious supports of privilege. The result is a much increased class mobility, again reducing tension. Scientific criticism has, more directly, undermined the bases of specific ideologies. Biology raises some difficult questions for social Darwinism. And social science, in identifying the rising, now dominant middle class, and noting divisions within the working class between the skilled and the semi-skilled and between men and women, has brought into question Marxian predictions about class solidarity and the increasing gulf between the proletariat and the owners of capital.

Another relevant development has been Keynesian economic thinking and policies, and acceptance of the necessary involvement and responsibility of the state in economic affairs to reduce fluctuations in business activity and even to promote development. The perception of this need has made management *étatist*, and, even in France, prepared to accept the trade unionist in consultation procedures with government as a not wholly hostile interest – sometimes even as an ally. As a corollary of the recognition of common interests, the factory manager, especially in the more modern enterprises, is prepared to see the union leader as an auxiliary personnel manager, and to see the worker as someone who may have something to contribute to improved factory management. This recognition is very general in Germany and Holland where company law requires worker participation up to the highest level.

As a concomitant of affluence, universal education has been prolonged and much greater equality of opportunity in this sphere now exists. It is argued that education, particularly if taken to the tertiary level, increases tolerance and scepticism and subjects a person to a wide variety of cross-pressures and intellectual and other influences. It increases pragmatism – again with damaging effects on ideological appeals in an environment of diminished class bitterness. There appears to be an inverse correlation between educational attainment and ideological commitment to party. Thus Hedley Cantril, looking at French and Italian party members, finds that the most loyal and unquestioning are those at the lower end of the economic scale, such as unskilled workers. Those higher up and better educated tend to be more critical.[6]

The effects of mass communication have been considered to have an effect on the appeal of ideology, particularly the development of television. The media present a *variety* of political views and arguments. Their charters often require it;[7] their monopoly position makes it desirable. They bombard their audiences with information. The appeal of *party* newspapers seems to have suffered a decline (which may be a consequence) but, in any case, the variety of views replaces the coherent ideological presentation of the party or party-linked newspaper as a dominant influence. The effects of the media in widening horizons and creating greater awareness of changing opportunities has played its part, in conjunction with improvements in transport, in increasing the mobility of persons within large regions and on an inter-regional basis. In 1911 only about 20 per cent of Frenchmen were born outside their department of residence. By 1962 it was approximately 40 per cent.[8] The effect of mobility is to increase cross-pressures and to induce attitudinal ambiguities and compromises.

Finally, there has been the rise of the middle class, the competition for whose allegiance is necessary to political parties which hope to govern. The new enlarged middle class in its attitudes and interests blurs the lines between right and left. It has bourgois, materialistic values. It values equality of opportunity and instruments of class mobility. It is exposed to conflicting pressures from left to right. The careers of many of its members lie with the state in the civil service, nationalised industries, the teaching profession, the armed services, and they benefit from the enlarged role of the state prescribed by the left. Others – members of the professions, managerial cadres – have an entrepreneurial orientation to the right. But their backgrounds, schooling, accents, living conditions are comparable with their salaried friends. Both sides of the political spectrum are drawn towards the centre to win their support.

It is plausible that these elements of change in advanced industrial society are linked to changes in political attitudes – changes which may very generally be described as a decline of ideology. The labelling of the phenomenon should not distract attention from its substance: an evident, actual diminution in the late fifties and early sixties of the popular strength and enthusiasm with which coherent alternative blueprints for societal transformation were proposed and supported. Affluent Western societies in the late fifties and early sixties were apparently marked by satisfaction bordering on complacency with their economic lot. They had 'never had it so good', Harold Macmillan told them.

This was an environment particularly favourable to the development of the corporatist society. There was no strong motive for rank-and-file participation in the activity of parties which had grown very much like each other, differing only slightly on the means by which agreed objectives could best be reached. Interest organisational elites, particularly where complex technical questions seemed to be important, could also be left to manage affairs without membership involvement and interference and, therefore, with only minimal accountability. To secure the agreement and co-operation of the different sectoral elites in formulating government policies designed to increase the prevailing affluence was the only real political problem and it did not seem a difficult one. It was managed by the creation of consultative bodies in which managerial, professional and union technocrats met with the appropriate government bureaucracies as the recognised representatives of groups within their sector and had an important, often decisive influence on policies affecting their sector. In the seventies, the popularity of the thesis of ideological decline has waned. With energy crises, problems of inflation, unemployment and troubled industrial relations, the advanced societies no longer exhibit anything like complacency or consensual unity. No major new ideology has emerged as a challenge to contemporary society, but disturbances 'on the fringe' are enough to provoke the question whether there are factors favouring, and actual signs of ideological resurgence. To this question we now turn.

NOTES

1 Philip E. Converse and Georges Dupeux, 'Politicisation of the electorate in France and the United States', *Public Opinion Quarterly*, vol. 26, no. 1 (1962), pp. 89–90. We have not cited actual figures because their accuracy has been questioned. The general point remains valid, however.
2 J. B. Christoph, 'Consensus and change in British political ideology', *American Political Science Review*, vol. 59 (September 1965), p. 629.
3 Daniel Bell, *The End of Ideology: On the Exhaustion of Political Ideas in the Fifties* (New York: Macmillan, 1972), pp. 399–400.
4 *The Times*, 14 May 1974.
5 P. Allum, 'Italy', in S. Henig (ed.), *European Political Parties*, PEP (London: Allen & Unwin, 1969), p. 219.
6 Hedley Cantril, *Politics of Despair* (New York: Macmillan, 1958), pp. 200–3.
7 See e.g. R. J. Harrison, 'The Broadcasting Corporation Act', *Landfall*, June 1962.
8 Olivier Guichard, *Aménager la France* (Paris: Laffont, 1965).

3
Radical Politics

The dominant 'consensus' politics of the democratic advanced industrial societies does not pass without some challenges. At one level
there are the critical academic analyses with reformist, occasionally
radical reformist, implications, like those of C. Wright Mills, M.
McLuhan, A. Toffler and J. K. Galbraith.[1] More dramatic in their
impact are the challenges which are accompanied by some political
mobilisation, often behind a purely negative destructive opposition
which offers no immediate alternative. These, it has been argued,
represent the burgeoning of the first heresies of the diffuse consensus
of liberal-capitalism. Moynihan,[2] for example, identifies three clusters
of heretical behaviour. There are the alienated – those who are in a
chronic state of identity crisis under the strains and cross-pressures of
urban society, victims of technological innovation, mobility, rootless-
ness, the break up of the family, of insecure, dull routine labour and
an inability to comprehend the system; the 'opt out' or 'Nirvana now'
cluster – people who reject and ignore the society which surrounds
them, perhaps forming small communal enclaves dedicated to an
alternative life style; and, finally, the New Left, as typified by the
SDS in the United States. Another analyst, Zijderveld,[3] offers three
somewhat different categories, which complement those of Moynihan.
He suggests two kinds of withdrawal behaviour: 'Gnosticism' – a
withdrawal from reality to a subjective Nirvana, searching for 'utter
reality' in one's own soul, often with the assistance of psychedelic
drugs; and 'Anarchism' – whose adherents launch a counter-culture
or life style which denies everything holy to 'straight' society. They
return to 'nature' in communes which are often communistic in
economics and sexuality. This is basically a cultural protest but it
may develop political manifestation in alliance with the third
Zijderveld category, the Activists, who are politically involved and are
equatable with Moynihan's New Left. Of the four basic categories
which emerge from these analyses – the alienated, the Gnostics, the
Anarchists and the Activists or New Left, only the last are regularly
involved politically but they may all, including the largest of these

clusters, the alienated, occasionally mobilise for political challenge. Such radical challenge tends, in contemporary politics, to take the form which is now quite often labelled 'the politics of protest'.

In general the advanced societies have stable political institutions, effective law enforcement, an established pattern of civil rights, institutionalised channels for the expression of individual and group demands, and specialised consensual mechanisms like the political parties. Government, indeed, is presumed to rest on the consent of the governed. Were this not so, very much larger instruments of coercion than the existing police forces would be necessary. There does not appear to be a halfway house between the heavy hand of dictatorship and the thin blue line of police in the democracy. While the condition of consent is fulfilled, the possibility of a revolutionary mass movement would appear to be remote. The one notion negates the other. In the time-hallowed cliché, the ballot is substituted for the bullet. However, most advanced democracies, in practice, experience, and also make allowance for the expression of, minority discontent outside formal political and legal processes. Indeed, certain ordinarily illegal acts are treated as legitimate for this purpose until they become a threat to public order. Thus, forceful picketing, marches and demonstrations, unauthorised bill-posting, sit-ins, work-ins are in this category – outside the law, but regarded as 'legitimate'.

RADICAL 'ACTIVIST' CATEGORIES

(a) *Minority interests with reformist goals*
A variety of social groups subscribe to these methods and to more extreme kinds of activism. Some of them are 'affected' as well as being 'disaffected'. For example, the squatters' movement, women's liberation movements, ethnic minorities, campaigners for homosexual law reform, claimants' unions, the US Draft Resistance, are groupings of those who conceive that their particular interests or values are flouted by, or neglected in, society, and that the usual channels of influence are closed to them. Such groups are often led, at least at their formation, by revolutionaries, but group aims are limited. An early example was the suffragette movement. Contemporary movements for women's liberation and equality bear the closest comparison with the suffragette movements. The large squatters' movement which has grown up in protest against speculative building clearance schemes, and against inadequate housing policies in British cities which leave areas due for rebuilding with houses empty for many years, is a hybrid of legality and illegality. On the one hand, it is illegal to break into a house. On the other hand, the law does define certain squatters' rights. Some councils are happy enough to be relieved of part of their

housing difficulties in this way, as it involves a minimum of obligations. The Squatters' Association with its able middle-class intellectual
(occasionally revolutionary) cadre can bring about a situation which
the local authority is not legally permitted to bring about itself – that
is, the temporary occupation of condemned houses, or of private
houses which would otherwise remain empty.

Some such groups will be found to have their social roots among
those strongly affected by the pace of technological change. People
on fixed incomes, downwardly mobile classes like parsons, male
clerical workers, teachers, university staff, small shopkeepers and small
businessmen, writers, as well as people outside the production system
like old age pensioners, have formed organisations and in some cases
taken, for them, unusual protest actions, such as strikes and demonstrations occasionally erupting into violence. Most have not been
assigned, and are unable to gain, an influential place in the 'corporatist' economic decision-making process, and so cannot otherwise
affect the terms of their own adjustment to the forces of social change.

(b) *Minority promotional groups*

Most other forms of protest action are also organised by radical
intellectual cadres. The Campaign for Nuclear Disarmament, SANE,
Amnesty International, and Half-Life are disaffected groups operating within a specific issue area, an area distinguished by the fact
that the political parties do not include it within their programmes,
and by the fact that, where the matter falls within the scope of state
action, the state operates within a massive permissive consensus.
Some are found on the extreme right in groups which feel that the
rules they perceive as necessary for the governance of society have
broken down. The National Front in Britain is one such group, while
the law and order theme in recent American elections is an attempt
by the orthodox parties to reap some of the appeal of this tendency.
The activity of these groups is overt – they aim at mass persuasion.
They espouse, however, systemic, not anti-systemic goals, largely
ignored by the main parties.

(c) *Conspiratorial groups*

Another category of dissent action is both illegal and perceived as
illegitimate. The advanced societies are becoming increasingly familiar
with assassination, kidnapping, hijacking, bombing and sabotage as
political instruments. This is the underground politics of an elite. The
conspiratorial terrorist organisation utilising these techniques is characterised by a high level of discipline and secrecy. One type is that
drawn from a high elite group which considers itself frustrated in its
rightful exercise of power. The Generals' plot against de Gaulle, who
had let them down by granting independence to Algeria, is an

example. Revolutionary left-wing groups are the other end of the spectrum. The outstanding examples have been the German Baader-Meinhof gang, the American Weatherman and the Symbionese Liberation Army, the British Angry Brigade, the Japanese Red Army Faction, the Italian group known as the Armed Nucleus of the Proletariat and the Italian Red Brigades – all of them exclusively intellectual in their composition. Some formerly conspirational non-violent groups, like the Communist Party in Britain, France and Italy, are co-opted by society, and their acceptance robs them of their character and to some extent of their dissenting value orientations. The co-opting process is normally a tribute to their influence by the orthodox left which seeks to capture their electoral or industrial power. The orthodox left, on the other hand, is likely to be a severe enemy of the uninfluential, potentially violent revolutionaries, most of whom are to be found as a tiny minority of the student population in the advanced society.[4]

Richard Clutterbuck has pointed out that the most dangerous element in the minority, the urban terrorists, claim 'to speak and fight on behalf of the working classes . . . Yet with very rare exceptions (such as the Provisional IRA) they are led and predominantly re-cruited from university students, graduates and the sons and daughters of the affluent.' They make very few recruits in the working class and these are mainly from the criminal or rootless and inadequate fringes of society, not from the farm or the shop floor. Though the working class reject their leadership they nevertheless retain a conviction that they are fighting in their interest.[5]

Powerlessness and repression are factors which appear to be favourable to conspiratorial leadership. Lack of public response, allied to police harassment, led many Blacks in America to desert the formal civil rights movement in favour of conspiratorial groups like the Black Panthers. 'Tokenism' (Black senators, women newscasters etc.) probably works in the other direction, since it allays the sense of powerlessness. University students are particularly sensitive, as dependents on grants and/or parents, and as non-producers, to their own powerlessness. Since also, in the arts and social sciences, they are being given the broad education which was the prerogative of a small ruling upper class, and society is incapable of offering them the status for which they are trained in such numbers, there are tensions created which find outlets in movements of moral protest.

These activist sub-categories, whether with systemic or anti-systemic goals, have in common, however, their occasional or habitual eschewal of the orthodox modes of groups and party activity in the democracies. Their dissent takes another course. That is to say that, even where no *legal* barriers exist to its political expression through ordinary constitutional channels, it does not follow such channels, tending to rely more on 'anomic' behaviour – likely to take the form of riots, marches and demonstrations – and, in the last analysis, relying on the conspiratorially organised exploitation of a higher level of violence than either the state or respectable opposition groups are prepared to use. In this extreme category of unconstitutional action, acts of terrorism of indiscriminate ruthlessness and brutality are used either to provoke authority itself to move beyond the accepted norm and so alienate other citizens, or to achieve some immediate aim (perhaps only publicity), by relying on the unwillingness of the state to retaliate in kind, in situations where this would be the only really effective immediate recourse. Anomic behaviour[6] serves similar purposes. It may be a means by which a protest group can extend the limits of state violence beyond the point of consensus by using various disruptive techniques of non-violent civil disobedience.

There are a number of other reasons why non-constitutional channels of action are preferred. First, for a relatively small extremist minority, unconstitutional methods serve to underline the rejection of contemporary democratic mixed capitalism by demonstrating a refusal to come to terms, even temporarily, with any of its institutions. Second, the efficacy of anomic and other forms of protest which turn on violence in some way has increased. The activity is widely publicised via the mass news media without any cost to the promoters. Technology has created critical points of vulnerability, furthermore, to violent attack or non-violent disruption. Third, radical protest of the anomic variety sometimes gains support from, and may be partially (but not primarily) explained by reference to, psychological malaise (anomie and alienation) which seeks some relief in the collective hysteria of dramatic and violent gesture, or in sporadic vandalism. Fourth, and finally, the groups which utilise such measures may be *relatively* deprived of access to ordinary channels because they do not have adequate financial resources, access to the communications network, or regularity of membership. They may be characterised by a loose or non-existent organisation and by a very low potential for consensus on explicit positive goals. They cannot exploit key positions of vital importance to the economy. They have no 'recognised' place on the official consultative bodies. They lack 'respectability' both in their personnel and goals. They lack the necessary skills but, even more, they lack the numbers and the possible social base required for an orthodox operation. Students, particularly, are in this 'powerless' position.

IDEOLOGICAL POTENTIAL

Only the activist, New Left cluster bears any resemblance to a new ideological movement. It does have a very low-level transforming goal. That is, it has the positive though rather vague conception of 'participatory democracy' and it proposes a number of humanistic values. It does provide an action commitment, for the most part of a negative destructive kind. It reveals occasional pretensions to a 'scientific' analysis of existing society.[7] But it does not offer a comprehensive, coherent vision of a new society, and the elements in society to which it appeals are still so apparently diffuse that its *revolutionary* potential must still be rated very low. Marcuse has made the point emphatically: 'In the contemporary period, the technological controls appear to be the very embodiment of Reason for the benefit of all social groups and interests – to such an extent that all contradiction seems irrational and all counteraction impossible . . . Intellectual and emotional refusal "to go along" appears neurotic and impotent'.[8] The May 1968 events in France showed how far diffuse intellectual and emotional refusals could be brought together for action. The bonds that were forged between revolutionary elements, and then between them and discontented non-revolutionary masses, proved very fragile. However, the 'events' and their legacy challenge Marcuse's view that 'The impact of progress turns Reason into submission to the facts of life . . . The efficiency of the system blunts the individual's recognition that it contains no facts which do not communicate the repressive power of the whole'.[9]

The group which most persistently and identifiably rejects this submission is the university and college student group.

It is plausible, as Bennett Berger has suggested, that 'the problem of student unrest is rooted in the prolongation of adolescence in industrialised countries',[10] – something which may be seen as, in a sense, a triumph of civilisation. It provides for an increased time for philosophical questioning and identity searching, contributing to personal and social development, and taking place at the period of peak intellectual activity, social energy and physical strength.

The social evils against which the protests of students are directed touch very few of them personally. Neither they nor their parents are likely to have had much experience of extreme poverty, bad housing, poor schooling, unemployment, harsh treatment by the police, inadequacies in the health and social services, or racial and sexual discrimination. Citing eleven studies conducted in the United States, Kenneth Keniston has summarised the characteristics of the student activist.

A large and still growing number of studies, conducted under different auspices, at different times, and about different students, present a remarkably consistent picture of the protest-prone individual. For one, student protesters are generally outstanding students; the higher the student's grade average, the more outstanding his academic achievements, the more likely it is that he will become involved in any given political demonstration.

The home backgrounds of student activists, the studies reveal, have a number of similar features. The families of such students tend to espouse liberal political views. Students, in fact, report that their parents share their views and accept or even support their activity. Many are liberal democrats, and among them there is a disproportionate number of socialists, pacifists and other minority opinions associated with the left in politics. Many protesters come from Jewish families, an ethnic group of generally liberal political tendency. Where parents are religious they are more often associated with the more liberal denominations such as Reform Judaism, Unitarianism or the Quakers. 'Such parents are reported to have high ethical and political standards, regardless of their actual religious convictions.'

A significant proportion of the activist group are drawn from upper middle-class families or professional or intellectual standing. Somewhat surprisingly Keniston finds that, in comparison with the active student conservative,

> members of protest groups tend to have higher parental incomes, more parental education, and less anxiety about social status (Westby and Braungart, 1966). Another study finds that high levels of education distinguish the activist's family even in the grandparental generation (Flaks, 1967). In brief, activists are not drawn from disadvantaged, status-anxious, underprivileged, or uneducated groups, on the contrary, they are selectively recruited from among those young Americans who have had the most socially fortunate upbringings.

Such students tend to be among the most committed to the values with which the traditional university disciplines are concerned – literature, the arts and humanities – rather than the more clearly vocational training in, for example, engineering, science, or business studies.

Rejecting careerist and familist goals, activists espouse humanitarian expressive, and self-actualizing values. Perhaps because of these values, they delay career choice longer than their class mates. Nor are such students distinctively dogmatic, rigid, or authoritarian. Quite the contrary, the substance and style of their beliefs and activities tend to be open, flexible, and highly liberal. Their fields of academic specialization are non-vocational – the social sciences and the humanities. Once in college, they not only do well academically, but tend to persist in their academic commitments, dropping out less frequently than most of their classmates. As might be expected a disproportionate number receive a B.A. within four years and continue on to graduate school, preparing themselves for academic careers.[11]

These survey findings help to explain why student political dissenters, ordinarily, are not revolutionaries. Small minorities of self-described revolutionaries are able to capitalise on the frustrated liberal idealism of the typical student body to generate various kinds of anomic behaviour, but the rank-and-file marchers, demonstrators, petition signers and occupiers of buildings do not seek to destroy the system but to protest against its more conservative, authoritarian and uncaring attributes in the interest of a rather vague humanistic liberalism. Student fidelity to revolutionary cadres has, consequently, proved ephemeral. But the nature of the dedicated revolutionary student leadership also helps to explain the temporary nature of this support.

Revolution in its most familiar historical form is for identifiable ends: to change leadership, to achieve specified reforms, to implement an alternative ideological blueprint of society and government. Its strategy is determined by the practical need to accomplish these ends, and the most familiar action, therefore, is to overthrow the government and capture its power, by the lightning coup in the capital, the assassination and the insurgency. Revolutionary action of this kind has given ground in the advanced societies to action which in many cases is not immediately motivated by any practical end or proposal for reform. This is one reason why the capture of government assumes less importance as an objective. Another reason is that historical revolutions, particularly the communist revolutions of the twentieth century which are the most influential, have not achieved their pre-revolutionary objectives with the capture of government. The example is of the 'revolution betrayed' by the new ruling group, or of the potential for survival of traditional ruling classes, traditional values and structures. The hate object for the contemporary student revolutionary is, therefor, 'the system', in any and all of its manifestations, not just the government. Disruption of industry, destruction of property, the capture of the control of a sector of society may all be rationalised by reference to anti-*systemic* objectives. 'Societé est une fleur carnivore' was one of the slogans of the May 1968 revolt in France. It is an indictment of the *whole* society. To accept any part of it, and to participate, is to support society and possibly be corrupted by what it has to offer. 'Je participe, tu participes, il participe, nous participons, vous participez, ils profitent!' The transformation objectives of this cluster are, therefore, more profound even than Marxism. Marxism, though revolutionary, was materialistic and realistic in the tradition of the society from which it sprung. But these are the very characteristics that the French students and the SDS in the United States rejected. In this sense – the anti-science sense – the revolutionary fervour is anti-ideological, even anti-rational, the political complement of Dali's surrealism. Its emphasis is creative rather than consumer oriented. The Port Huron statement (1962) emphasised *human* relationships: love, generosity, creativity, participation. The SDS challenged the materialistic values of contemporary society like Xtians arriving in second-century Rome.

The events of May 1968 in France provided the opportunity for expression and development of New Left idealism. For most of the enormous crowds of people drawn into these events there were, of course, no revolutionary aims but a variety of different, potentially conflicting aims and grievances. As a prelude to the revolt there were disturbances in the universities which were dealing with three times the number of students in 1968 in comparison with ten years earlier without a corresponding increase in facilities. The high degree of centralisation in education hindered any local reforms of authoritarian teaching, outdated curriculum and highly competitive examination system. Another generally alienating factor was that the National Union of French Students (UNEF) was not accorded recognition as a negotiating body. This helped to ensure that it remained weak and militant. These conditions provided an excellent opportunity for revolutionary intellectual cadres to spark incidents which, brutally dealt with by the police, served to enlist moderate but already disgruntled students in protest action against the authorities. This action, in its turn severely repressed, led to more widespread sympathetic reaction by other social groups, including workers. Action committees provided diffuse leadership.

There were many elements in the intellectual vanguard of May but some generalisations are possible. First, their basic appeal was to the instincts of the individual and to emotions and their expression. One very small chance aspect of this helped to draw thousands of people on to the streets from all sectors of society. It was play rather than work. Glorious weather and a carnival atmosphere succeeded in challenging the drab routines of the industrial society. Second, there were no specific organisational aims designed to replace existing political structures. To quote from an article which appeared in the student magazine *Le Point* the day after the night of the barricades (this English version is from CAW!, the magazine of the American SDS):

No definite goals: these always open the way for laying down arms, for the rhetoric of compromise and concessions, for conciliatory demobilizations. This time we reject and we contest, so as to be sure of having nothing to receive, thus to avoid anything likely to smother the movement of revolution and radical transformation of society. We aim at shaking up the most stable, the most public, the most necessary structures of what makes up the basis of the social existence of capitalism.

and:

> This revolution . . . is . . . outside of all orders of rationality since the bourgeoisie has taken over all existing rationalities . . . all reason is on the other side, on the side of paternity, of the law.[12]

This helps to explain the importance of slogans rather than theories. They could make destructive points, but they did not have to point in any definite direction: 'L'imagination au pouvoir'.

The role of the French Communists in 'les événements' tended to confirm the student view of 'all orders of rationality'. The communist CGT, with other unions, called the national one-day strike of 13 May. They supported the extension of striking on subsequent days in the factories, but they sought to channel the demands into claims for higher wages and other material benefits, attacking the irresponsibility of the student leaders. Their position was in many ways like General de Gaulle's own, summed up so graphically in his immediately famous phrase: 'Les reforms, oui, la chi en lit, non!'

In 1968 the New Left offered no positive structures or policies then: these were to emerge from chaos. One positive idea that did emerge was the idea of participatory democracy – through personal involvement at the local level. This was the intellectual product of the linking of diffuse, vague, revolutionary negativism and diffuse, vague, non-revolutionary idealism. The links were not strong enough to hold together a movement. Since 1968, and with a considerable debt to it, a more general concern which has developed with the quality of life in industrial societies is reminiscent of early, but soon defunct, socialist expectations of the rewarding leisure opportunities, including cultural enrichment, which would be enjoyed by the working man emancipated from long hours of routine labour as a result of planning for increased productivity. Student *mass* protest and other non-conspiratorial forms are partly, therefore, the dramatic political revival of liberal-democratic humanistic ideals. They are once again finding some outlets in the world outside the university within the political parties on the intellectual left wing. Today, most left-wing parties in the advanced industrial democratic societies are sensitive to pressure on the kinds of issues which students raise, though disturbed by the threat to party unity and electoral appeal which they constitute. The French Socialists, for example, have to contend with their CERES group – the Cercles d'Etude et de Recherches et d'Education Socialiste.

They were successfully excluded from the Secretariat of the party, on which they had previously had three members, because they refused to have one of their motions composited with that of the majority at the Pau conference in February 1975.[13] In Germany similarly, the Young Left has provided a challenge to which the Socialist Party has proved sensitive. In early 1974, in the last few weeks of Herr Brandt's Chancellorship, Herr Schmidt, then Finance Minister, thought it necessary to deny that the decline in the SPD's electoral fortunes was a result of disillusion with economic management and the rise in un-employment and inflationary pressures. He thought it more likely that it was due to popular anxiety about the influence within the party of the left-wing Young Socialists (JUSOS).[14] He mounted, thereafter, a successful campaign to undermine their position in the party and was, apparently, vindicated by electoral gains for moderate Socialists and FDP candidates in the nine ensuing state elections in the following fourteen months. In general, the unity of French Socialists, German Social-Democrats, Dutch Labour and British Labour has been strained by issues like Vietnam, women's rights, homosexual law reform, foreign immigration policy, racial discrimination, environmental de-gradation and educational opportunity. Even among the parties of the right there is a conception of 'the ugly face of capitalism' and increasing concern about 'the quality of life'.

There is, in fact, an increasingly pervasive critique of industrialism and urban civilisation. The idea of progress itself in material terms is questioned. The popular catch-words of this questioning exercise are pollution, environmental conservation, urban renewal, population control, the responsibility of science and scientists, devolution, poverty, ghettoes, participation, and even 'spaceship earth'.

These are conceptions and questions which challenge, in effect, not merely the values of industrial society but the ancient injunction in Genesis to 'increase and multiply, and fill the earth, and subdue it, and rule over the fishes of the sea, and the fowls of the air, and all living creatures that move upon the earth', perhaps the longest respected and the most energetically fulfilled of all biblical commands. As yet the challenge has had little effect on existing political structures, but the relevant questions are being raised in universities and intellectual circles. The encroachment of ideas upon the minds of pragmatic elites who believe that their experience and developed judgement is the basis of their policies and decisions, should not, however, be overlooked. As John Maynard Keynes put it, 'the ideas of economists and political philosophers, both when they are right and when they are wrong, are more powerful than is commonly understood. Indeed the world is ruled by little else . . . Madmen in authority, who hear voices in the air [he is referring to Nazi leaders in 1935, the time of writing] are distilling their frenzy from some academic scribbler of a few years back . . . [and] the power of vested interests is vastly exaggerated compared with the gradual encroachment of ideas.'[15]

Keynes's own ideas had a profound influence on subsequent policy making – an influence which, it might be argued, is rivalled in recent history only by the earlier ideas of Karl Marx. No single work of contemporary social criticism as yet looks like assuming the prominence of the great works of Marx or Keynes, but a very large critical literature, nevertheless, has already made a significant impact.

There exists as a result of it an alternative conception of progress, opposed in many respects to technological developments and increased consumption – emphasising the *quality* of life, and working to establish itself within existing structures in the reformist tradition.

It has not assumed the character of a political movement, but it challenges Marcuse's extreme conception of 'a truly totalitarian universe in which society and nature, mind and body are kept in a state of permanent mobilisation for the defence of this universe'.[16] That is too extreme an account of the end of ideology.

There is no question that radical protest, in character, though not in explicit formulation, can be seen as a protest against aspects of contemporary society which are symptomatic of corporatism. Evidently, 'the system' against which revolutionary protest is directed is not the liberal society of meaningful participatory pluralism in which, through their active involvement, citizens are themselves the authors of the laws which govern them. It is, rather, one which is distinguished, in the elementary rhetoric of the radical, by the division between 'us' and 'them'; one in which conventional participation is pointless since only 'they' profit, as the May 1968 slogan averred. 'They' are the elite, and they quite specifically include the established leaders of the proletarian organisations who have, allegedly, 'sold out'. It is not, therefore, surprising that participatory democracy emerged as a positive goal in 1968, or that the values and institutions singled out for the most violent attack were those of what have been called the 'commanding heights' of the economy of industrial societies. It is in this sector, we shall argue in the next two chapters, that corporatism is most advanced.

NOTES

1   Bell's thesis, according to C. Wright Mills, is 'a slogan of complacency, circulating among the prematurely middle-aged, centred in the present, and in the rich Western societies': 'Letter to the New Left', in P. Jacobs and S. Landau (eds), *The New Radicals* (New York: Random House, 1966), p. 104. See also his *Power Elite* (1959), McLuhan's *Understanding Media* (1965), Toffler's *Future Shock* (1970) and Galbraith's *Economics and the Public Purpose* (1974).

2   Daniel Moynihan, 'The New Left and liberal values', abridged version of the Phi Beta Kappa lecture (Harvard, 6–7 June), in *Dialogue*, vol. 2, no. 3 (1969).

3   Anton C. Zijderveld, *The Abstract Society* (Harmondsworth: Penguin 1972) pp. 93–117.

4   'Trade unionists society want law to curb student militants', *The Times*, 16 February 1974.

5   Richard Clutterbuck, *Living with Terrorism* (London: Faber, 1975), p. 27.

6   What G. A. Almond and G. B. Powell define as 'Spontaneous penetrations . . . such as riots, demonstrations, assassinations and the like' in their *Comparative Politics: A Development Approach* (Boston: Little, Brown, 1966), pp. 74–9.

7   See e.g. D. G. Cohn Bendit, *Obsolete Communism* (London: Deutsch 1968) and his comments in *Magazin Litteraire*, 19 July 1968.

8   H. Marcuse, *One Dimensional Man* (London: Sphere Books, 1968), p. 25.

9   ibid., p. 26.

10 Bennett M. Berger, 'Student unrest and prolonged adolescence', *Dialogue*, vol. 3, no. 4 (1970), p. 63.

11 Kenneth Keniston, 'The sources of student dissent', in Walt Anderson (ed.), *The Age of Protest* (California: Goodyear Publishing Co., 1969), pp. 232–3.

12 op. cit., Issue 3, pp. 1 and 47.

13 See *The Economist*, 8 February 1975, p. 33.

14 *The Economist*, 10 May 1975, p. 55.

15 J. M. Keynes, *The General Theory of Employment Interest and Money* (New York: Harcourt Brace, 1936), p. 383, quoted in J. K. Galbraith, *The Age of Uncertainty* (London: BBC, Deutsch, 1977), p. 11.

16 Marcuse, op. cit., p. 31.

4
The Political Economy

The development from primitive, hunting society to contemporary industrial society, considered in terms of human satisfaction, has not been a 'progress', it has been argued, but a maintaining of place. Scarce resources and population changes have necessitated, though they may not have directly brought about, more intensive exploitation of natural resources. Man the hunter, 'an animal that had carefully and beautifully prepared itself through millions of years of natural selection to range and gamble, lounge and play, feast and forage'[1] gave way to the agriculturalist. A surplus agriculture may have provided the basis for cities and the various facets of a 'civilised' life, but for the majority it was a condemnation to the trivial round, the common tasks of agricultural toil. 'It left us . . . insecure and at the mercy of those who were able to maintain the predatory life. Finally it created slaves and serfs who were robbed even of restricted territory and autonomy.'[2]

In the last two hundred years, mostly in Western Europe and the Americas, the agriculturalist has given way to the industrial labourer, living in the great urban centre some way from the workplace where he performs a specialised task related to a relatively remote end-product. It is not clear that the physical, social and psychological costs have been outweighed by the gains of these developments. 'The main features of economic development, including changes in the resource-base, the division of labour, the development of trade and industry, increasingly intensive agricultural methods and many other aspects of a society's changing productive activity, are all predictable responses to the growth of need. They cannot be understood as attempts to increase economic efficiency . . . development is accompanied – as often as not – by a decrease in the real efficiency of societies.'[3] Whether efficiency, measured by man-hours worked to supply basic needs, or whether costs of all kinds have outweighed gains, may not be clear, but there is no doubt that the developmental process has made the individual man increasingly dependent on more and more people in larger and larger societies. The self-sufficient hunter, clothed and sheltered by the skins of the animals which provided his food, has given way to the urban dweller, clothed in synthetic fibres, living in a unit built by numerous skilled specialists and supported by a range of community services. Human interdependence has steadily increased with industrialism and has brought in its wake needs and conflicts which governments have been expected to satisfy and regulate.

The advance of trade and industry, consequently, has been accompanied by changes in the relationships between, and mutual relevance of, governmental and economic activity. A crude summary of this development since the beginning of the industrial revolution in Europe in the late eighteenth and early nineteenth centuries would include (1) a *laissez-faire* phase of minimal governmental intervention; (2) a transitional period in the late nineteenth and early twentieth centuries characterised by increasing government involvement and regulation, usually with 'welfare' objectives but with some attempts at management of the economy (sometimes with the result of exacerbating the business cycle by meeting depression with government 'economies'); (3) the macro-economic management of the Keynesian era, beginning with the New Deal in the thirties in the United States; (4) a transitional period to the late sixties in which macro-economic management was slowly complemented by micro-economic measures; (5) concern with micro-economic aspects of management: sectoral and regional problems and so on in the seventies.

The changes have had profound political consequences. State paternalism gave way to *laissez-faire* because, as it had operated in the sixteenth and seventeenth centuries, it stood in the way of innovative entrepreneurial behaviour and of the development of a free labour market. The demand of economically powerful new classes for political opportunity saw the introduction of liberal democratic constitutions. In practical policy terms, any theoretical conflict between notions of liberty and equality was resolved by measures to promote equality of opportunity, variously, through extension of the franchise, universal education, and through welfare provisions for those who, through no fault of their own, were unable to compete. Socialist parties, coming to power in the postwar era, did not seriously challenge the capitalist, free-enterprise economic system. Their planning was minimal. In effect, in the postwar period, up to the end of the sixties, the common, and the operationally most significant, feature of economic policies throughout Western Europe, vaguely Keynesian in inspiration, was their concern with demand management. Governments laid heavy emphasis on maintaining a high level of demand in order to achieve the primary policy goal of full employment. Micro-economic targets, for which nationalisation, controls and indicative planning were supposed to be instruments, were specified occasionally – for example, in Britain and France – and were sometimes achieved in absolute terms. But this was not because they achieved their intended place on a scale of defined priorities for economic reconstruction and development. They were encompassed rather within the broad framework of general economic growth within a continuously stimulated free market in which specific targets of regional or sectoral improvement were lost sight of.

The success of this macro-economic approach can be measured by reference to the almost continuous expansion in *per capita* output for nearly thirty years from the end of the war. Everywhere it surpassed what was achieved from 1870 to 1913 and 1918 to 1939.[4] This postwar growth was achieved with only relatively minor interruptions. The words 'depression' and 'slump' were found to be too violent to describe them. The term 'recession' was coined. It connoted some increase in unemployment and a reduced rate of growth, normally induced by government action to check inflation. GNP rarely actually fell. Reflation restored the impetus. Economic management in this vein, far from weakening free enterprise capitalism seemed to have dealt with its one periodic failing – the depression.

By the seventies, however, alarm bells were being rung by many economists, and the term 'stagflation' was used to denote the phenomenon of runaway inflation up to double figures, coupled with continuing or rising unemployment. There are many explanations: wages are 'stickier' because unions are stronger; gearing ratios for financing industry have changed – away from equity and variable-interest sources of investment to fixed high-interest loans and retained profits; raw material prices, though they may fall in some cases with recession, are nevertheless kept generally high by producer agreements like OPEC. Overall, costs are less variable downward, and so, therefore, are manufacturing prices. At the same time, governments have taken the dangerously attractive course, sanctioned by the stimulation to growth it provided, of continually increasing government expenditure through the simple expedient of running a budget deficit. The pressure to spend has been increased by the need to provide compensatory payments through various social security measures to match the effects of inflation on people with fixed incomes, savings, and contractual long-term financial obligations, and the need to deal with increasingly evident sectoral and regional unemployment – pockets of depression amid the general growth.

In effect, the limitations of crudely applied Keynesian policy have become apparent. Keynesian policy applied only to short-term general problems of the economy. It was a macro-strategy providing a general stimulus. It did not obviate the need for policies to deal with specific micro-economic problems. The macro-economic management principle had evidently been too enthusiastically synthesised by economists with the principle of a free market economy in a pluralist society.

The growing concern with micro-economic problems, general by the seventies, has inevitably been accompanied by some revision of attitudes to a question at the heart of political debate – the distribution of the fruits of economic activity – in Laswell's terms, 'who gets what, when, where and how?'. Laswell's formulation, offered as a definition of politics, does allow for consideration of other social values than material goods and services, but the religious conflicts that racked European societies before the nineteenth century, and conflicts over duty, honour and loyalty, have assumed less and less importance in comparison with material values since the industrial revolution. The concept of social justice is now conceived in largely material terms.

What the historical record shows is that questions about the distribution of material goods cannot be considered entirely apart from the economic activity which engenders them, as though they were a kind of consequent but separate ethical problem. Capitalism as an economic system connotes certain assumptions about economic distribution. It assumes that the possession and use of productive resources – land, capital, energy, talents – will bring differential rewards to the degree that they are needed in the market-place. Though all society benefits from the stimulus which economic incentives provide to an expansion of productive activity, any notions of justice in the sense of 'fair shares' or 'equality' are out of place. In terms of social values achieved, 'liberty', loosely conceived, stands higher than 'equality', its historical societal rival. Centrally planned economic systems, on the other hand, have to face directly the ethical aspects of economic distribution as they relate to the governmentally defined overall goals and to ideologically based definitions of the 'common good'. The development of the 'mixed economy' with its element of central planning presents, increasingly, the same ethical problem.

In practice, perhaps needless to say, there never have been 'pure' versions of the two kinds of economic system. Compassion, notions of justice and the pressures of powerful economic interests on government have modified a simple market distribution of resources (though not always in the direction of equality),[5] and in central economic planning in Eastern Europe ideas of distributive justice are muddied in practice by strategic, incentive considerations in the pursuit of immediate economic growth targets. But the development of the mixed economy of the advanced industrial societies and the planning role of the state which it subsumes, brings the rivalry between liberty and equality to the forefront of political dispute. Different, albeit *vaguely* different, attitudes to them divide the political parties of the left and right. And the attempt to reconcile the two principles is the underlying rationale of much of the complicated law, and administrative interpretation of the law, which is the framework for government activity in the economic arena. Thus in a capitalist system, according to its apologists, social security can be provided within the limits set by the need to preserve incentives in the labour market. To eliminate exploitive monopolies, to maintain certain industries in difficulties, or certain kinds of employment, or types of local community which are thought to have social value though they are declining economically, industries can be regulated, or even nationalised, so long as the private sector remains large enough to provide a yardstick for wages, prices and profitable operation. The governments of the advanced industrial societies, however, as well as most economists disagree as to where the critical boundaries lie, and whether alternatively they ought decisively to be crossed and the consequences accepted. In this chapter we shall offer an account of, and profit from, the debate between the leading protagonists of different schools since it provides a searching analysis, not only of the nature of the mixed economy of the advanced industrial societies but of the political problems associated with it.

There are some writers who have argued that the mixed economy *mélange* of the two types of economic system is particularly dangerous and, in the long term, impossible to maintain. Hayek argues, for example, that the move towards central planning supplants competition by a different and irreconcilable principle. He argues that the incremental progress of the democracies towards central direction would result, during its course, in something which in many respects would be even worse than comprehensive central direction: 'a state of affairs which can satisfy neither planners nor liberals: *a sort of syndicalist or "corporative" organization of industry, in which competition is more or less suppressed but planning is left in the hands of the independent monopolies of the separate industries*'.[6] In this situation (essentially 'corporatist' and readily identifiable as the contemporary 'mixed' economy), neither planning nor competition, according to Hayek, can work effectively.

Hayek's critique of central planning extends to the Keynesian demand-management policies which seemed to satisfy for a time so many of the requirements of a conception of market determination of economic activity while avoiding the penalties of cyclical fluctuation. He maintains that inflation can only temporarily absorb unemployment, and it must inevitably make it worse in the long run, since it postpones adjustment to long-term changes in demand patterns. Furthermore, he insists, inflation is an accelerating process which can only end by getting out of hand, destroying the currency and monetary institutions and endangering the stability of society itself. Hayek argues that the alternative to full employment policy is falsely seen to be general unemployment, reminiscent of the Great Depression of the thirties. That was an exceptional state and in such circumstances monetary expansion could, he admits, only be beneficial. However,

Hayek points out: 'It is by no means evident that a policy which will be beneficial in such a state will also always and necessarily be so in the kind of intermediate position in which an economic system finds itself most of the time, when significant unemployment is confined to certain industries, occupations or localities.'[7]

The danger of demand management is that sectional or localised unemployment may well be the last to be stimulated by general increases in the money supply, and if the major inflationary policies which do finally mop up such unemployment are instituted they will hinder a redistribution of labour appropriate to the distribution of demand. Hayek believes that the best inducement to move, for labour, is not the attraction of a higher wage elsewhere, when the money supply and general demand is rising and the worker still has the relative security of his existing job. It is rather the inability to earn the accustomed wages or find any employment in his locality or in his old occupation when the total demand is held more or less constant.

The role of trade unions is also significant when full employment policies are being pursued. 'As soon as government assumes the responsibility to maintain full employment at whatever wages the trade unions succeed in obtaining, they [the trade unions] no longer have any reason to take account of the unemployment their wage demands might have caused.'[8] Nevertheless, the success of any particular union in raising money wage beyond an increase in productivity is opposed to the interests of those seeking employment, who will as a consequence not find it in that industry. In so far as action by powerful unions of the relatively unskilled reduces differentials and otherwise distorts the effect of demand on the remuneration and distribution of labour, the effect must be to 'reduce the productivity of labour all round and, therefore, also the general level of real wages . . . This is certainly true of most countries of Europe, where union policy is strengthened by the general use of restrictive practices of a "make-work character".'[9] Unions in effect 'are using their power in a manner which tends to make the market system ineffective and which, at the same time, gives them a control of the direction of economic activity that would be dangerous in the hands of government but is intolerable if exercised by a particular group. They do so through their influence on the relative wages of different groups of workers and through their constant upward pressure on the level of money wages, with its inevitable inflationary consequence.'[10]

From the vantage point of the seventies, Hayek appears to have been a remarkable prophetical analyst of the effects of Keynesian policies. He provided, it may be conceded, an 'explicit framework of analysis within which the nature of the troubles [of inflation and unemployment] can be explained and a comprehensive approach to them developed'.[11]

Hayek's positive prescription is for a movement away from planning, to establish the conditions for free competition. He rejects the assertion that modern technological progress makes central planning inevitable. He points out that monopolies, against which controls have been argued necessary, are a product of legal protection rather than unrestrained competition, based on questionable presumptions about the virtues of size. For small firms are no less efficient necessarily than large – if anything the opposite.[12] Then, the complexity of modern economic activity, far from recommending planning, makes a synoptic view impossible and recommends the decentralised mutual-adjustment economic decision-making and co-ordination mode that the price mechanism provides. His argument, therefore, is that a 'carefully thought-out legal framework is required',[13] within which competition would be preserved and would work beneficially. Hayek's is not, therefore, a dogmatic *laissez-faire* opposition to all central planning. 'The successful use of competition as the principle of social organisation precludes certain types of coercive interference with economic life, but it admits of others which sometimes may very considerably assist its work, and even requires certain kinds of government action.'[14]

What is precluded is legislation interfering with the free movement of prices and equal entry into trades or professions, and what is required is that the law should not tolerate attempts by individuals or groups to restrict either. The maintenance of competition does not preclude measures which affect all producers equally – for example, to combat pollution, to improve working conditions – 'nor is the preservation of competition incompatible with an extensive system of social services'.[15]

This dismissal of central planning is not merely, or even primarily economic. More important in his own view is Hayek's assertion of the primacy of a threatened liberty over equality and his rejection of any absolute conception of social justice.

Liberty, Hayek believes, is threatened when there is a collective goal which justifies repression of individual autonomous goals. It is threatened when parliaments come to be regarded as 'talking shops', overburdened with the legislation necessary for planning, so that 'the conviction grows that if efficient planning is to be done, the direction must be "taken out of politics" and placed in the hands of experts, permanent officials or independent autonomous bodies'.[16] Liberty is threatened further when the rule of law is eroded by the state's selection of one group rather than another for negotiation and consultation, and then also by its legislating in the interest of a particular identifiable group of specific persons rather than by general legislation whose 'effect on particular ends or particular people cannot be known beforehand'.[17] In sum, 'most planners who have seriously considered the practical aspects of their task have little doubt that a directed economy must be run on more or less dictatorial lines. That the complex system of interrelated activities, if it is to be consciously directed at all, must be directed by a single staff of experts, and that ultimate responsibility must rest in the hands of a commander-in-chief, whose actions must not be fettered by democratic procedure, is too obvious a consequence of underlying ideas of central planning not to command fairly general assent.'[18]

Hayek rejects forcibly the argument that planning and this degree of instrumental control are prerequisites for the achievement of social justice. The chimeric concept of social justice necessarily incorporates some conception of 'desert'. But desert can only be *socially* defined unless some absolute moral standard of deserts is posited. Prevailing morality is unable to define any such standard, but in any case the prior question arises, Hayek argues, as to whether it is moral to subject people to the degree of central direction of their lives that realisation of some concept of deserts would require for its fulfilment. Lamentably, in spite of this, an appeal to 'social justice' is an effective weapon of contemporary political discussion and is 'at present probably the gravest threat to most other values of a free civilisation'.[19] It is 'simply a quasi-religious superstition of the kind which we should respectfully leave in peace so long as it merely makes those happy who hold it, but which we must fight when it becomes the pretext of coercing other men'.[20]

Hayek's insistence that liberty is threatened by central planning is an echo of the view of his fellow-Austrian, L. Von Mises,[21] who sees *laissez-faire* capitalism as the only bulwark against 'the barbarism of Moscow'. It is, in turn, echoed by Milton Friedman[22] who regards competitive capitalism 'as a system of economic freedom and a necessary condition for political freedom', and thinks the notion of democratic socialism is a delusion. Other writers have stressed or echoed Hayek's doubts about the synoptic capacity of human beings to encompass the central planning of the complex economic life of the industrial society, arguing the superiority of a human capacity for mutual adjustment of which the free economic market is an outstanding demonstration.[23]

Counter arguments in favour of the central planning alternative are equally numerous. Leaving aside Marxist-Leninism because of its vision of the eventual withering away of the state, many other writers defend an extension of state central planning as a desirable and necessary path to take away from the ambiguities and allegedly consequent problems of the mixed economy. Oscar Lange, for example, a contemporary of Hayek's, writing when the latter offered some of his first warnings against planning in the mid-thirties, pointed out that the market regulation of investment and of the supply of goods and

services could be matched, to the extent that the sufficing of demand
was the ideal of the planners, by their allocating resources and setting
prices as was necessary to compensate for the readily measurable
building-up or running-down of inventories. Central planners, in
other words, accepting the limits of the human synoptic capacity,
could bring into operation their own automatic regulator.[24] Planners
could raise prices to rebuild inventories or allocate capital resources
as efficiently and in virtually the same manner and with identical
effects on investment as under a market system, if they so chose.[25]
But they had the option, not available to unplanned capitalism, of
putting aside the effective demand criterion to some extent, to set a
higher level of capital accumulation for more rapid growth, or to
provide better welfare services and public utilities than capitalism
could achieve.

More recently, democratic socialists like H. Laski, Anthony
Crosland, Stuart Holland and J. K. Galbraith are among those who
have argued the possibility and desirability of much greater centrally
directed planning and asserted its compatibility with democratic
freedom.

With occasional roots spreading into but not firmly planted in
either libertarian or orthodox socialist criticism of the mixed economy
is a mixture of criticisms of the mixed economy from the 'New Left'.
Among the salient elements of these is the rejection of the market
mechanism for its inefficiency and its lack of concern for social justice
and environmental quality, with, at the same time, a distaste for the
massive bureaucracy which is a necessary instrument of central planning. The preferred alternative is a decentralised political decision-
making and economic system. Small producer co-operatives would
constitute the basic unit of economic enterprise, within local com-
munities, locally governed.

Another New Left criticism is the assertion that the advanced
societies are indulging in overconsumption, dangerously depleting
resources for which no obvious replacement exists and at the same
time creating environmental hazards of pollution and waste. It is also
argued that private consumption (of commodities) is too high relative
to public consumption. Private consumption, furthermore, does not
represent a true element of choice, as the libertarians argue, but is
manipulated through advertising so that demand responds to production and not vice versa.[26] Higher *public* consumption, it is argued,
might achieve general aims of social justice in spending to alleviate
poverty, poor housing and policing, shortcomings in the school system,
transportation, health and recreation services. Many of these criticisms have some basis but, together, they do not as yet, coming as they
do from such a variety of New Left sources, constitute a coherent
critique and alternative to the mixed economy. Thus the New Left

ideal of decentralised economy of producer co-operatives seems to imply, in spite of the intention to avoid it, the overall working of the market as regulator and as incentive to quality, cost-efficiency and innovation, and as tacit co-ordinator of local activity, since it is inconceivable that a pattern of local self-sufficiency could be maintained throughout the densely populated advanced industrial societies. The only alternative to the market as regulator of such a system is the central bureaucracy, for which there is an almost equal distaste. A possible escape from the horns of this dilemma, the market socialism of Lange, has not attracted the attention of New Left thinkers. Instead, as Lindbeck has pointed out, 'it is safe to say that the Marxist influence in the New Left has increased in recent years . . . If this trend continues, the intellectual distance between the revolutionary old Left and the New Left may diminish substantially.'[27]

On neither side of this divide, however, does it appear to have been found possible to demonstrate empirically the validity of much of the indictment of the mixed economy. In spite of Friedmann's unsupported assertion that 'historical evidence speaks with a single voice on the relation between political freedom and a free market',[28] we do not know, nor is it obvious, that a market-based socialism after Lange's conception would involve the impairment of 'freedom' characteristic of the centrally planned economies of Eastern Europe.[29] It is not clear that either fullscale *laissez-faire* competition, preserved, if that were possible, against monopoly by legislation, would ensure more rapid growth (assuming that that is the general interest), or that central direction would do so, since the existing socialist bureaucratic states, responding to economic discontents and to bottlenecks, breakdowns and other productivity problems, have been experimenting (*à la* Liberman and, until the 1968 invasion of Czechoslovakia, *à la* Ota Sik) with decentralisation of the planning apparatus and with greater use of the market mechanism as a regulatory agent, while the capitalist states move from the opposite direction towards the same middle ground.

Both extremes of criticism of the mixed economy are themselves subject to a further criticism. While they offer relatively simple and attractively clear theoretical alternatives to the mixed economy, without the latter's confusion of opposed principles, they assume, unwarrantably, that because the principles are in theoretical opposition they are incompatible in practice. They assume further that the faults and weakness of the mixed economy can be put down to that presumed incompatibility, rather than to problems which are not directly of systemic origin at all – for example, oil producer pricing or the advance of science and technology. This latter is by no means an exclusive product of the mixed economy, but one which subjects all societies to constant shock, necessitating continuous major adjustment.

Then, the theory of drift towards socialism, common to both critiques, though differently evaluated, must also be treated with scepticism. Human behaviour, whether individual or social, is characterised by inconsistency, and by simultaneous adherence to contradictory and incompatible principles. This is normality. Consistency in extra-ordinary.

If this is, in a limited sense, a defence of the contemporary position between capitalism and socialism, denying the inevitability of its imminent collapse, questioning the desirability of deliberately bringing about its demise through political action, it is not a denial of the value of the libertarian or socialist critique. From these sources, it may be argued, has come some of the most penetrating theoretical analysis of the actual contemporary system. Without it, as Lowe has pointed out, we have a prevailing economic theory, the contemporary orthodox neo-classical economics, but it refers to conditions where there is automatic regulation and so no need of guidance.[30] It does not refer to the real world. Even of one of the works of the notable Paul Samuelson it has been said, 'A careful examination of the papers both on theory and on policy yields only the most oblique suggestion that neoclassical price theory is descriptive of the real world. Of course, there is no denial, but Samuelson's attitude is clearly guarded and agnostic.'[31] Not all economists are as careful as Samuelson in this respect, but it is in general true that 'one of the most unfortunate tendencies in the teaching of economics, particularly in Britain, is that of making a clear split between economic theory and applied economics. All too often economic theory is taught merely as logical analysis, and is, at best, only vaguely related to the world, while applied economics becomes description unenlightened by any theoretical framework.'[32]

The writer who, following Hayek, has made the most ambitious attempt to break free from the confines of neo-Marxist and neo-classical analysis in assessing the contemporary economic system of the advanced societies is J. K. Galbraith. His critique of the mixed economy could, particularly in his earlier books, *American Capitalism, The Affluent Society* and, to a lesser extent, *The New Industrial State*, just barely be regarded as a defence, but he does argue for important modifications in the direction of a 'New Socialism' in *Economics and the Public Purpose*. Developed, then, over a number of important works, much criticised by neo-classicists,[33] his thesis is that in the modern economy, two systems exist side by side. The first, the 'planning system', consists of the very large corporations which can seek, feasibly, to control their environment, by persuading consumers as to products, and the state as to products and needs, by contracting with suppliers of their raw materials or other requirements, or expanding vertically to control them directly. The second system,

'the market system', exists where large-scale organisation is inapplic-
able or ineffective – the area of the small firm: garages, restaurants,
small shops, builders, small manufacturing firms, farmers etc. In
general, in the market system, firms try to maximise profits as neo-
classical analysis suggests; but in the planning system the primary
aim is growth, since control of the environment is served by the
growth of the enterprise, even beyond the level of technical operating
efficiency, enhancing 'power over prices, costs, consumers, suppliers,
the community and the state', enhancing thereby the long-term
survival prospects of the firm and also rewarding in a personal way
the technical-managerial elite – the 'technostructure'. Profits are not
irrelevant, but they are seen over a very long time scale. Within the
'planning system' 'industries control prices in response to protective
need – in response to the heavy capital investment, long-term horizons
. . . and higher proportion of overhead costs . . . These firms set
prices with a view to expanding sales – to growth . . . the antithesis
of monopoly pricing . . . The neo-classical model describes an
ill that does not exist because it assumes a purpose that is not
pursued.'[34]

Though the classical economist's model of perfect competition was
modified to take account of the actual development of monopoly and
oligopoly and it was recognised that suppliers could determine prices,
it was still assumed that they did so in order to maximise profit, and
that they were subject in doing so to consumer preferences, elasticities
and inelasticity. The consumer was still king and the firm was also
assumed to be subordinate to the state. The state in turn was assumed
to be primarily responsive to the needs of the public as a whole and
not primarily to the big firms and unions. Neo-classical economics is,
therefore, hostile to tariffs, price supports and anything which supports monopolies. It favours anti-trust legislation. It readily adapted
itself, we have pointed out, to the Keynesian concept of demand
management policy. The market mechanism was still regarded as the
efficient regulator and co-ordinator of the economic system. In
Galbraith's analysis, however, the 'planning system' exists in the
closest association with the state. The state is a major procurer of the
products of the planning system: for example, of atomic energy and
its application, modern air transport, modern electronics, computers.
It provides the educated, qualified manpower. It provides the necessary supplementary investment: highways, postal services, telex,
public transport for workers. Its military expenditure is a major
stimulus to technological innovation in the 'new technology' industries.
It supplies capital, including government plant and equipment, progress payments as working capital, and loans. Finally, its bureaucracy
identifies with the interests of the firms in the planning sector. It
does so, increasingly, at the expense of the public 'welfare' sector and

the market sector, which is relatively neglected in government expenditure.

The relationship of the planning sector to the government bureaucracy is an important aspect of Galbraith's thesis. 'Public regulatory bodies tend to become the captives of the firms that ostensibly they regulate.'[35] Parliamentarians, losing power generally, chose 'to become allies of the public bureaucracy . . . the spectacularly successful choice of the Armed Services and Appropriations Committees [of the United States]. They derive power in Congress, patronage, public construction and weapons contracts for their constituencies . . .'[36] The bureaucratic relationship with the technostructure (or technical-managerial elite) is summed up as 'symbiotic'.[37] The mode is, in other words, corporatist.

The attempt by the large corporations to control their environment extends to the international arena. 'The function of the multinational corporation is . . . the accommodation of the technostructure to the peculiar uncertainties of international trade.'[38] It does internationally what it does in the domestic environment: controlling prices, contracting with suppliers, establishing relations with the government bureaucracies. There is the additional advantage that foreign competition in the international market which might benefit from lower costs can be met in most cases (the Japanese market is an exception) by producing internationally where the costs are lowest.[39]

In the absence of the free market price regulator and co-ordinator of economic activity there is, in the planning system, an efficient co-ordinating mechanism within a product field. It is the pattern of contracting and subcontracting – a 'vast web' – which 'goes far to solve . . . the problem of vertical co-ordination'.[40] This is Galbraith's answer to the criticism that 'no satisfactory explanation relating the plans of one firm to those of others is forthcoming'[41] in his analysis. There remains a problem of end-product co-ordination, for which no efficient mechanism, according to Galbraith, exists. 'The modern planning system is, in fact, plagued by such problems of co-ordination.'[42]

Problems also arise in the planning system because there is no mechanism to equate saving and investment. Excess saving represents a falling off in demand, which may well lead to unemployment and a reduction of output, though not of prices and wages. The fall in demand reduces investment. The effect is worst on the market system. There, incomes do fall with falling demand though the small entrepreneur goes on working.

In his earlier work, Galbraith had seen the trade unions as a countervailing power to the corporations, tending to harmonise their effects with the public interest. But he now finds in the contemporary industrial society the goals of the unions are consonant with those of the corporations and there has been an easing of the conflict between them. The exploitation of workers occurs in the market system. 'In the planning system, workers are defended by the unions and the state and favoured by the market power of the employing corporation which allows it to pass the cost of wage settlements along to the public . . . [consequently] the American trade unionist disavows socialism. His European counterpart hears it advocated, applauds, but wants no action.'[43] In conditions of reduced demand, then, union action to increase wages continues in the planning sector, the costs being passed on in increased prices. If steps are taken to reduce inflation by further reducing demand – raising interest rates, restricting lending etc. – this, again, hits the public sector, particularly local government, and the small entrepreneur in the market system both of whom do borrow. It does not hit the corporations which finance investment from their own resources and profits. The economy therefore is continuously distorted in favour of the great corporation (the planning system) and affected by its wages and prices spiral. The effect is to make only one apparent course open to government – namely, wage and price control,[44] (though this technique, Galbraith notes dryly, tends to be abandoned, under pressure from the planning system, as soon as it starts to work).

It is the distortion of the economy in the direction of the planning sector, taking into account the basic problems of the lack of end-product co-ordination, instability of savings and investment, and cumulative inflationary tendencies that lead Galbraith to the advocacy of what he calls the 'New Socialism'. It is also the extent to which the interests of the planning system, though 'by some miracle of accident or design'[45] they may be the same as those of the public, are 'in the absence of such miracle or arrangement' different from the public interest. The interest of the planning system does differ from that of the public in its tendency to promote an imbalance of government spending in defence, space research, highways and other planning system directions, rather than welfare, the arts, environmental improvement, recreation and weaker parts of the economy, like the railways. This reflects the power of the planning system over the state.[46] The same power is also reflected in the way in which, unhampered until very recently, certain costs of production in the planning sector are passed on to the community as air, land and water pollution and aesthetic degradation of the environment.

Galbraith's proposals for modifying the system in order to meet these problems take the form of what he calls 'A General Theory of Reform'. An important part of the 'theory' is the argument for the emancipation of the state. While the symbiotic relationship between public bureaucracy and technostructure exists there is little point in considering such solutions as public ownership of the great corporations. 'Before the state can regulate in the planning system, it . . .

must be broken free from the power of the planning system.'[47] Galbraith sees the legislature as the primary instrument of this emancipation. Though to some extent already much influenced by the planning system, its members 'are open to countering persuasion – and the people who elect them are subject to the pressure of circumstances hostile to the persuasion of the planning system . . . So, as viewed by the planning system the legislator is not reliable.'[48] Galbraith's specific proposals for strengthening the legislature relate primarily to the Congress of the United States. He points out, for example, that the seniority system and the specialist committee system operate at the moment to produce long-term unwarrantably friendly relations with the corporations which could be prevented if committee assignments and chairmanships were rotated. He discounts the alleged importance of the 'experience' of the long-term committee member.[49] The basic argument, however, is capable of more general application. Legislatures should be strengthened, made more independent of the bureaucracy and the technostructure and members should be dependent on electoral processes in which the presumption is much more against re-election than in favour of it. This will 'greatly enhance the likelihood that legislators will reflect contemporary public attitudes'.[50] Galbraith's thesis reflects an unusual conception of the potential relationship between constitutional rules and political and economic behaviour.

Emancipated through legislative and other constitutional reforms, what direction does Galbraith believe the state should take in its assumption of control of the economic system? The 'New Socialism' he insists is not ideological; 'it is compelled by circumstance'. Specifically, because the 'market system' is weak, it must be strengthened, if necessary by public ownership, for 'there are industries here which require technical competence, related organisation and market power and related command over resource use if they are to render minimally adequate service'.[51] Galbraith singles out here the housing construction industry and medical and hospital care, but he admits 'a presumption in favour of public intervention anywhere in the market system'.[52] The case for public ownership accompanied by wage and price control, following emancipation of the state, is also strong in the commanding heights of the 'planning system', where the change would be one 'of form rather than substance'. Galbraith argues, 'The case for socialism is imperative in the weakest areas of the economy. It is also paradoxically compelling in the parts of exceptional strength. It is here the answer, or part of the answer, lies to the power of the planning system that derives from bureaucratic symbiosis . . . For unduly weak industries and unduly strong ones – as a remedy for an area of gross underdevelopment and as a control on gross overdevelopment – the word "socialism" is one we can no longer suppress.'[53]

It cannot really be claimed that Galbraith's proposals for reform comprise a coherent, unambiguous programme. But any straight-forward and neatly consistent set of solutions would be suspect in view of the enormous diversity and complexity of the problems. Galbraith, however, in spite of his critics, does offer some provoca-tively vague pointers towards reform, and they do arise out of a coherent description of contemporary economic activity. The descrip-tion is offered at such a high level of generalisation that there is little difficulty in finding apparent examples of major exceptions to the behaviour he describes, but there is, equally, little difficulty about recognising the main features of the economic landscape as he paints it.

The American, Dutch, West German, French, British and Japanese economies all exhibit their well-developed planning sectors as well as the residual market sector. Their great corporations seek, with con-siderable success, to control their environment. Since this environment does vary somewhat from society to society, strategies vary, and governments are more or less 'emancipated' and in a position to exercise control.

In Britain, the ideological and attitudinal climate is least favourable, it may be argued, to a really forceful governmental control over the planning system. Government-directed enterprise is probably larger *in toto* in Britain than among the others, but it is, on balance, the least 'managed' of the states mentioned. Shonfield has explained this by reference to British traditions. They have resulted in 'the accept-ance of a slower rate of technical progress than in those countries which were not trammelled by inhibitions on the use of public power in the private sector'. Industry has a stronger tradition of self-reliance and independence from the state and from financial institutions. In industrial relations, too, Britain has been the unpaternal state. The trade union tradition has been, equally, outside the framework of law.[54]

Industry has not responded to the appeals of, and incentives offered by, successive governments to invest. The trade unions for their part have defied attempts to provide a legal framework for industrial relations. Instead, through 'concertation', disjointed sectoral bargained planning has eventuated, in which, as Shonfield points out, the 'new corporatist organisations bypass the ordinary democratic process – neither throwing their own deliberations open to the public nor sub-jecting the bargains . . . to regular parliamentary scrutiny'. It is assumed indeed that 'agreed action by communal organisations them-selves is to be preferred to the exercise of governmental power. The Government's role is essentially that of a long-stop'.[55] As a result, in the sixties and seventies planning in Britain has been less successful than elsewhere. Great corporations like Rolls Royce, British Leyland

and Chrysler have collapsed, or would have collapsed, without last-ditch government rescue operations.

In France, in some contrast, 'a set of institutions which were largely pre-capitalist in design', Shonfield has argued, 'could be adapted more readily than others to serve the purposes of the new capitalism with its large built-in segment of public power in the second half of the twentieth century'.[56] French economic planning has been based on the use of government contracts, tax and financial concessions to influence business choices. Over 50 per cent of capital investment can be influenced by government, and this power has been used forcefully. The state has also pushed large firms into each other's arms to create companies of international size and to push out foreign competition. Trade unions are not as well integrated in the planning system as elsewhere, but they are relatively weak and the *patronat* has manifold and influential links with government. It may be a consequence that output per man hour in manufacturing, hourly earnings and wage costs per unit have improved since 1963 more than in the UK or Germany.

In Germany the involvement of the state and the development of the 'planning system' was given a fillip by reconstruction after the war. Government policy was to encourage the free market economy but to protect it against economic crises and inhibit cartelisation. Large state-owned enterprises like Volkswagen were in part de-nationalised by sale of shares to the public, but tax reduction and investment privileges encouraged economic expansion to the point where West Germany became the third largest industrial country until overtaken by Japan in 1968. Industry, in spite of decartelisation, is concentrated. About 30 per cent of economic activity is publicly owned and managed. Three per cent of all taxpayers own 42 per cent of taxable wealth. There are many small firms in the sizeable market system, but 1 per cent of firms produce 40 per cent of the total industrial turnover. Their strong position affects small business. Their prosperity and expansion is necessary to the state itself. 'Large industrial concerns in the Federal Republic are not only able to make the most profits and to control the market, but they also have a sort of guarantee . . . since the state is forced to preserve these concerns in the interest of full employment.'[57]

Within the planning system the banks, particularly the big three, are a key factor. They have an important influence on the non-banking sector, partly through direct holding of shares and partly through the exercise of small shareholders' proxies. A 1964 inquiry showed that at the average company meeting the banks represented over 50 per cent of the voting capital present – 9 per cent directly owned, 41 per cent in the form of proxies. The banks are also widely represented in seats on the supervisory boards of major companies, quite frequently as chairman of the board.[58]

Note should be taken also of the role of the Federation of German Industry, particularly its leading elements (*Spitzenverbände*) within the economic system. Their role, added to that of the banks, helps produce what has been called 'the characteristic flavour of collective purpose in German industry'. They are represented with major interest groups on the Standing Advisory Councils (*Beirat*) set up by ministries for each of their main activities. The pattern is distinctly corporatist. 'The officials in Bonn seem often to regard the *Beirat* not as an instrument for outside intervention in departmental business, but rather as providing them with an umbrella under which they are able to shelter in their dealings with parliament . . . all that seems to be missing in order to bring these disparate pieces of an embryonic planning exercise together into a working system is a plan.'[59]

A similar flavour of collective purpose is evident in Japan. It is given shape in government plans for the private sector. The main sanction for these is a moral and psychological one. Private corporation planners ensure the predictability of their economic environment by using, quite voluntarily, the state Economic Planning Agency projections as the basis for their own planning. They preserve a close liaison with the agency. They send their employees on secondment to it to train at their expense. Committees of government and industry, something like the French Commissions, are consultative pre-plan mechanisms. Their use is pervasive in all sectors of industry. Not too surprisingly, Japanese planning is essentially formulated to maximise private gain.

In Holland, governmental influence is sanctioned not only by consensus but by the ultimate threat of price control. Industry is highly concentrated. Royal Dutch Shell, Phillips and Unilever employ 12 per cent of the work force and exercise a dominant influence in the economy. Enterprises of 1,000 employees or more employ 40 per cent of the work force. Government itself had already before the Second World War acquired the railways and mines. It has a controlling interest in KLM and the exploitation of natural gas. It also runs the public utilities and the ports. The coalition of religious and liberal parties which dominated politics until the seventies was averse to extending the scope of public ownership but it was forced by economic circumstances and business influence to guarantee, subsidise, make allowances for investment and help areas of regional large-scale unemployment. The Social and Economic Council on which are represented government, employers and unions plays an important consensual role in economic matters, contributing to the high level of integration of unions, evidenced in the infrequency of strikes. Price control, imposed notably after 1969 to combat strong inflationary pressures, is used more readily in Holland than in most other advanced capitalist societies. It is advanced as a threat to stiffen the resistance of firms to wage demands. Nevertheless, predictability within the planning system depends largely on consensus, arrived at with little apparent difficulty in a small country where close, almost intimate, relationships between government departments and the major firms in which industrial activity is concentrated, are relatively easy to achieve.

Variations upon this Galbraithian theme could be played by reference to other advanced societies in Western Europe, vindicating his very general and impressionistic, common-sense assault on yesterday's logically elegant economics. In fact, the difference between these societies is one merely of degree. The analyses of Hayek and Galbraith, in basic agreement in spite of their very different prescriptions for reform, apply to them all. And it is the mixed economy which they describe, and the planning problems which they identify which have provided the main stimulus to the growth of societal corporatism. In particular, the increasingly apparent need to plan sectorally rather than simply manipulate overall demand, has led to the creation of the complex of government and interest group institutionalised consultation which so easily acquires corporatist character. To this consultation process, or 'concertation', we turn, specifically, in the next chapter.

NOTES

1 Lionel Tiger and Robin Fox, *The Imperial Animal* (St Albans: Paladin, 1974), p. 155.
2 ibid.
3 Richard G. Wilkinson, *Poverty and Progress* (London: Methuen, 1973), p. 90.
4 See M. M. Postan, *An Economic History of Western Europe 1954–1964* (London: Methuen, 1967), pp. 16–17.
5 See David Miller, *Social Justice* (Oxford: Clarendon Press, 1976), Part 3.
6 See F. A. Hayek, *The Road to Serfdom* (London: Routledge & Kegan Paul, 1944), p. 30 (my italics). (Hayek here is very close to Galbraith.)
7 See F. A. Hayek, *A Tiger by the Tail* (London: IEA, 1972), p. 55.
8 See F. A. Hayek, *Full Employment At Any Price?* (London: Institute of Economic Affairs, 1975), Occasional Paper No. 45, p. 23.
9 *A Tiger by the Tail*, p. 72.
10 ibid., p. 73.
11 *The Times*, 4 January 1975, cited in Hayek, *Full Employment At Any Price?*, Preface by Arthur Seldon, p. 8.
12 There is impressive empirical evidence on European firms in support of this. See Alexis P. Jacquemin and Henry W. de Jong, *European Industrial Organisation* (London: Macmillan, 1977). pp. 149–56.
13 *The Road to Serfdom*, p. 27.

14   ibid., p. 27.
15   ibid., p. 28.
16   ibid., p. 46.
17   ibid., p. 57.
18   ibid., p. 66.
19   F. A. Hayek, *Law, Legalisation, and Liberty* (London: Routledge & Kegan Paul, 1973–6), pp. 66–7.
20   ibid., p. 66.
21   See his *The Anti-Capitalist Mentality* (Princeton: Princeton University Press, 1956), p. 112.
22   *Capitalism and Freedom* (Chicago: University of Chicago Press, 1962), pp. 4 and 8.
23   C. E. Lindblom, *The Intelligence of Democracy* (New York: Free Press, 1965).
24   Oscar Lange, *On the Economic Theory of Socialism* (University of Minnesota, 1938) reprinted in Oscar Lange and Fred M. Taylor *On the Economic Theory* of Socialism ed. E. Lippincott (McGraw Hill, 1964), pp. 57–142.
25   The problem with this solution is that unless there are alternative suppliers of the same product, producers can lower the quality of their product at its centrally set price, negating the effect of the reduction. See Assar Lindbeck, *The Political Economy of the New Left* (New York: Harper & Row, 1971), pp. 50–1.
26   As Galbraith makes the same point, 'When houses and health care are unavailable and male deodorants are abundant, the notion of a benign response to public wants begins to buckle under the strain': *Economics and the Public Purpose* (Harmondsworth: Pelican Books, 1975), p. 25.
27   Lindbeck, op. cit., p. 92.
28   op. cit., p. 9.
29   As Lindbeck has pointed out *vis-à-vis nationalisation* of capital, 'In all communist dictatorships today, dictatorship came first and nationalisation afterward': op. cit., p. 64.
30   Adolph Lowe, *On Economic Knowledge: Towards a Science of Political Economics* (New York: Harper & Row, 1965), p. 98.
31   Kenneth Arrow, *Journal of Political Economy*, 1967, cited by Heilbroner, op. cit., p. 120.
32   R. G. Lipsey, *An Introduction to Positive Economics* (London: Weidenfeld & Nicolson, 2nd edn, 1966), p. xiv.
33   The impact of Galbraith can readily be appreciated by an examination of the reaction of Milton Friedmann to his work in *From Galbraith to Economic Freedom*, IEA Occasional Paper 48 (1977). I would count myself among the admirers of Professor Friedmann but this essay contains not one single argument that really negates the thesis in *Economics and the Public Purpose*, written in 1973, and published the following year. Friedmann begins his attack by quoting Adam Smith, in an expression of opinion, not a reasoned argument, excusable in itself as a literary flourish but the first of a number of what, in the list of logical fallacies, are ordinarily termed 'arguments from authority'. He goes on to say that the theme of private affluence versus public squalor due to government financial neglect of the public sector is 'an absurd claim. Anybody who studies the statistics knows that government spending has grown apace.' (Galbraith's argument is not that government spending has not grown but that it serves the purposes of the planning system rather than welfare and the market system where it is needed.) Friedmann goes on to argue that it is a mistake to suppose

that big business and big labour are always on different sides (p. 16)–as though Galbraith still held to a simple 'countervailing power' thesis, when he says specifically, 'The affirmative goals of the technostructure have become consonant with those of the union' and 'the conflict between labour and capital has been greatly eased' (p. 177). 'A high rate of growth, which means steady employment, extensive access to overtime, perhaps even promotion, rewards the working force as well as the technostructure' (pp. 177–8). Sharpe had pointed out in 1973 that the 'countervailing' argument was rapidly dropped. Then, in yet another argument, on Galbraith's assertion that the defence industry is a prime example of one that seeks to control its own destiny by its relationship with government (the main client for its products) Friedmann refers to a study by Demetz on the real return from investment in defence industry stocks as against 'the average of all other stocks' (p. 22), finding that the former is more variable from year to year. Friedmann's argument implies that comparative stock market value trends are a reliable indicator of successful relationship with government (ignoring such factors as a firm's own major policy decisions) and misrepresents Demetz who did not compare all other stocks but 'randomly selected portfolios of 13 stocks per portfolio' (selected quotations from Demetz printed on p. 25 of Friedmann). Friedmann's essay is a useful account and example of the responses of many other neo-classists to Galbraith.

34 Galbraith, op. cit., p. 136.
35 ibid., p. 176.
36 ibid., p. 177.
37 ibid., p. 62.
38 ibid., pp. 182–3.
39 ibid., see pp. 184–6.
40 ibid., p. 143.
41 M. E. Sharpe, *John Kenneth Galbraith and the Lower Economics* (London: Macmillan, 1973), p. 45.
42 op. cit., p. 144.
43 ibid., p. 294.
44 See ibid., pp. 195–214.
45 ibid., p. 19.
46 ibid., pp. 216–17.
47 ibid., p. 236.
48 ibid., p. 265.
49 ibid., p. 268.
50 ibid., p. 267.
51 ibid., p. 295.
52 ibid., p. 300.
53 ibid., pp. 301–3.
54 A. Shonfield, *Modern Capitalism* (Oxford: OUP 1965): see especially pp. 160–6.
55 ibid., pp. 162–3.
56 ibid., p. 387.
57 See ibid., especially pp. 239–97.
58 See G. Denton et al., *Economic Planning and Policies in Britain, France and Germany* (London: Allen & Unwin, 1968), pp. 69–70.
59 Shonfield, op. cit., p. 263. Shonfield notes that 'One official explained to me that he had deliberately avoided establishing a *Beirat* in his sphere of activity, because he was dealing with problems which required the exercise of administrative initiative in the public interest'! (pp. 263–4).

5

'Pluralism' and 'Concertation'

The basic argument of this chapter is that 'concertation', or institutionalised consultation between interest organisations and government, brings the 'pluralist' society somewhat closer to corporatism, and into potential conflict with behavioural standards which are fundamental to the ideal of representative democratic government.

The classical formulations of the ideal of representative and democratic government postulate, in one form or another, the need to achieve some expression of the common interests of individuals. In Rousseau's conception, the common interest, or general will, could only properly be represented by itself. It ought to come from all and be applied to all. In practice, he recognised this meant majority rule. The social contract, which brought the state into being, needed unanimous consent, but 'apart from this primitive contract, the vote of the majority always binds all the rest'.[1] This might not achieve a perfect expression of the general will but, except where the citizens were truly virtuous, nothing less was acceptable. Certainly, no partial associations should be formed in the state to promote their partial interest.

In James Mill's and Bentham's models of representative government the community interest does not have the almost mystical corporate quality of the 'general will', being simply an aggregate of the diverse interests of individuals, the majority determining the rest. Bentham does not specifically forbid 'partial associations' but he is adamant that 'No member of this House [the legislature, in this case the House of Commons, which was to be the supreme legislative authority] can, otherwise than by a notorious fiction, be styled a representative of any part of the people, other than of the part composed of such individuals as have, or might have, voted on his election. And that, by the general appellation of representatives of the people, is, and ought to be understood, representatives of the whole body of the people.'[2]

Madison is so determinedly opposed to partial associations or 'factions' that he cannot accept the majoritarian compromise without severe qualification. He defines a faction as 'a number of citizens, whether amounting to a majority or a minority of the whole, who are united and actuated by some common impulse of passion, or of interest, adverse to the rights of other citizens, or to the permanent and aggregate interests of the community'.[3] He recognises that they are inherent in a free society and that they cannot be eliminated. As a defence against their tyranny, therefore, he proposes constitutional checks and balances, to control the violence of factions.

All the democracies have, in practice, fallen short of the ideal of the theorists. All have developed parties and interest groupings which, though they may individually profess the common good, may be perceived as factions in the Madisonian sense, or 'partial associations'. Madison's checks and balances, embodied in the American constitution, have, ironically, provided an especially favourable environment for the development of powerful 'lobbies'. Working outside the formal constitutional provision for the expression of the citizen's interest through elections and the legislative assembly, they are at first sight even more at odds with the classical ideal than parties. Yet, it has been asserted, in all advanced democratic societies they 'are a far more important channel of communication than parties for the transmission of political ideas from the mass of citizenry to their rulers'.[4]

This development has its eloquent apologists. They are of two kinds. Arthur Bentley in *The Process of Government* (1949), Earl Latham in his article 'The group basis of politics' (*American Political Science Review*, 1952), David Truman in his article 'The American system in crisis' (*Political Science Quarterly*, 1959) (though not in his earlier *Governmental Process*), William Kornhauser in *The Politics of Mass Society* (1959), Robert Dahl in *Who Governs?* (1961), Giovanni Sartori in his *Democratic Theory* (1965) all propound an essentially elitist theory of democracy. It is a theory of group activity and competition in which a low level of participation by group members is seen as a positive advantage. 'Democracy is terribly difficult. It is so difficult that only expert and accountable elites can save it from the excesses of perfectionism, from the vortex of democracy.'[5] This theory of democratic elitism claims, tortuously, a classical heritage going back to Madison's distrust of majority tyranny and his recognition of the existence of factions.[6]

Elitist theory is democratic in the sense that there is elite competition, a competition that takes place within and between organisations. With the essential electoral mechanism the ordinary citizen has a choice between elites.

This conception, however, has not been easily accommodated within the framework of British liberal democratic theory which regards citizen participation as an important and desirable element. John Stuart Mill, Sir Ernest Barker, A. D. Lindsay, G. H. Cole, Harold Laski all stressed its vital place, not only to secure governmental responsibility, but because political activity was an aspect of man's intellectual and moral development.[7]

In this tradition Hobhouse, who recognised group activity as a fact of political life, welcomed it as something which could serve to increase the potential for active citizenship. 'The individual voter feels himself lost among the millions. He is imperfectly acquainted with the devious issues and large problems of the day, and is sensible how little his solitary vote can affect their decisions. What he needs to give him support and direction is organisation with his neighbours and fellow workers. He can understand, for example, the affairs of his trade union . . . Responsibility comes home to him, and to bring home responsibility is the problem of all government. The development of social interest – and that is democracy – depends not only on adult suffrage and the supremacy of the elected legislature, but on all the intermediate organisations which link the individual to the whole.'[8]

H. R. G. Greaves was expounding the same view in 1958 (*The Foundations of Political Theory*), Graeme Duncan and Steven Lukes in 1963 (*Political Studies*). In the United States versions of the same argument are offered by Roland Pennock (1962) in *Democracy Today*,[9] and by Bachrach and Baratz in 1962,[10] Bachrach in 1967 (*Theory of Democratic Elitism, a Critique*), Amitai Etzioni in *The Active Society* (1968) and, in a modified form, by George Beam, *Usual Politics* (1970), and finally by Dennis F. Thompson in *The Democratic Citizen* (1970).

Most recently, in Britain, Carole Pateman in *Participation and Democratic Theory* (1970) defends the concept of the participatory democracy vigorously and effectively.

It seems, in fact, that it is the participatory apologia which has gained ground in the past ten years, perhaps because of the evident collapse of the real or imagined, vaunted and deplored 'one-dimensional society', characterised by a consensus of tyrannical scale. And the academic reflects a wider sentiment. 'Participation', as Carole Pateman points out, has become an important word in the popular political vocabulary of the western democracies.[11]

It was taken up in France after 1968. It is the principle, in the UK, underlying the Bullock Report (both in the majority and even more, perhaps, in the dissenting minority view); the American anti-poverty programme stresses its importance. The ideal of the participatory pluralist society in one which is, then, distinguished by a more involved citizenry, active in politics not merely at infrequent parliamentary elections but through membership of political parties and of a variety of groups. Groups (and here there is common ground with democratic elitism), though they do not seek to capture government, are actively involved in the formulation of policy through lobbying. To the objection that a group which lobbies government is seeking to satisfy its narrow particular interest and not that of the community as a whole, there is the answer that competing, and therefore, countervailing interests make themselves felt. Policy, therefore, is influenced by direct communication between government and a variety of affected interests, and so is likely more faithfully to reflect a true 'community' interest. The apologia recognises that, in practice, pressure politics takes a variety of forms, ranging from the spontaneous demonstration to the highly organised group effort to influence government policy at every possible pressure point in the formulation process. The character of the group helps to explain differences in this activity between groups. Between countries, differences are explicable in terms of the avenues of access which are available and the differences in the focus of decision-making power.

Almond and Powell have offered a simple but comprehensive typology of pressure politics: anomic activity, non-associational, institutional and associational.

The 'anomic' category refers to 'more or less spontaneous penetrations into the political system from the society such as riots, demonstrations, assassinations, and the like'.[12] It may be set off by an incident or by an inflammatory speech, or an explicitly organised group may engineer the reactions.

'Non-associational' interests refer to kinship groups, ethnic and regional interest groupings and other identifiable but unorganised groups. Typically, their activity is sporadic and expressed either by informal delegations or, occasionally, by anomic activity. However, 'important non-associational groups with continuing interests soon develop organised structures',[13] and thereby assume a different character.

'Institutional' interests are those of the members of formal organisations with designated political or social functions other than the articulation of the interests of their members. Legislatures, bureaucracies, the churches, the great industrial corporations, the army, are institutions which create a professional corps with their own specific interests different in some cases from those of the institution. The organisational structure of the latter may provide a vehicle for the expression of the group interest.

'Associational' interest groups are the specialised structures for interest articulation: trade unions, employers' federations, ethnic organisations, civic groups. The *raison d'être* of the association may not be exclusively political but it can adapt itself to the task of reaching compromises among its members which can be expressed as policy goals. This category has the superior competitive position. The role of such associations is perceived as legitimate to a greater degree than the 'institutional' interest grouping. They tend to employ full-time professional staff for their specialist activity. Otherwise their

influence depends on the size of membership, its potential for mobilisation for action, including voting discipline, the resources of the
members, and their perceived 'respectability'. Another important
factor determining effectiveness is the autonomy of the organisation
in relation to other institutions. The autonomy of a trade union, for
example, may be prejudiced by religious, ethnic and ideological associations with a church, ethnic association or political party, the actual
basis of associational interest being subordinated occasionally to the
needs of the dominant institution. Such linkages may also fragment
the expression of an interest, weakening it.

Superior numbers, or intensity of commitment, or single-minded-
ness rather than divided loyalties, are not, however, at odds with
realistic expectations about a working democracy, and these four
types of pressure politics, though they may offend the classic conception of the democratic process, may be, and generally are, perceived
in contemporary political theory as practical necessities. Rather
crudely in the case of what Almond and Powell call 'anomic' activity,
but with increasing precision in the best financed and organised
associational activity, groups are seen to define a particular interest
for the government. The communication process, furthermore, is a
two-way process. The integration of citizens into groups permits the
values of the intergroup-defined 'community' interest to be established
among the citizenry through group socialisation. This is implicit in
the notion of 'feedback' in the self-stabilising systems of David
Easton.[14] In Etzioni's language, the groups are 'specialised consensual
mechanisms' shifting some of the burden of consensus formation from
elected legislative assemblies. They resolve individual differences
through discussion and progressive compromise within their organisational hierarchy. They help to sustain the policy outcome of group
competition by defending the procedure through which it was reached.
They maintain its legitimacy and so make effective government
possible without a massive apparatus of controls.

This idealised view of a modern pluralist democracy seems to have
affected the practice of government in the advanced societies. Governments are less and less willing to listen to the self-appointed spokesman or the *ad hoc* deputation, preferring to hear the single voice of
the official representative of interest associations. The process of
consultation with association officials has, in most democratic societies,
become highly institutionalised. Consultation, that is, is regular, the
nature and weight of representation of groups and government is
established, procedure is agreed, and the status of the inter-group and
governmental body is recognised through the provision of meeting
facilities and services, and the necessary finance by the government.
It is promoted with the fervour of the recent convert in continental
Europe as the politics of 'concertation'.

Unfortunately, the reality of pressure politics does not entirely conform to the ideal upon which this development rests. It falls short of it in important respects:

(1) Pressure groups do not compromise and channel the demands of their members. They have, in many cases, become remote oligarchies, and the mass membership is neither involved nor committed, thereby, to procedures for conflict resolution.

This early critique of the pluralist model is best known under the 'iron law of oligarchy' label – the law which ensures that leaders of organisations retain their power with little or no internal competition and without necessarily being representative of, or accountable to, membership opinion and interests.[15] This critique is increasingly relevant as a result of structural developments in the advanced societies. It is clear that oligarchical tendencies will be positively related to the increased size of associations because of the correspondingly greater need for organisational efficiency and the physical difficulties of submitting leaders and their decisions to critical review by all members.

(2) Countervalency does not operate. Some groups are very much more powerful than others. Some interests go virtually unrepresented.

The doctrine of countervailing powers is a critical pluralist assumption. But the most long-standing objection to democratic pluralism is that some sectors are much richer and better organised than others, and some interests are virtually excluded. The vector sum of group pressures is not, consequently, the community interest. In particular, the ubiquitous consumer interest is so poorly organised that governments have in some cases thought it desirable to promote consumer organisations.[16]

These two criticisms of the pluralist model go some way towards establishing a different model of contemporary society – 'elitist' but not democratic – opposed to, or at least a sinister version of, the pluralist. If there is introduced the idea of the importance of bureaucratic, scientific and technical expertise in modern conditions, yet another contra-democratic model is suggested: that of the technocracy – a version of the elitist conception.[17] The trade union provides an example, for as the technology of production and control has become more complex, leaders have to have knowledge and communications skills which ordinary members do not have. So differences in language, educational background and vocational origins and, therefore, of personal interests between leaders of trade unions and rank and file have increased.

(3) The institutionalisation of pressure group consultation with government accentuates both these tendencies. Group leaders, through their association with government, develop a different viewpoint from their members. The recognition of one group rather than another for consultation accentuates the disparity of power between groups. It may even effectively shut off the voice of dissent.

(4) Group organisations with a partial monopoly, strengthened by official recognition, tend to acquire, in co-operation with departmental bureaucracies, the right to make authoritative policy decisions within their functional sector.

Let us examine these propositions more closely and consider how they relate to each other.

First, we have suggested, groups do not compromise and channel demands, and involve their members. They do not, therefore, help to maintain the general commitment to national procedures of conflict resolution. The leadership has become too remote. This argument applies primarily to the groups which Almond and Powell label 'associational' in their classification of interest group activity. These are the important groups from the pluralist and neo-functionalist standpoint, being defined as 'the specialised structures for interest articulation'. They include the trade unions, business federations, farmers' organisations, civic groups. This is the category whose attempts to exercise political influence are most likely to be regarded as legitimate and acceptable. In comparison with institutional pressures like those of the church, the army or the bureaucracy, or attempts to use family influence, or in comparison with so-called 'anomic' activity like the riots and demonstrations of aggrieved students or French winegrowers, the activities of associations are respectable and 'properly' organised.

Their organisation and their respectability is, at the same time, their strength, and in our argument, their weakness. The group with all the potential weight and financial resources of a large membership is able to employ full-time professional and expert staff for its specialist activity. It elaborates an organisational hierarchy for formulating policy and administering it. It enjoys, in fact, the advantages of bureaucratisation. But it begins to experience also the well-known bureaucratic dysfunctions: the remoteness of top leadership, the failure to communicate expertise, the development of impersonal rules and procedures (popularly known in their negative aspect as 'red tape'), cumbersomeness, and, therefore, delays in decision making – even, at worst, a lofty and authoritarian manner with its clientele members.

As a result, in some of the very large and most important organisations acting as pressure groups in the advanced industrial societies, it is not at all clear that they do articulate the views and attitudes of their members. It is even less clear that the membership is involved and active. Typically, in Britain, it has been said, 'the active membership of many groups is so small that policy determination has become largely a matter for paid officials who are subject to little check from the rank and file. Consequently, those who claim to speak for a group may be speaking mainly for themselves.'[18]

Large companies, for example, which are associations of employees and shareholders, are controlled by a small managerial elite and, to a very limited extent, by very big institutional shareholders who are themselves directed by a small managerial elite. Only in Germany and Holland is there more than a show of employee participation. Shareholders' meetings are poorly attended and easily dominated by management. This is common to virtually all advanced industrial societies. A report by Ralph Nader on giant corporations in the United States finds that they are secretive in their affairs. They are cumbersome and inefficient. Shareholders and even top directors have little influence over the decisions of the managerial elite, while the decisions themselves are often taken without any concern for their social impact, an impact which, of course, extends to their own small shareholders, and which includes political activity.[19]

If we extend the analysis beyond the level of the company to the industrial confederations, the same problems of representativeness and bureaucratic dysfunction exist. In the United Kingdom the CBI has been coming under a great deal of criticism from its members. In 1975, in May, the Central Council (this is the CBI assembly – some 400 strong) set up a committee of inquiry under Lord Plowden to examine the complaints. It reported in January 1976 'a strong conviction in some quarters of its membership that the CBI was not dealing as effectively as it might with the problems now facing British industry' . . . 'We do not think that the essential cooperation between the CBI and the main industrial sectors can be secured until the organisations representing them are brought into a closer relationship with the CBI's planning and policy making.' To assist the professional executive it suggested an inner cabinet of top industrialists to meet regularly and consider policy, and, of course, to represent the various sectors better.[20]

The trade unions are another set of very important organisations where this representative, consensual failure is apparent. Except for France, where a low level of membership and participation in organisations is probably endemic, trade unions in all European countries include a very large proportion of the people employed in industry (excluding the service sector). Since industrial relations figure so largely among the politically debilitating problems the advanced industrial societies have to face, the consensual efficacy of the trade unions is evidently of great importance. It appears to be rather low, given available evidence on membership participation and attitudes to leadership and official policy.

CONCERTATION

In these circumstances, and considered in relation to the basic 'specialised consensual role' of groups, the practice of 'concertation', that is, the institutionalisation of government consultation with groups, is also dysfunctional in its present forms. It is a *consequence* of a common evolution of controls in the advanced societies. All have experienced a growth of influence by their bureaucracies and executives, and a corresponding decline in parliamentary control. To this, pressure groups have responded by concentrating their efforts upon the bureaucracy and the executive and reducing their attention to the legislature. In France, this change was marked in an especially striking fashion, because the move away from parliamentary dominance was abrupt, as the Fifth Republic succeeded the Fourth, and, like other countries, France has encouraged this development by a proliferation of formal institutions of consultation.

The first of the associated problems is that institutionalised links, or concertation, between associational groups and government bureaucracies may result in a loss of autonomy and of representative character for the groups. Consultative committees with sectoral and governmental representatives, particularly when they are given regulatory and administrative functions, can acquire a corporate viewpoint. Though not an instrument of unified and coherent state control like their counterparts in totalitarian societies, they do become part of an apparatus of somewhat disjointed government. Group demands are, of course, compromised in such bodies – that is part of their function – but there is also the possibility that group representatives suffer an attitudinal compromise and so even less faithfully represent their sectors. The further problem is that, to the extent that leaders are perceived as more remote, detached from members' views and aspirations and associated with government, membership involvement declines and becomes apathetic, or, because of a reduced commitment to the procedures thitherto recognised for defining the group's position, it becomes anarchically militant.

The reduced commitment extends to other, higher, elements of the societal consensual hierarchy, including parliamentary procedures. To the degree that parliament and the political executive are bypassed or are perceived to have a reduced role in the policy-making process because of the increased role of bureaucratic and group organs of 'concertation', this decline in commitment is understandable.

Another consequent problem is that disaffected elements are, increasingly, prepared to challenge directly the policy decisions of an elected government in parliament using group power, even illegally deployed. This effect can be seen in most advanced industrial societies. It increases doubts about the apologia for the pluralist society in so far as it depends on the doctrine of countervailing powers, since, it may be argued, the power of certain groups is enhanced roughly in proportion to their ability to disrupt the essential social and economic functions of society.

RECOGNITION

Another problem of institutionalisation – a corollary of concertation – is the question, which organisations are accepted as partners in the consultation process with government – the problem of recognition. Within sectors there are rival organisations with representative claims. Concertation, in practice, involves recognition. Taken far enough, recognition can virtually shut off the main challenge to established elites – a freely formed new association, denying the representativeness of the old. Free association is a vital assumption of the pluralist model, distinguishing it from corporatism.

The importance of the freely formed association is something which stems from the restricted character of the internal life of associations, a life in which what we tend to regard as the institutional norms of democracy cannot be realised. First, basic policy formulation by majorities is ordinarily constrained by the constitutionally defined objectives of associations. These are not subject to constant modification by discussion, and they are ordinarily interpreted authoritatively by leaders. Second, the responsibility of executives is not ensured by any continuous process of supervision by an elected assembly, nor even by widely diffused information and publicity about their activities. Third, the existence of an *institutionalised* opposition by an organised faction or factions, criticising policy and offering an alternative executive, is out of the question and, by the same token, anything approaching the guarantee of the rights of individuals, taken for granted as a necessary condition of democratic government at the state level, is ruled out by counter notions of solidarity, loyalty and discipline for defensive action against opposing interests. It is through the new association, then, that dissenting views or important unassimilated minorities are able to find expression. But increasingly, without recognition, new associations labour under severe disadvantages.

The acceptance by government of one group rather than another as the official spokesman for a sector may have important consequences both for policy and for overall sectoral commitment to policy. Recognition favours one group and, possibly, one set of attitudes rather than another. It gives the favoured group a superior recruitment potential.

It may serve to suppress effectively a demand for reform swelling from some genuine discontent. To the degree that it confers a sectoral monopoly it thwarts the expression of individual or minority group dissent within the sector. Henry Ehrmann has raised the question as to whether this kind of sectoral domination by one organisation – in effect, a set of leaders of the organisation – in very close association with a corresponding section of the bureaucracy, does not constitute 'neo-feudalism'. 'A creeping pluralism', he argues, 'has rendered the right to an isolated existence very precarious. In many cases, of which the cartel situation is only one of the better known, an individual or a subgroup wishing to balk the decisions made in their name by the leadership of an interest organisation can do so only at the risk of ostracism and economic ruin. Where citizens owe their livelihood and security to the groups, their primary loyalties will easily belong to the interest groups rather than to the state. Thereby a situation reminiscent of feudal arrangements is created.'[21]

Recognition takes a variety of forms. It may be effected by selective invitation to participate in consultative committees and commissions. It may be recognition for negotiation with the firm or the industry or the state as employer. It may be recognition by wage arbitration tribunals or courts. It may be indirect, via an obligation laid on employers to negotiate with certain unions or kinds of unions.[22]

In France, as one example, in industrial relations the notion of 'syndicat le plus representatif' is sanctioned by legislation (as it is in Belgium). The same notion is recognised in practice in Holland. The French law allows full liberty of association – there is no question of a 'closed shop' – but it lays down criteria of representativeness which favour the biggest, longest established unions both for access to consultation procedures with government and for legal right within enterprises. Thus for *priority* representation in legally defined Works Committees the requirements are that a union should have at least one year of existence in the enterprise; 10 per cent or more of employees as members; a certain minimum membership subscription, and a degree of success in elections within the enterprise. In addition to these requirements a law of 1971 gave the big five industrial confederations – the CGT, FO, CFDT, CFTC and CGC – special rights in order to ensure that 'house' unions (sponsored by the company) did not monopolise the benefits of the law (which include financial benefits and organising-time allowance). They could create a syndicate within an enterprise or accept an existing independent syndicate, and even if it had only one member, he would automatically be the *délégué syndical* to which each 'representative' union is entitled on the Works Committee. In other words, these unions by virtue of national legal recognition have a privileged status in any enterprise.

Additional advantages affect elections to Works Committees. The election is by *scrutin de liste à deux tours*. On the first ballot, which requires a quorum of votes, only representative syndicates have the right to put up candidates. Other unions or independents have to wait for the second ballot.

Divisions between the big five, the withdrawal by the biggest union, the CGT, and the most radical, the CFDT, from some of the most important consultative bodies, and above all, the deliberate and widespread evasion of the law by employers, have reduced the importance of privileged recognition in France, but it is nevertheless valuable enough to be strongly contested by excluded unions and jealously guarded by the big five.

In Britain, commenting on consultation, on the growth of large industrial corporations and on concomitant trade union development, especially 'the recent and accelerated implementation of closed shop agreements' and the legislation which recognises and sanctions them, Paul Nicholson has suggested that 'any man who dares to act upon normal ideas about the human rights to join, not to join or to resign from any organisation which is legally, morally and socially acceptable, like a trade union, will experience the fierce heat and heavy weight of legislation which unleashes corporate power against him'.[23]

The dangers to which Ehrmann and Paul Nicholson refer are particularly well illustrated by the case in 1975 in which a British trade unionist, president of his union, was dismissed from his job as an employee of the Central Electricity Generating Board (a nationalised industry) because he did not belong to one of the unions recognised by the Board. Six other members of the same union had already been dismissed from another power station, while some 300 members of the union were reported to have been warned that failure to join a recognised union would result in dismissal. Most of these joined an appropriate union, the Labour Relations (Amendment) Act of 1974 having repealed earlier legislation which had made the closed shop illegal. The dismissal of the president of the union gave a publicity *succès de scandale* to the fact that unemployment benefit had been withheld by an assessor of the Department of Health and Social Security. The minister, in reply to a letter from the secretary of the Confederation of Employee Organisations on the subject, declared that unemployment benefit was intended for people who became unemployed through no fault of their own. 'A person who declines to fall in with new conditions of employment which result from a collective agreement may well be considered to have brought about his dismissal . . . In view of the independence of the insurance authorities neither the Prime Minister nor any other minister has power to intervene in their decisions in any way or to pay benefit except in accordance with their decisions.'[24] In the House of Commons on 2 December the minister, Mr Foot, re-emphasised the point. 'I have no powers whatever over the decisions of the Commissioners and others concerned with unemployment benefit. That does not enter into my power and province in any way'.[25] This is a case, therefore, in which consultation procedures, legally sanctioned as exclusive, between vocational interest groups and an arm of the state (the nationalised industry employer) have very important consequences for any group which is in conflict with the dominant interest organisation. Its members lose their jobs, they may lose customary compensation for wrongful dismissal, they may, as in this case, not be allowed unemployment benefit for up to six weeks[26] and they may very well lose the possibility of employment elsewhere in their trade. The case provoked accusations of 'fascism' but it is certainly not an example of *state* corporatism, i.e. a process *dominated* by the state and used as an instrument of its control. In this case the recognised trade unions are not simply compliant allies of the state employer in securing the obedience of workers. But whether the agreements between the state-employer and the recognised unions are a product of conflict or of amicable connivance, their consequences are the same for the dissenter. The distinction between the unified hierarchy of state corporatism and the institutionalised bargaining structure of the advanced pluralist society could conceivably become blurred. The blurring is where there is a considerable development of institutionalised consultation, with official recognition of specific organisations, and a vocational closed shop. Where, in addition, the consultative body can be seen to have the dominant regulatory role within a sector then the dividing line is very hazy. Whether the decisions of the body concerned emerge from conflict or from the amicable connivance of the participating organisations and bureaucrats is all the same to the would-be dissenter if there are no effective, permitted ways of making his views felt within the organisation. Where there are, also, clear indications of widespread dissatisfaction with particular representative organisations enjoying a monopoly of governmental recognition, the situation is more serious. The consensual apparatus is put in jeopardy. Elitism reinforced by concertation is conducive not to a vital and active membership participation but to apathy and alienation. There is some evidence of this.

GOALS OF MILITANTS

Another factor related to concertation and contributing to elitism, at least in employee organisations, may be the changing goals of militants. Concertation seems desirable and becomes feasible when industrial society has reached a particular phase. In this phase the associations of the relatively underprivileged – the trade unions – have attained strength and status and cannot be ignored or suppressed. At this stage their activity is not characterised by the pursuit of radical reformist or revolutionary goals. Their leaders have largely abandoned ideology for claims. Today, generally speaking, the values of the old 'growth and struggle' period of unionism have declined. This was the period when the union was not simply considered as an association for the pursuit of immediate economic claims, but also, a friendly society of 'brothers' (the still current residual terminology), many of its leaders inspired by the idea of a different, better society, attached to a religious creed, an ideology, a political party, with the members finding much of their social life within the union. There was a 'solidaristic' rather than 'instrumental' view both of work and the union. Unionism is now more 'instrumental'.

But the two different kinds of unionism have different organisational implications. When conceptions of brotherhood, class solidarity and ideological unity are important to union leaders, participation is a necessary instrument of these goals. Workers have to be mobilised to be persuaded. Rank-and-file activity, therefore, is deliberately stimulated by leaders. They submit themselves, their views and their actions for judgement by members in meetings, conferences, study groups. They produce and distribute journals and tracts. They organise marches and demonstrations. But mobilisation of active participation, important for ideological persuasion, is not conducive to the definition of a coherent set of pragmatic claims, to be pursued incrementally; the element of local direction which it entails is not conducive to the development of an integrated nationwide strategy. But it is precisely such a strategy that modern unionism is strongly impelled to enunciate. Government asks the unions for views on broad issues of economic policy. Leaders are in contact with civil servants and politicians who themselves have to view individual policies or proposals within a broader policy context. They cannot avoid, especially in the biggest national unions, confrontation with issues like regional and structural unemployment, multinational corporations, intergovernmental collaborative projects, and the international competitive position of British industry and their own skill competitiveness in particular.[27] This is a demanding intellectual and expert task. The unionism of claims, therefore, enhances leadership and discipline as an organisational value rather than membership participation, though few union leaders would want to admit this.[28]

INDICATIONS

I have argued that the development of large-scale organisations, of concertation techniques, of recognition practices, and of pragmatic aims, are factors which reinforce existing tendencies towards unrepresentative 'elitism', consequent dissatisfaction with, and a low level of participation in, associational life, and I suggested that there is some evidence of this. If we take as an example the sector where organisations 'represent' the largest number of people and where the allegation of developing corporatism has been laid – the trade union sector – the indicators are fairly clear. They are to be found in public expressions of discontent with national leadership, survey data on participation, the incidence of 'entryism' (or leftist takeover of in-active organisations or sections) and sporadic deviant behaviour from national 'official' policy by local rank-and-file sections.

In this sector membership figures are not a good indication of the viability of organisations because of the variety of affective inde-pendent environmental factors, not related to commitment and quite apart from the inertia already referred to. In some cases sustained membership could be explained by the fact that opportunities for recruitment have been improved during the period since the war, either through removal of legal restrictions as in Italy, France and Germany, or as a result of changed attitudes on the part of employ-ers. Elsewhere, union membership is a formal condition of employ-ment; otherwise, especially in Belgium, the unions are agents for a wide range of welfare functions; or the work force has increased through normal population growth or by immigration. In fact, total membership of trade unions has not declined, and in some cases has increased in the period 1963–77. A comparison of available member-ship figures for the UK, Netherlands, Belgium, France, Germany and Italy reveals an overall pattern: a decline in the already small art and craft unions, little change in the manufacturing, construction and extractive industries, but gains registered in the white collar unions.[29]

Belgium leads the EEC countries in unionisation with over 65 per cent of employed being organised. Italy would appear to be next, with over 55 per cent unionised, but reported figures here are particu-larly likely to be exaggerated. Luxembourg and the UK record just under 50 per cent, the Netherlands just over 40 per cent, Germany just under, while France has about 20 per cent. Membership figures have to be seen in the light of industrial structures in these countries. Since they have substantial service sectors (35–50 per cent) member-ship is quite high for the established organisable sectors of extractive and heavy industry. French unions are the main exception, notoriously, and in spite of recent gains, fragmented and weak. The particularly high figure for Belgium is explained by the fact that the trade unions are agents for social welfare payments and services.

Membership figures are unreliable to a degree, dependent as they are on reports by the unions themselves. Estimates of participation and commitment are very difficult except on a survey or an impres-sionistic basis. The prevailing impression is that there has been a general decline in active support for voluntary organisations in general and of trade unions in particular. Routine meetings are badly attended and there is widespread discontent with many aspects of union activity, on the one hand, among more conservative members who dislike the apparent loss of control by the union and the eruption of locally organised stoppages, and on the other hand there is the more widespread disaffection with the national leadership of which the unofficial local action is an indication. In France, a low level of participation is endemic but the role of unions has been affected by post-war legislation to promote concertation. They are given a place in planning through representation on the Modernisation Commissions, the Regional Economic and Social Committees (CODERS), the Economic and Social Council, and many other bodies. Their status in collective bargaining is defined by the Labour Code, and the scope of bargaining was enlarged by the Act of June 1971 to include 'the worker's security in a wider social context'.[30] This includes such matters as retirement and training. They may also negotiate the profit-sharing contracts which, since August 1967, are compulsory for all firms with more than 100 employees.

Half the members of National Prices Committee are trade union representatives and half the members of the directing boards of Social Security and Family Allowance officers are appointed by national unions. Other important committee and ministerial commissions in which the unions play an influential part include the Higher Committee of Employment, which assists the Minister of Labour, the departmental employment commissions, the regional training, social promotion and employment committees. The unions are represented on the boards of nationalised or mixed-economy enterprises and further legislation has been recommended which would require one-third worker representation on the boards of large companies.[31]

The trade union position in France, however, is weaker than in most other industrial societies. One explanation of this weakness is to be found in the structure of French industry. Small enterprises employing less than ten workers account for over one-third of the total work force. In such firms only 10–15 per cent of workers are organised. In establishments with more than 50 employees, 41 per cent are organised. A second explanation of trade union weakness is that the climate of legal rights and conventional practice, considered together, is relatively unfavourable. Though statutory rights have been added to during the life of the Fifth Republic, unions still labour under disadvantages which, in a cultural climate generally unfavourable to associational life, they are unlikely to be able to overcome without further legal measures. Union meetings, for example, cannot be called on the shop floor during working hours. Evasion of the law which requires management, in specified conditions, to proceed to the election of workers' representatives (obligatory in firms with more than ten workers) and Works Committees (obligatory in firms where there are more than fifty workers) is widespread. So too is illegal discrimination against, and intimidation of, union representatives.[32] Management-favoured right-wing unions like the CFT (Confédération Française du Travail) are improperly recognised in elections when they do take place. Intimidation of ordinary workers by management or by management-favoured unions is widely reported. This is another factor helping to account for low membership and low participation.

Another factor is the relative ineffectiveness of union activity because of the divisions within the union movement. The CGT and CFDT have reached a formal accord and do maintain a considerable degree of co-operation (though this breaks down seriously from time to time). CGT is by far the largest agglomerate with 45 per cent of trade union membership, and CFDT is second with 24·5 per cent. But Force Ouvrière, the third largest confederation, not without considerable internal dissension, usually takes a separate position under the leadership of André Bergeron. It stands aloof from action on which the other two, often in conjunction with FEN (the fourth largest), have agreed, and on which they have attempted to secure all-union co-operation. A recent example is the general strike called for 8 October 1976 which the national leadership of Force Ouvrière condemned, though some of the constituent unions and sections took part. Strike solidarity is very difficult to achieve in these circumstances and strikes tend to be relatively ineffective. Notoriously, for example, strikes on the Paris Metro usually result merely in a reduced service and free travel for the passengers. It took the rigours of the Plan Barre and the government's abrogation of the 1971 agreement guaranteeing an annual 2 per cent rise in real wages to bring all three unions together in the two-day strike of 14 and 15 December 1976 of gas and electricity workers.

Trade unionism in France would appear to be still in its growth and struggle period. In some of its aspects, therefore, it gives an appearance of greater vitality than unionism in other advanced societies, particularly in the ideological sense. The three big unions, CGT, CFDT and CGT-FO, are formally committed to the class struggle and the elimination of the *patronat*. In the case of the Force Ouvrière this is a formal and perfunctory commitment. As far as the other two unions are concerned, relations with the Patronat are hostile on both sides.

All three unions are, however, involved in the politics of concertation, though the CGT and CFDT leaders are wary of appearing too committed to it. The Force Ouvière leadership which is, in practice, the exception, genuinely committed to making concertation work, is severely criticised within its own ranks for 'un Syndicalisme de senateurs'. To avoid the same stigma, George Seguy, Secretary General of the CGT, attempts to distinguish between 'concertation' or joint policy formulation, which he rejects, and 'negotiation', more in harmony with the concept of class warfare.[33] Both CGT and CFDT suspended their participation in the work of the Seventh Plan in early 1976.[34] Their involvement in concertation in general, however, is too deep to escape critical comment. Thus, the *gauchiste* *Lutte Ouvrière* complained that the role of the state in the syndicalist conception appears to have changed. 'For the syndicats of today, the state is not an instrument of the capitalist system, helping to perpetuate the domination of the *patronat* . . . but an arbiter to whom they can appeal and to whom they will submit, for the regulation of industrial conflict . . . This is the conception which has led them to accept the idea of co-operation at all levels with the state . . . and even a more or less complete fusion between the highest levels of the trade union bureaucracy and certain state organs . . . This collaboration is detrimental to the interests of workers.'[35]

Ideological emphasis and divisions within the trade union movement can be seen as characteristic weapons and products respectively of mobilisation activity in a growth and struggle situation. The unions confront an almost solidly hostile *patronat*. Having had very little experience of an unambiguous period of 'labour' government they find themselves in a state of natural opposition to government and to the political objectives of governing parties. Leaders will negotiate but have no real incentive to assume the image of responsibility – unlike British union leaders with a Labour government in power. It is consequently possible for the *patronat* to castigate them for their irresponsibility. This helps to perpetuate the unreconciled hostility of the two estates of the economy. The advent of a left-wing government to power in France, particularly a government coalition including communists, would do a great deal, probably, to strengthen in France the conception of social partnership which is the Giscardien goal.

For the present, however, surveys indicate that workers regard union leaders as people sincerely devoted to their ideological goals and the class struggle in general, and not as self-seeking opportunists. But this perception of their idealism does not succeed in engendering active commitment and enthusiastic participation among rank-and-file members, nor even a conviction that the intense activity of their leaders directly serves their interests as workers. In a survey of 1,116 workers in 1969 it appeared that only a little less than a quarter of workers had attended a union meeting in the previous six months. More than half of the total had never been to a meeting at all. Of the actual union members (346, or less than one-third of those surveyed), some 182 – over half – had not been to a meeting for more than a year.[36]

A small majority of workers (57 per cent) appears to have some very general confidence in unionism as a way of defending their interests but there are evident doubts about the actual pattern of union activity. Fifty-four per cent think that workers should no longer follow their unions because they are too much occupied with politics and not enough with the professional defence of workers. Finally, if it can be considered an indication of confidence in union direction generally, the idea of union direction of enterprises is unpopular enough to confirm a somewhat sceptical view of leaders. Union direction proved the least popular of a number of alternatives offered in the survey for reform of company structure. The actual preferences were as shown in Table 5.1.

Table 5.1

State direction	16%
Union direction	11%
All personnel direction	21%
As at present	46%
Don't know	5%

CGT members and sympathisers showed the strongest preferences for trade union direction, and, presumably, confidence in the union leadership. Twenty-one per cent of them favoured union direction.

One of the factors, it was noted, which helps to cut leaders off from the rank and file in the conditions of advanced industrial society is the need for the bureaucratisation of large organisations. This is particularly so when they have pragmatic, complex aims. This is very evident in French trade unionism. The managing personnel and the organisation of trade unions has to be adapted to the problems of dealing with the bureaucracy of large firms and of government in furtherance of a policy of economic claims. The intellectual and verbal talents required for organisational roles are to be found primarily among the more highly skilled and better educated workers. In the case of the CGT this factor is less divisive than for the other unions. The elite of skilled workers who forged the union movement in the last quarter of the nineteenth century are still able to identify with it. The confederation is at its strongest in the older industries of medium size where the work force is relatively skilled, rather than in the larger and newer production line enterprises. A strong educational training programme makes up deficiencies and helps identify leadership capabilities. Militants and rank and file in the CGT, therefore, are more alike in their workplace and worktype origin than is the case in the other unions. The CGT is found to be 'the main depository in France of traditional working class values', in a survey by Erbès–Seguin.[37]

Both CFDT and Force Ouvrière in comparison are, proportionately to their total membership, well established in the mass production industries. Force Ouvrière is also strong proportionately in very small establishments of less than fifty employees in sectors of relatively unskilled employment such as food, packaging and transport. Ordinary members and sympathisers, therefore, are unskilled and semi-skilled operatives, while union officers are recruited from the more highly qualified workers, the technicians and engineers.

The somewhat greater similarity between rank and file and CGT militants is a factor which facilitates, though it does not ensure, participation. The CGT, in any case, places a great deal of emphasis on promoting participation. There is, as we have noted, a subtle relationship between militant devotion to ideology and the energy which will be expended in the effort to involve the rank and file of sympathisers and members of a syndicate. It is possibly as a consequence of this that the CGT does have a higher proportion of members to sympathisers than the other two unions.[38] There is another product of this effort in a very slightly superior participation record over the other unions. There is though, according to the Erbès–Seguin survey, a price. Within the CGT, as a direct product of the emphasis on shop floor participation, there is a divergence of aims between shop floor local militants and the national officers. The shop floor contact with members and sympathisers, though ideologically motivated, produces much more preoccupation with petty claims in comparison with the political objectives pursued through party and government channels at the federal summit. In the sixties, too, the shop floor militants were, on average, younger than previously, while at the federal level the same people retained power.

There is a greater uniformity of personnel within the ranks of the militants in the other two unions and, unlike CGT officials, they may have responsibilities at several levels within their organisations. There is also rather more frequent turnover of responsibilities except at the very summit. The co-ordination of action, therefore, between different establishments in the same industry and the programmatic incremental negotiation of claims is accomplished more easily.

In addition to the survey evidence of low participation as an indication of apathy there is the evidence of sporadic deviant behaviour by union sections and of 'entryism'. The incidence of both is greatest in Force Ouvrière. This is the confederation in France which best conforms to the model of a unionism of pragmatic, non-ideological aims and activities, with a leadership whose representativeness is perceived to be compromised by concertation procedures. The Confédération Générale des Cadres has the same characteristics but it has a much smaller membership (less than half that of FO), it represents a more uniform professional interest, closer to management, and it is, therefore, less vulnerable. Within the ranks of Force Ouvrière, however, major instances of deviant behaviour by local unions or by particular professional unions are common; and more than any other confederation, Force Ouvrière is subject to 'gauchiste entryism' or left-wing capture of more or less inactive sections. The OCI (l'Organisation Communiste Internationaliste) and LO (or Lutte Ouvrière) are the principal groupings, though anarchists of various kinds are also strong. André Bergeron, the Secretary General, possibly benefits personally from their presence as a way of staving off any challenge to his moderate leadership from within the ranks of the moderates themselves, many of whom would prefer greater unity of action with the other syndicates. Known as 'le père tranquille du syndicalisme', he is the only leader who has, apparently, good relations with the gauchistes and does not publicly attack them. But though Bergeron's personal position above the divisions seems secure enough, Force Ouvrière does present the strongest aspect of internal disunity.

The CGT is not as susceptible to gauchism mainly because orthodox devoted communists among the militants are quick to attack any deviant political tendency, if necessary by expelling the members concerned. A bitter dispute in October 1974, for example, within one constituent union, the CGT-UAP, ended with the expulsion of eight delegates for their gauchiste activity within the union.[39] CGT leaders are quick also to attack signs of gauchism in other unions, particularly the CFDT. The CFDT, however, is vulnerable. Its ideological preference for 'un socialisme autogestionnaire' readily forms part of an elite-sponsored nationwide strategy of negotiations for economic goals rather than a strategy of mass persuasion. With the ideology of autogestion, especially since the events of May which added hope to wishes, it is natural enough that the principal organ of militant involvement at the base of the confederation is the *section syndicale d'entreprise* – the professional branch on the shop floor. This leaves the interprofessional local groupings (the UIB, or *unions interprofessionelles des bases*, the UL or *unions locales*, and UR or *unions régionales*) relatively inactive – 'an easy prey for those who practice entryism'.[40] Krivine's Revolutionary Communist League, and gauchistes of May 1968, are strong within CFDT. The continued majority of Edmond Maire, Secretary General of the Confederation, now depends on the proportionate strength of the FGM (Fédération Générale de la Metallurgie) and FUC (Fédération Unie de la Chimie) and on the continued support of certain powerful and fairly active regional unions like those of the Loire and Lorraine. Smaller regional unions have been infiltrated by the left because, as one member of the national executive put it, 'the true unionist is active in the enterprises, pursuing claims of a professional kind. He is not attracted by responsibility in the local, regional or departmental organisation so this is left to gauchistes who transform the branch into an arena for political debate.'[41]

Apathy, local deviance and entryism are also features of British unions. A well-known study of the affluent worker in the UK offers a number of insights into worker attitudes which suggest why this part of the consensual apparatus has developed faults. The researchers were able to identify three 'ideal-type' orientations to work which they labelled (a) instrumental, (b) bureaucratic and (c) solidaristic. In the first case, work is regarded simply as a means of acquiring the income necessary to support a way of life of which the work is not an integral part. The involvement of the worker with his organisation is primarily a calculative one – to minimise effort and to maximise economic returns.

The bureaucratic orientation is one in which the work is regarded as a career and the involvement of the worker with his organisation 'contains definite moral elements rather than deriving from a purely market relationship'.[42] Work plays an important part in the worker's self-conception. 'His "position" and "prospects" are significant sources of his social identity . . . Work represents a central life interest . . . workers' lives cannot be sharply dichotomised into work and non-work.'[43]

In the solidaristic orientation work is, again, not just a means to an end but also a meaningful group activity. The group may be the enterprise as a whole. Alternatively, it may be the work group or shop, in which case there may be a negative orientation to the enterprise, fortified by the group. In either case, personal involvement in the work situation is strong and carries over into social life outside the enterprise.

Each of these orientations may be associated with different kinds of work. The first is characteristic of the unskilled affluent worker, performing the routine production or assembly line task, relatively mobile from job to job and employer to employer. The bureaucratic orientation is more characteristic of the salaried employee; the solidaristic, of the worker with craft skills. The categories helped to define union orientation. Only in the case of the craftsmen was there a committed attitude to union principles and routine activities. A very low level of attendance at union branch meetings was found among the semi-skilled. Though 22 per cent of craftsmen attended 'regularly', the overall attendance including craftsmen was as shown in Table 5.2.

Table 5.2

Regularly	7%
Occasionally	14%
Rarely	19%
Never	60%
Don't know	1%

The survey suggested that indifference, the demands of home life, and either satisfaction with, or hostility to, the union were explanations of non-participation.[44] There was, however, a significant difference between the unionism of the branch and the unionism of the workplace. Thus, though very few voted at union branch elections, 83 per cent of the total voted regularly in shop steward elections.[45] Simple convenience is one explanation of this high figure, since elections take place on the spot. But reasons for regular voting show the importance also of a conception of the greater importance of shop stewards in comparison with branch officials, of better knowledge of the candidates and of an overall sense of the superior relevance and interest of shop affairs over union affairs. It was, furthermore, evident that 'the unionism of the workplace is very largely *dissociated* from what they regard as the official activity of the unions to which they happen to belong'. More recent surveys show no improvement in this low level of commitment and some evidence of a worsening relationship.

The Gallup Poll Index Report No. 182, 1975 (August survey) revealed that, of a representative sample of 912 electors, 73 per cent thought that trade unions were becoming too powerful. (This compared with 61 per cent in 1974 and 52 per cent in 1973.) To the question, 'Do you think the views of the trade union leadership are or are not representative of the views of the ordinary trade union members?' a clear majority, not only of the general public but of trade unionists, thought they were not, as shown in Table 5.3.

Table 5.3

	Total sample	Trade unionists
Are	20%	28%
Are not	61%	59%
Don't know	19%	13%

Sixty-five per cent of the total sample were opposed to the idea of the 'closed shop', compared with 56 per cent of trade union members.

The poll, taken as a whole, shows that while the idea of trade unionism is accepted by a small majority, there is, even among trade unionists themselves, a widespread suspicion of those aspects of union activity that smack of compulsion or which conceivably threaten democratic government. Only a minority of trade unionists (39 per cent) would accept the view that it should be compulsory to join a union if the worker is receiving union rates of pay. Only 35 per cent of unionists thought their unions should be concerned with political matters,[46] only 28 per cent favoured sponsorship of MPs. These attitude surveys complement other evidence of the gap between the shop floor worker and the leadership.

Many strikes are unofficial. Unofficial strikes are sometimes adopted by the union because they have to be – the leadership, in effect, concedes in order to conciliate. But the initiative comes from the shop floor. There are, notably, local revolts against the union, either by the more traditional workers disturbed by the disruptive activity of the larger shop floor, or, in other cases, local groups reacting against remote control by national leadership. Thus, twenty-three craftsmen who did not take part in a union meeting during working hours at the Vickers shipyard at Barrow-in-Furness refused to pay fines imposed by their union under threat of expulsion in autumn 1975. The men were members of the National Union of Sheet Metal Workers, Coppersmiths and Heating and Domestic Engineers, and were engaged on defence contracts. They did not attend a meeting held to discuss overtime arrangements. They were fined £50 each, ordered to work no overtime, and told that if they did not pay the fines by 27 December they would be expelled. One of the men said that they had not attended the meeting because they did not want to disrupt production for the thirty minutes that the meeting lasted. He said the fines had been imposed by a 'kangaroo court'.[47]

At the same time, in Peterborough, seventy test shop workers at the Perkins Engines voted at a meeting to instruct the company not to deduct union subscription from their pay packets. The firm employs more than 6,000 shop floor workers, and the Amalgamated Union of Engineering Workers has sole negotiating rights. The men were protesting about the introduction of a new pension scheme. One of them said: 'It was steamrollered through by the Union after it had been rejected by a mass meeting. This is our retaliation.'[48]

Some unions in the UK seem to be able to effect changes in national leadership. However, this is not usually so directly a product of membership disaffection as is shop floor militancy. It may be, rather, a product of 'entryism' by political radicals like Communists, the Workers' Socialist League, the Workers' Revolutionary Party and the International Marxists. It is not revived participation in union structures, but a strategy dependent on the non-participation of the majority. It represents no improvement in consensual efficiency. The moderate reply, as this kind of takeover has become prevalent, has been to attempt to introduce the postal ballot. This would seem to be based on a realistic assessment of the poor possibilities of attracting large numbers of moderates to union meetings to recapture control. There is no reason to suppose that associational groupings like unions will be able, in the affluent society, to revive the activism which was characteristic of the early years of the struggle for higher wages. But the minimal effort of the postal ballot is conceivable. It is unlikely, however, to have the effect on the consensual apparatus of the union that the general election has in the country as a whole –

namely, to stimulate alternative conceptions of a majority interest and the emergence of alternative leaderships. It is more likely to consolidate the position of existing leaders, and to make any kind of challenge almost impossible.

The problem is that British union structure is a complex of local and, for the most part, of craft unions, which developed during a period of gradual industrialisation. Trade unions were dealing at first with relatively small enterprises and were concerned collectively, both at the branch and higher levels of organisation, with the conditions of employment within a trade, not with those in an enterprise. Today, in an era of very large enterprise, with works in different parts of the country, this pattern of organisation is anachronistic. It is the conditions within large enterprises which give rise to a common interest. What would seem to be required is a consensual apparatus at the level of the enterprise, and beyond that, at the higher level of the group of similar enterprises, able to resolve conflicts over demarcation and pay differentials between workers in the industry. Its multi-tiered structure might ultimately be capable of stating positions on national economic policy, preferably in public debate with other sectoral interests in a quasi-parliamentary forum like an economic and social council, which did represent a genuine consensus to which workers in the industry could generally be prepared to accept a commitment. The pattern of union representation has been rationalised to a very limited degree on such lines with the development of large unions of amalgamated trades, but most enterprises encompass several unions, union branches are not enterprise based, and only a still very loose co-ordination (via the TUC) is achieved between the individual unions. The National Economic Development Council which since 1961 brings together a small group of ministers, trade union leaders, employers and independents, and, since 1974, the Advisory, Conciliation and Arbitration Service which also has TUC and CBI representation, are not large enough to meet the need for *public* debate in an assembly widely representative of major interest organisations. Such an assembly has been suggested on a number of occasions. It was recommended by the National Industrial Conference of 1919 and more recently by Eric Wigham in *Strikes and the Government, 1893–1974*.[49]

The recommendation may seem to have corporatist implications but these are superficial. Concertation is not of itself corporatist. It can be public, representative and participatory, and allow for competition. And narrow functional specificity of interest intermediation may be as corporatist – secret, noncompetitive, oligarchic – as any other. There is no particular liberal-democratic 'pluralist' quality about inefficient and ineffective interest intermediation. The division of union representation within an enterprise or an industry according to narrow, often obsolete 'craft' specialisms, productive of jurisdictional squabbles and unco-ordinated action, does not indicate a state of free association and competitiveness, or of representative leadership and participation and commitment by members. Rather it reduces their likelihood.

Countries which, apparently, come a little closer to the rationalised conception above are the Netherlands, Sweden and West Germany. West Germany's trade union structure and industrial relations have been much admired. Throughout the sixties, only the Netherlands and Sweden (which have a similar pattern) had a smaller number of days lost in strikes: see Table 5.4.

Table 5.4

Working days lost through strikes/ 1,000 employees	1973	1974	1963–7
Germany	563·1	1,051·2	34
France	3,914·6	338·0	347
Italy	20,402·3	16,747·3	1,045
Netherlands	583·8	6·9	16
Belgium	866·0	578·3	166
United Kingdom	7,173·0	740·0	184
Ireland	206·7	551·8	not available
Denmark	3,901·2	184·2	104

Source: Eurostats, Basic statistics of the European Community, No. 10, 1975, p. 93, and Donovan Report 1968.

It can of course be argued that Germany enjoys a number of advantages conducive to good labour relations in comparison with France, Italy and the UK. There is, arguably, a tradition of deference to authority,[50] yet a far less rigid and marked class distinction, and there has been a postwar spirit of redemption and desire for recovery. There has been sustained growth which has led to full employment and high wages. The latter has in turn attracted large numbers of foreign workers who provide a cushion against the difficulties of small cyclical fluctuations in employment, since they are the first to be made redundant.

In addition to these factors, however, there has been, since the war, a completely new organisation of the trade unions into sixteen large industrial unions, all affiliated to the national confederation (DGB). This has been seen as a great advantage in rationalising wage negotiations and avoiding inter-union rivalry and demarcation disputes. Furthermore, since the 1952 Works Constitution Act, there has been an agreed legal framework for trade union activity. It gives trade unions the primary role in collective bargaining within an industry, but, in matters not determined by union contracts such as work organisation and conditions, Works Councils, elected by the whole staff of plants (union and non-union), act and negotiate on behalf of the employees. Trade unionists play a major part in these. They comprised 77·6 per cent of the membership in 1972. This is becoming a specialised aspect of union activity, with union experts in 'ergonomics' to be found in many enterprises considering how working conditions may be 'humanised'. The negotiation of wage agreements remains the prerogative of the unions *per se* but so integrated is the Works Council and union activity that most workers fail to make a distinction between them. One study indicated that 90 per cent of employees identify the Works Council with the trade union.[51] This may well contribute to the general satisfaction (71 per cent), expressed in the survey, of union members. Lockouts or strikes are illegal during the period covered by an agreement. Labour courts decide on disputes arising from contracts. Their procedures are not costly and legal aid is available if either party employs a lawyer.

In this environment of participation and controls, the German trade unions regard striking as an undesirable procedure. They are ardent apostles of the principle of co-determination in industry. The main instrument of this is the Works Council which has wide powers of co-decision with management on working conditions. Control, however, is also affected by the requirement under German Company law of one-third union representation on the supervisory boards of all joint stock and limited companies with more than 500 employees, and one-half representation in the coal and steel industries. The supervisory boards determine grand policy and they appoint the management board which is responsible for day-to-day activity.

The unions are not affiliated to the political parties, there is no official closed shop and union leaders seem to be very satisfied with co-determination. They seek co-partnership as a logical extension of co-determination and the unions themselves are considerable entrepreneurs, following something like the trading principles of British co-operative societies. The satisfaction of the unions has ensured their co-operation in a generous non-statutory incomes policy, in which it has always been conceded that pay rises should exceed price rises.

This is not to say, of course, that the German worker is entirely at one with union officials at the opulent Confederation headquarters in Dusseldorf. Surveys indicate satisfaction with union activity but it is not clear whether this extends to the national activity relevant here or merely reflects general satisfaction with Works Councils which are identified with trade unions in people's minds. There are some indications that the local–national distinction needs to be made. First, as the comparative figures in the Table 5.4 show, the remarkably low strike record has occasionally been broken. There were major strikes in 1969. There was a wave of strikes in February 1974 initiated by massive majorities. Members of the Public Service and Transport Union were 79 per cent in favour of their strike, the success of which left the pay policy in ruins. Of unionised railwaymen, 89·9 per cent voted for stoppage, 90·9 per cent of clerical, canteen and other workers employed by the police force voted for strike action, as did the postal workers.[52] Part of the explanation would seem to be in the results of concertation activity.

Explaining the wave of unauthorised strikes in the autumn of 1969 Willey points out that trade union leaders had achieved their objective of top level involvement in national economic planning when the Konzertierte Aktion working group was set up by the SPD government in 1967. 'But their participation was a two-edged sword. Sharing in planning also involved behaving responsibly in the light of group findings.' Moderate wage settlements were, therefore, accepted in 1968 for eighteen months rather than the usual twelve. The wave of unofficial strikes in 1969 against these contracts were the result. Union officials were abused as traitors to the working class and whistled down at meetings.[53]

A second possible indicator of dissatisfaction is that, in spite of a shorter working week than his British counterpart, twenty-one days more holiday per year and numerous fringe benefits, the health of the German worker is, prima facie, very much worse. For every three days lost through sickness in Britain, four are lost in West Germany. The difference in 1972 mounted to four times the number of days lost through strikes in Britain (though 1972 was a very bad year in the UK). It is difficult to believe that comparative ill health rather than deliberate absenteeism (on general sickness pay) is entirely responsible for the difference. It may be at least marginally linked to dissatisfaction which union leadership is failing to reflect.

There would certainly not appear to be any greater enthusiasm for participation in formal union activity in West Germany in comparison with other countries. An average of about 10 per cent of members attend union meetings, but almost all of these are salaried or honorary elected union functionaries. The large number of offices are filled with some difficulty.[54] The DGB convention meets every three or four years and, again, a large proportion of the delegates are salaried or honorary officials. At the 1954 convention, for example, 53 per cent of delegates were salaried officials.[55] In these conditions, though there are occasional upsets, leading members of the executive retain their seats year after year. 'At six DGB conventions from 1951–62, 56 positions in the inner executive board were filled by election. In only three cases did a candidate for re-election have opposition [although both were defeated] . . . At 62 industrial union conventions in the period 1950–60, 469 inner-board positions were filled by election. In only 36 cases (7·7 per cent) were elections contested. In only seven cases (1·5 per cent) was either an incumbent or candidate suggested to the convention by the executive board defeated.[56] This suggests that the union outside the factory is in the same state of oligarchy, reinforced by apathy, as the trade unions of other countries, while the system of representation within the enterprise is working relatively well.

The German record must be seen, in any case, in the light of continued economic prosperity. It remains to be seen whether the incomes policy role of the unions and their involvement in national economic planning will not provoke unofficial militancy and strikes if and when economic conditions worsen and more stringent pay guidelines are attempted.

In Italy too the unionism of the shop floor is becoming a major force of change in what has hitherto been a confused pattern of union activity. Reported union membership has been high, but the dichotomy between leaders and rank and file is apparent. Smouldering shop-floor discontent flares up frequently enough to give Italy the worst record among the nine members of the EEC of damaging stoppages. Fragmentation of the unions based on ideological and religious differences which have little or nothing to do with the pragmatic concerns of the workers and weaken their bargaining power is generally seen as a contributory factor to their discontent, though in recent years the unions have made efforts to combat this weakness and to combine for collective bargaining purposes. Faced as they are with a number of very large firms which dominate industrial life and by the two great state companies, the IRI and the ENI, this development of union co-operation was long overdue. At the same time, the framework of law, which also restricted the scope of union activity, has been altered. Within enterprises, until 1966, internal elected 'commissions', weakened by heavy restrictions, had been responsible for bargaining. This function was taken over by unions in 1966, and the Workers' Statute of May 1970 has led to further changes. There has been, since then, the emergence of a system of Works Councils. A novel mode of elections to the Councils has had its effect on union activity. 'Candidates do not have to have syndical backing. The elections are open: one delegate to every 25 workers. Groups of workers in similar conditions and jobs are asked, individually, to designate the worker in their group in whom they would have most confidence as a representative. The process is secret. Once elected the mandate of a delegate may be revoked by the group. Unions, as a consequence, are obliged to consider pressures from the ordinary worker, including non-unionists, and to join forces to secure the election of a union member. Ninety per cent of the delegates are in fact union members, but their major preoccupation has to be conditions of work.'[57]

It remains to be seen whether these changes in practice amount to a major improvement in the Italian consensual apparatus which, as comparative strike figures show, has been relatively inefficient.

A general picture emerges from this evidence. In France, Britain, Germany, Italy, Holland and Belgium the indicators point in the same direction. Surveys show that most people regard trade unions as an integral and acceptable part of democratic industrial society. All six countries have proliferated organs of concertation on which recognised trade unions have a place. Surveys also show, however, considerable disquiet about contemporary union activity so that even where, as in France, workers feel that, on the whole, union leaders are working sincerely enough for their members, they are not convinced that the efforts they make do actually serve rank-and-file interests.

None of these countries has a good record of membership participation in union activity. Branch meetings are very poorly attended. Typically, only those holding some kind of office are likely to be present. Office holders are very difficult to recruit; so too are occasional helpers for canvassing, dues collecting and demonstrations.

In Britain, France and Italy especially, 'entryism' is a problem. A variety of radical left-wing groups have profited from the quiescence of many territorial units of the unions, to take them over. Even a union like the French CGT whose militants still have relatively strong ideological aims and ardently seek participation by the rank and file, succeeds only to the extent of having a slight superiority over the other confederations in membership activity. The CGT's successful resistence to 'entryism' is based on tough action in expelling dissidents more than on its superior record of participation.

Everywhere, the unionism of the workplace is the most active. In Britain it is very largely dissociated from what workers regard as the 'official activity' of the unions to which they happen to belong. In Germany too, workplace and national union activity must be distinguished. In most workers' minds, the survey shows, Works Councils *are* the union.

Throughout Europe, the contribution made by unofficial action, at the local, shop floor level, to the number of working days lost in strikes is impressive. Official strikes are, themselves, often reluctant recognition by national leaders of local initiatives.

Rank-and-file union members regard wage negotiations as the prime objective of union activity. Governments use concertation procedures as mechanism for achieving wage restraint agreement which will help reduce the pace of inflation. It is not surprising that distrust of 'concertation' procedures is widely expressed at shop floor level, in left-wing union journals, by breakaway unions, and even by leaders involved in the process. Study of the rate of growth in working-class incomes since 1948 in the United Kingdom tends to demonstrate an objective basis for this distrust since the periods of maximum union commitment to concertation, that is, when Labour governments have been in office, have been the periods of lowest percentage rate of growth in real incomes of manual workers.

Paradoxes emerge in this chapter. The embracing paradox is that we have all kinds of evidence that most citizens will not participate actively in the life of associations unless that participation is made very very easy for them (for example, on the shop floor of the factory during working hours). Most citizens are not knowledgeable nor do they have clear views on the issues with which national leaders have to struggle. The views they do express tend to be conservative, even authoritarian, in comparison with those of their leaders. Their passive behaviour and their ignorance only serve to reinforce tendencies to oligarchy in organisations.

However, oligarchy in organisations which are involved in corporatist decision making represents a threat to the stability of the Western-style democracies – because, ultimately, these democracies depend (in the absence of the massive apparatus of controls which characterises the Eastern 'democracies') on consensus, even if only a permissive consensus. The behaviour of very strongly oligarchical associations risks the breakdown of that consensus and an eruption of dissident sentiment in very damaging forms, including economic disruption, community violence, widespread evasion of the law and criminal behaviour, and extremist political parties.

There is, therefore, some point in searching for ways in which levels of participation can be increased, with a cynical eye to the very limited possibilities. Of these, the development of shop floor industrial democracy through Works Councils seems the most promising; capable of involving large numbers of people in that sector of the population which is least active through the other existing channels of political participation and whose withdrawal of consent is potentially the most damaging.

A way of raising shop floor democracy above the level of concern with petty claims would be by making it the base of a larger framework, democratically structured, of professional representation. Corporatist potential, however, inheres in any system of institutionalised professional representation, so that appropriate rules would be needed to inhibit tendencies towards singular recognition, secrecy, sectoral autonomy and non-accountability. Of equal importance would be the appropriate conditions of party and parliamentary viability as specialised consensual mechanisms and as instruments of public accountability. We turn to this question in the next chapter.

NOTES

1 *Social Contracts*, IV, ch. 2.
2 *Resolutions on Parliamentary Reform*, Bowering edn (Tait, 1843).
3 *The Federalist Papers*, No. 10.
4 R. T. McKenzie, 'Parties, pressure groups and the British political process', *Political Quarterly*, vol. 29 (1958).
5 Giovanni Sartori, *Democratic Theory* (Detroit: Wayne State University Press, 1962).
6 See Robert A. Dahl, *A Preface to Democratic Theory* (Chicago: University of Chicago Press, Phoenix Books, 1963), *passim*.
7 See e.g. J. S. Mill, *Representative Government* (London: Dent, Everyman No. 482, 1910), pp. 203–4, and G. H. Cole, *Social Theory* (London: Methuen, 1920), especially p. 208.
8 L. T. Hobhouse, *Liberalism* (London: Butterworth, 1911), pp. 232–3.
9 Edited by W. N. Chambers and R. H. Salisbury.
10 'Two faces of power', *American Political Science Review*, vol. 56 (December 1962), pp. 947–8.
11 Carole Pateman, *Participation and Democratic Theory* (Cambridge: CUP, 1970), p. 1.
12 G. A. Almond and G. B. Powell, *Comparative Politics: A Developmental Approach* (Boston: Little, Brown, 1966), pp. 75–6.
13 ibid., p. 77.
14 *A Systems Analysis of Political Life* (New York: Wiley, 1965), pp. 382–429.
15 See Roberto Michels, *Political Parties*, trans. E. and C. Paul (New York: Free Press, 1962).
16 In the UK a Minister of Prices and Consumer Protection has been created. In other countries, France and Holland, for example, there is an attempt to encourage consumer organisations by providing for their representation on regional planning councils and in the Economic and Social Councils. On the European scale the Economic and Social Committee of the EEC makes similar provision. These arrangements provide only minimal protection against the power of major interest groups like the agricultural lobby. At Community level, therefore, a Consumers' Consultative Committee has been set up, which is pressing for each producer minister in the Council of Ministers to be matched by a consumer minister, on the grounds that Council meetings of, for example, agricultural ministers legislate largely in the interests of their farmer clientele.
17 This is only to take Michels's observations on the 'technical indispensibility of leadership' (op. cit., p. 364) a stage further.
18 A. H. Hanson and M. Walles, *Governing Britain* (London: Fontana/ Collins, 1975), p. 162.
19 *The Times*, 26 January 1976.
20 *The Times*, 15 January 1976; see also W. Grant and D. Marsh, *The CBI* (London: Hodder & Stoughton, 1977), especially chs 3 and 5.
21 H. W. Ehrmann in M. Dogan and R. Rose (eds), *European Politics* (London: Macmillan, 1971), p. 351, and see Ralph Dahrendorf, *Conflict and Contract* (Liverpool: Liverpool University Press, 1975), p. 14, and Robert Moss, *The Collapse of Democracy* (London: Temple Smith, 1975).

22 On this see A. Gladstone and M. Ozaki, 'La reconnaissance des syndicats aux fins de la négociation collective' *Revenue International du Travail*, no. 2–3 (September 1975), pp. 185–214.
23 'The state and the individual', *The Times*, 8 December 1975.
24 *The Times*, 3 December 1975.
25 *The Times*, Parliamentary Report, 3 December 1975.
26 This is an effect of the Social Security Act 1975, s. 20 (1) (*a*).
27 Typically the British Aerospace Joint Unions Executive Committee begins its October 1976 report: 'Union members wish to see a healthy aerospace industry . . . This report examines the overall position of the British industry in relation to both the EEC and the World, and concludes that Britain possesses distinct cost and other advantages over international competitors.' *Finance and Projects Sub-Committee Report 1*, Issue 1, para. 1.
28 Ernest Bevin and George Woodcock came audaciously close to doing so, however. See T. Lane, *The Union Makes Us Strong* (London: Arrow Books, 1974), pp. 254–5.
29 See the *Europa Yearbook*, 1963, pp. 4ff.
30 *An Outline of Trade Unionism* (London: French Embassy Press and Information Service, 1975), p. 11.
31 ibid., p. 18.
32 See Hubert Lesire-Ogrel, *Le Syndicat dans l'entreprise* (Paris: Sevil 1967), pp. 3–110.
33 *Le Monde*, 10 June 1974; see also George Seguy's apologia for negotiation combined with class warfare in *Cahiers Français*, January-February 1972, pp. 24–5. The union ranking and percentages given above are derived from the total reported membership of the 'Big Six' in 1974. The figures reported each year by the Ministry of Labour in France for elections to *comités d'entreprises* correspond very closely, in the seventies, to the membership percentages shown for the CGT and CFDT. However, neither FO, CGC nor CFTC maintain their proportionate membership strength in factory elections over the whole country.

   For an account of efforts to achieve joint CGT–CFDT action since the signing of a joint programme of minimal co-operation on 26 June 1974 see Henri Tincq, 'Un an de rapports CGT–CFDT', *Projet*, no. 98 September–October 1975), pp. 960–8.
34 *Le Monde*, 14 February 1976.
35 'Syndicats-état: des rapports de plus en plus étroits', *Lutte Ouvrière*, 10 January 1976, p. 9 (my translation).
36 G. Adam *et al.*, *'L'Ouvrier français en 1970'* (Paris: Colin, 1970), pp. 21–2.
37 S. Erbes-Seguin, *Démocratie dans les syndicats* (Paris: Mouton, 1971), pp. 112–15, and see Adam, op. cit., p. 25.
38 The distinction is between paid-up 'members' and those 'sympathisers' who regularly support a particular union in meeting and factory elections.
39 See *Lutte Ouvrière*, 22 October 1974.
40 *Rapport général*, CFDT 37th Congress (Annecy, June 1976).
41 *Témoignage Chrétien*, 3 June 1976, p. 6.
42 J. H. Goldthorpe *et al.*, *The Affluent Worker: Industrial Attitudes and Behaviour* (Cambridge: CUP, 1968), p. 41.
43 ibid., p. 41.
44 ibid., Table 40, p. 99; see pp. 99–100.
45 ibid., pp. 102–3.

46   In France the comparable figure was 32 per cent: Adam, op. cit., p. 157.

47   *The Times*, 6 December 1975.

48   *The Times*, 6 December 1975.

49   Eric Wigham, *Strikes and the Government, 1893–1974* (London: Macmillan, 1976).

50   What L. J. Edinger describes as 'highly formalised patterns of polyarchic elitism and mass passivity' in his *Politics in Germany* (Boston: Little, Brown, 1969), p. 198, cited by G. Smith, *Politics in Western Europe* (London: Heinemann, 1972), p. 67.

51   Richard J. Willey, *Democracy in the West German Trade Unions: A Reappraisal of the Iron Law*, Sage Professional Papers 2 (01–023), (Sage, 1971), p. 11, citing *Die Quelle*, December 1962, pp. 550–1.

52   In Sweden also there have been major problems. Thus, in 1971 professional groups and government employees struck for a restoration of pay differentials *vis-à-vis* manual workers. The strike was widely disruptive and damaging and resulted in emergency legislation.

53   Willey, op. cit., p. 40.

54   ibid., p. 18.

55   ibid., p. 23.

56   ibid., p. 24. Willey argues that German trade unions are, in fact, democratic. He is impressed with the openness of the formal structures and with occasional electoral dismissal of important leaders who have failed to 'anticipate adverse reaction'. The weight of the evidence he presents, however, shows well-developed oligarchical tendencies.

57   My summary translation from 'Dossier: Représentants du personnel', *Intersocial* (Paris), 20 January 1974, p. 3.

Parties

Though pressure groups now tend to be regarded by governments as the main channel from people to rulers for the expression of interests, it is the contention of this chapter that interests and views are still articulated more faithfully and fully, and at least in bipolar party systems, aggregated more equitably, through parties than through the cacophony of pressure politics. This is the case even though interest representation is not the prime function of the political party, and though articulation and aggregation are conflicting goals. What distinguishes the political party from the pressure group is that it seeks to capture political office rather than influence office holders. Though parties may in some cases have their origins in something very much resembling the pressure group – that is, they were formed to advance a particular set of interests or attitudes – their *raison d'être* in the democratic advanced society has become the organisation of the electorate for the purpose of gaining a majority of the vote or whatever else the electoral system requires.

The requirements imposed by the electoral system in any country tend to become the dominant factors determining party organisation and platform. While most parties have a core social basis of support which indicates their origins as champions of particular religious, ethnic or socio-economic values, electoral systems and other control structures determine the extent to which these values have to be compromised.

TYPOLOGIES

Nevertheless, differences between parties within a particular system are primarily to be explained by reference to their core support. For this reason a typology of parties in the advanced pluralist societies could be founded on this element.

In the advanced societies, the major parties tend to be those with a socio-economic base. Though some electoral systems protect a variety of class parties, and though the survival of a peasant class in some places complicates the situation, the class parties tend towards one major party of the left and, with less force, a major party of the right or upper class.

Religious and ethnic factors complicate this division. However, for the most part, parties with a Christian foundation are to be found on the right of the political spectrum. Whatever their original complexion the need to oppose the extension of the role of the state in areas in which the church seeks to remain active (especially in education) forces the move towards the right and to an aggregative compromise with parties in that part of the political spectrum. Ethnic parties are less predictable.

However, a typology based on social supports is subject to the objection that class strengths, attitudes and party loyalties do change; parties of the right in some electoral systems need to attract a very large working-class vote, and succeed in doing so. In one instance, the Gaullist Party in France, a party of the right, for a time became the most popular party of the working class, attracting a larger proportion of its vote than any other party.

Organisation characteristics, therefore, form a more reliable basis of classification. One variant of this form of typology is offered by Duverger. He differentiates between the cadre party and the mass party. *Cadre parties* are those which depend on a group of leading political figures whose known views and whose judgements on current problems are the cues for their supporters. Such parties are not, ordinarily, distinguished by elaborate organisation and a party bureaucracy. At general elections they rely on the automatic publicity that attaches to the leading figures of the group. In general they are parties of the right, of the conservative or liberal tendencies, since an existing basis of privilege within a society is the source of leadership status which may be exploited politically. Such parties are not, however, oligarchical in a strict sense. Though one or some members may be particularly influential and/or have outstanding electoral appeal, the basic relationship between the members of the group is likely to be egalitarian, each having his own basis of support. Permanent bureaucracies are small and non-influential. Cadre parties, too, may have a very important aggregative role among parties in a multi-party system, providing, with their attachment to office rather than doctrines, the compromise position of leadership between larger parties more attached to principle. An ideology or doctrine in a cadre party would impose a strain on the loyalty of the disparate elements which support the leadership. Such support is characterised by a good deal of local independence of view.

The cadre party is distinguished from the *mass party*. The latter seeks to develop a mass membership from which leaders are recruited, organised in a hierarchy of elective offices and powers. Mass membership is essential for a party which cannot rely on wealthy patrons to finance its activities, particularly its electoral activities. The membership provides financial support through subscriptions and fund-raising activities. Parties of the left are the most likely to seek a mass basis for this reason. Characteristically, support is mobilised by the propagation of a party doctrine, or ideology of reform. It is, consequently, a source of inherent tension in the mass party that the ideology which helps to recruit a militant membership is too extreme for the mass of voters and has to be 'toned down' for electoral purposes. Mass parties, therefore, tend to exhibit a division between the parliamentary representatives and the constituency members whose attitudes are expressed in annual party conferences or congresses.

FUNCTIONS

This tension does not in fact impair the performance of the main systemic function fulfilled by the parties – that of aggregating, through a process of progressive compromise, the conflicting interests of the electorate. Rather, it productively narrows the gap between the politically motivated, 'available' activist and the ordinary citizen with an only marginal interest in national issues and with an on the whole apprehensive, negative attitude towards major change. The parliamentarian responds to the latter, forced to do so by the electoral process. In doing so he imposes a check on the extreme views of the militant, highly motivated political worker. Policy is, thus, a compromise between the two. The permanent bureaucracy, therefore, is not influential. Within the party itself, compromise is effected between the conflicting views of pragmatists and doctrinal purists. As a mass party ages, and tastes the fruits of office, and as these are more widely dispersed following increasing electoral success, the tendency within the party towards pragmatic, non-doctrinaire goals develops, though lip-service is still paid to doctrine. Modern mass parties, therefore, aggregate interests rather well. They do so at the price of failing to articulate any specific interest at all clearly: that is, in official party programmes or manifestos. Any doctrine or ideology stands in need of interpretation and the mass parties of the advanced pluralist society tend to blur rather than clarify doctrine in appealing to the general electorate.

The aggregative function depends for its continued fulfilment on an overall consensus within the party on constitutional processes, on the limits of political action and obligation and on basic economic and social values. Whenever any aspect of this consensus is strongly challenged from within one of the major established parties there is a tendency for the aggregative process to break down. There may be – for example, particularly when the economy is faltering – a challenge to the actions of leaders who are shifting party goals to the centre. The tension between the party outside the legislative assembly and that within the assembly becomes more acute. The product of this tension may well be a formal split between the established and the challenging elements within the party.

ELECTORAL SYSTEMS AND PARTY SYSTEMS

The nature of the electoral system will be one important determinant of when this split takes place. Systems of proportional representation and second ballot majority systems provide a stronger incentive than first-past-the-post plurality systems, since they afford better opportunities for smaller parties to gain seats in the assembly. The effect of party fragmentation, however, is to add to the consensual burden of parliament.

In the electoral system which requires a plurality of votes, of which the UK is the most prominent example, a party split is likely to be a much later product of this tension. For this reason, it could be argued that such a system, typically a two-party system, cannot tolerate, within the framework of a unitary state and of government by parliamentary majority, the same degree of dissensus as the multi-party state. The two major parties which the system tends to produce are able to establish a near monopoly of power. Any third party attempting to mount a countrywide challenge is at an enormous disadvantage in having to break traditional voting habits and fight powerful organisations and sitting members, as well as the very strong feeling on the part of the elector that by not making his choice between the two major parties he may very well be wasting his vote. Challenges to the prevailing consensus, therefore, are likely to be expressed within the major parties rather than through third parties. They find their most inviting home in the mass party of the left, partly because such parties normally have the most directly democratic structures (many mass parties of the right having emerged from cadre origins of which there are behavioural and organisational residues), and partly because such parties do pay lip-service to a reformist ideology in the name of which a challenge may be made (where mass parties of the right, like the German Christian Democrats, the French Gaullists and the British Conservatives, have no such ideological baggage to carry). Most large socialist parties in Europe, therefore, have their left wing, varying in strength from country to country and from time to time. To the degree that a left wing is successful in taking over the main administrative and decision-making structures of the party outside parliament, it becomes a thorn in the side of a parliamentary party charged with the final aggregative task of incorporating views and interests wider than those of the party active membership. The situation is worsened still more by the phenomenon which has been called 'entryism'. This is the deliberate infiltration of the moderate party by an extremist group. Two factors are favourable to 'entryism'. One is a degree of apathy among rank-and-file supporters of the party. The same apathy serves the left wing, enabling it to capture the party machinery. This is the second factor favourable to entryism, for the left wing is tempted to accept as its ally, in the effort to capture party leadership, an infiltrating organisation. Faced by this kind of challenge, and recognising that a mobilisation of the moderates is inherently impossible, parliamentary parties have two options between which, disastrously when they are in government, they may, with irresolute leaders, vacillate. On the one hand, rather than take action within the terms of the prevailing electoral consensus to deal with problems like inflation, unemployment, balance of payments adversities or disruptive industrial relations, they may do nothing, or take only half measures, in order to hold off the left-wing challenge. On the other hand, they may concede from time to time to the pressures from the left by adopting legislation or policies within existing powers which, because they are outside the prevailing electoral consensus, win the immediate promise of repeal or reversal by the opposition and are divisive and demoralising for the country as a whole. The multi-party system with coalition government has had at least the merit, while there is little or no economic or international problem to face, of allowing continuity of policy, along centrist lines, in societies marked by a very clear dissensus.

This is not, however, a conclusive argument for electoral schemes favouring third and fourth parties. The experience of centre-based coalition government suggests, still, weakness and instability in comparison with other forms. Some comparisons will serve to illustrate the above argument.

France, under the Third and Fourth Republics, provides an obvious example. There were at least five main tendencies in party activity, most with subdivisions. Two of these were the anti-democratic extreme right and the extreme left. Between these were the democratic parties of the right and of the left. Subdivisions of the right have emerged around interests like those of farmers, entrepreneurs, conservatives, nationalists, liberals and catholics. The left has been divided by moderates, catholics, intellectuals and working class. Between the democratic left and right was the other main tendency, the centre, the marshland of French politics.

The compromise between these tendencies and their subdivisions had to be effected in parliament. The party system itself was better suited to the articulation of a wide variety of views and interests than to their aggregation. A very wide range and large number of alternatives, therefore, had to be considered at the top level of the consensual apparatus – the decision-making stage – parliament itself. Within parliament, the main burden of achieving some kind of compromise between the alternatives was on the shoulders of certain members of parliament who could feasibly be asked to form governments – governments subject in every detail to, and highly vulnerable to, erratic parliamentary voting. The consequences for French government were clear.

First, there could be little chance of disciplined government majorities. Governments had to be coalitions of parties and they broke up frequently on matters of principle or party advantage. Deputies had no reason to fear the dissolution of parliament as a result of their manoeuvring. The dissolution of 1955 was the first to have occurred in eighty years. The average life of a ministry between 1875 and 1934 under the Third Republic was less than nine months, while in England in the same period it was approximately three-and-a-half years. In the period of economic difficulties and military threat between February 1930 and February 1934 there were fourteen ministries. Coalitions were most likely to collapse in conditions of stress and crisis, precisely when strong government was most urgently needed.

A second political consequence was that the situation favoured people who were devoted to office and cynical about policy. The Radical Socialists, the party of the centre *par excellence*, filled the bill admirably. The Radicals were a cadre party without any clear unifying principle and, therefore, ready to enter into alliance with other parties without too many qualms. When Mendes-France became the leader of the party in 1955 he found it a party 'without funds, files or soul'. But this is the party which scored twelve of the twenty-nine premierships of the Fourth Republic, though their most favourable position in the Assembly was in 1951 when they had 76 of the 627 seats. They played a vital, compromising role.

Other political consequences followed. In times of crisis or stress there was policy stalemate. Attempts to initiate strong action carried the risk that a party to the coalition would be alienated from it. The bureaucracy could not fill the gap in leadership; it could only carry on routine tasks along established policy lines.

All too frequently in these circumstances there was resort to the use of special emergency powers. Though the Fourth Republican constitution had tried to inhibit this by forbidding the delegation of the powers of parliament, hoping to avoid the experiences of the Third Republic, emergency powers were nevertheless often used because this seemed to be the only way to ensure some resolute action in a difficult moment. The use of emergency powers helped to dramatise the relative failure of the political system, with the consequence that there was widespread disillusion with politics. Parties could not be held accountable, nor could governments – there were too many of them between elections. No simple governmental alternatives were offered at elections.

The successes of the Fourth Republic in the economic field, in so far as they depended on government action (other explanations of the generally successful performance of the Western European states after the war, as well as of the differences of performance within the general pattern, are much stronger), may be ascribed to mechanisms which removed the responsibility largely from parliament – namely, the establishment of the Planning Commission and of the various Modernisation Commissions which were designed to exploit the consensual potential of interest groups rather than the party system and parliament.

The Fifth Republic constitution, and the important precedents for its interpretation created by General de Gaulle, have now provided a synthesis of the strengths of the Republican and Autocratic traditions in France. The excesses of unbridled parliamentary power (which the undisciplined parties were unwilling to reduce) have now been curbed, and the power of the executive over parliament much increased. The incompatibility rule which requires ministers to resign their parliamentary seats on appointment, and the reality of the threat of parliamentary dissolution, are important disincentives to errant behaviour on the part of members of the governing coalition.

These reforms, in conjunction with the requirement of direct election for the Presidency, since 1962, have not only transformed the decisiveness of French government but have contributed to the development of something like a bipolar party system. There is still a multiplicity of parties, but two, the Gaullists and the Socialists, have become dominant and are poles of attraction for the other parties. Most significantly, in 1972 the division of the left was, though not healed, patched up more effectively than ever before in French Republican history. The Socialist–Communist Alliance formed at that time resulted in a joint programme to which, in spite of strains, both parties remained committed until 1977.

Italy provides an example which from the standpoint of governmental decisiveness and stability is more detrimental to the multiparty multi-polar system. There are nine parties with regular parliamentary representation. The party organisations outside parliament have been able to control the electoral lists (because the electoral system is a straightforward proportional representation system in multi-member constituencies with proportional allocation of remainders), and parliamentary members are, therefore, subject to the discipline of the outside body of the party. Thus, consensus formation is left to the highest level – parliament – but the parliamentarians themselves are not really autonomous. In a truly multi-party, multi-polar system this has proved a major impediment to resolute government. The Xtian-Democrats, who have been the party of government since the war, have come very much under Vatican influence. The party membership is united on little other than religion, and there are deep divisions between left and right. Electoral organisation is undertaken by Catholic Action, a body of doctrinaire Catholic laymen. Until the accession of Pope John XXIII, this influence kept the party on the right of the political spectrum. John, however, encouraged the left wing of the party to come to terms with the Socialists. From November 1973, therefore, Socialists participated in government coalitions. The effect of this was to strain the unity of the Socialist Party, and as various Socialist ministers have found it necessary to resign from governments to avoid alienating their own left wing, they have contributed to the chronic instability of Italian government.

Italy has also suffered from the fact that electoral systems which encourage multiplicity and multi-polarity of parties serve also to preserve old-style ideological orientations within the realm of political debate, since they reduce the incentive to compromise. In Italy, as in France, a Communist Party has survived as an important organisation, mobilising a large working-class vote. The party is solidly in power in a number of municipalities, including large cities. It is also a party of advanced organisation and able leadership, as indeed is the French Communist Party. Both parties are relatively wealthy and they have a controlling hand in the largest trade union confederations, so that, as Giovanni Sartori observed, 'We thus come to the uncomfortable paradox that the communist party would make an excellent opposition if it were an opposition, i.e. a possible alternative government, but since it would replace the system as well as the people the net result is that the country is deprived of its best potential elites which form under the Communist pole of attraction and cannot really profit from the mechanism of alternation to power. On both accounts the working of the policy is paralysed to a very large extent.'[1]

The Italian constitution provides no effective safeguards. There is no scope in the constitution for the President to play a major role as there is in contemporary France. He is elected for seven years by an electoral college of both houses, plus delegates from the thirteen regional councils. His limited political and constitutional powers include a veto, which can be overridden, the power to dissolve both houses after consultation with their presidents, and what is, in the consequential conditions of instability of government, his most important role, the power to ask someone to form a government. The fall of Signor Moro's government in January 1976 was the end of the thirty-fourth government since the Second World War. The Presidential office has, therefore, only slightly more formal powers than that of a constitutional monarch. The office is sufficiently prestigious to attract key political figures but it cannot be the base for strong government and continuity of policy in default of parliament and the party system. Some improvement in the situation in the long run may be expected through the recent modification of the Communist Party, which has officially abandoned its anti-systemic stance and thus is theoretically available as a possible alternative government or as a coalition partner. However, its democratic promise is, as yet, un-proven, and uncertainty about it remains a source of the continued and long-standing weakness and instability in Italian government.

One place where the effect of this weakness may be seen is in Italian influence within the European Community. In spite of a wide-spread attachment to the ideal of European integration among Italian parties (now extending also to the Communist Party), Italian ministers have not been able to press their views with the vigour that a strong domestic base might have made possible, nor have they been able (with the notable exception of the Communist Party which has the strengths of irresponsibility in opposition) to be very specific about their goals within the Community. Within the Community, therefore, Italian support for integrative measures has been taken for granted, but Italy has not herself played an influential promotive role. Thus, commenting on the post-de Gasperi period and the record of the dominant Christian Democrats, F. Roy Willis has argued that 'the struggles of the currents within the DC itself, the constant bargaining for the formation of a governmental coalition, the frequent changes of personnel in the principal ministries, all tended to increase the incoherence, or rather the stasis of government. While Europeanism remained the cardinal principle of the DC's foreign policy, it became a general belief rather than a practical programme.'[2]

West Germany has nothing like the same problems. The Bonn constitution gave the country a much better legal basis for party activity than Weimar. This, in conjunction with such factors as the near elimination of old class barriers and the shedding of the strong regional influence of Prussia, has allowed the formation of a simplified and consensually more promising party system. For the multi-polarity of Weimar has been substituted a bi-polar multi-party system. There are two dominant parties – the CDU and the SDP. Each acts as a pole of attraction for the next two most important groupings, the CSU, quite closely integrated with the CDU, and the FDP, the recent allies of the SDP in government. Considering the CDU and CSU as one party for electoral purposes, the three main parties (the FDP increasingly outdistanced as a third runner) have obtained since 1949, when they had 72 per cent of the total, an increasing propor-tion of the vote. The electoral system has helped to ensure this. Each voter has two votes, one for an individual in a single-member con-stituency, the other for a party list for the Land. A plurality wins the constituency seat. The Land list votes are pooled nationally and apportioned between parties, each Land getting its voting proportion of seats for the party. A rule which requires at least 5 per cent of the vote or at least three constituency seats before any party is entitled to a proportion of the nationally pooled vote has worked, as intended, against minority parties. An inhibition against the parties' jostling for office and creating governmental instability is the constitutional requirement that the federal Chancellor can only be removed from office by a majority vote in the legislature which, in dismissing him, elects his successor.

There do remain tensions within the system which are a source of apparent weaknesses. Cabinet responsibility is not a constitutional requirement so that coalitions with the FDP since 1965 have often exhibited some divisions of opinion within government. After Adenauer's withdrawal from active politics, Germany seemed unable to define clear policies towards her Eastern neighbours nor was it very specific about its goals within the European Community. During the period of CDU/CSU ascendancy the course of economic policy meandered vaguely between planning, with some nationalisation (to 1947), Erhard's market economics (to 1952), then increasing protectionism and cartel orientations (to 1963). There are many forces within the CDU/CSU alliance, some of them at odds with each other. The alliance was originally a rallying point for any groupings opposed to socialism and it includes both labour and business elements, Protestants and Roman Catholics, centrists and devolutionists, civil servants and agriculturalists. Its leader, therefore, has to be the kind of person who is prepared to play a fairly passive role in policy promotion and who, without any very strong association with any of the constituent elements, can play the role of honest broker between them.

In 1966, right and left combined in the somewhat surprising coalition of Christian Democrats and Social Democrats. The ambiguity of this combination was reflected in policy. It limited government to a rather weak role, particularly in economic management. Even with the eventual assumption of power by the SPD in harness with the FDP there was little disturbance of the rather passive governmental stance in economic, Community and foreign affairs. The stance, however, in a period of economic strength and expansion probably did represent a genuine amalgam of electoral views and marked the responsiveness of party government to shifting supports. Germany, nevertheless, in this more 'streamlined' party system has enjoyed more stable government than it had during the Weimar period, and policy anaemia has been tolerable during a period of continuing economic success, and sustained by a permissive consensus.

In Holland, the electoral system is undoubtedly favourable to party diversity, a diversity so extreme that Holland is an exception to the contention advanced in this chapter about the aggregative role of parties. The 150-member lower house is elected by proportional representation over the country as a whole as one constituency. There are five main parties but, in all, fourteen have representation in the house. The upper house is also elected by proportional representation, in this case by the provincial councils.

In spite of the number of parties, reflecting as they do Catholic, Protestant and secular divisions which cut across the socio-economic boundaries, a high degree of elite consensus on practical policy issues is achieved. This is partly an effect of the very strong traditional need for continuing effective action on land reclamation and defences. Doctrinal differences have been subordinated to this practical end. More generally, co-operative goals and methods of achieving them are worked out in an elaborate committee structure in which the representation of different interest groups and views is effected. At the head of this structure of 'concertation' stands a Social and Economic Council with constitutional standing. Very large public industrial organisations also have extensive management functions in their various spheres of Dutch economic activity, and they too are instruments of consensus formation, reducing the burden on the party system, but blurring the lines of democratic accountability.

Within the consensual framework, in an era of widespread decline of parliaments, the Dutch parliament plays a somewhat unorthodox consensual role. The Dutch government is outside parliament so the latter controls its own agenda, its proceedings are televised, there is considerable freedom of voting, and, since the major interest group leaders are members of parliament, there are frequent 'smoke-filled room' negotiations, away from the floor of the House, in which major policy decisions are taken.

What the Dutch have done, in effect, with their notable pragmatism, is to bypass the fragmented and consensually ineffective party system, and develop the informal elitist and corporatist consensual infrastructure. Even so, the multi-polar party system has been, latterly, a source of political and administrative weakness.

Cabinet coalitions are very difficult to form in Holland. The process is protracted because the doctrinal preoccupations of the parties come to the fore at such times. Caretaker governments can carry on in a routine way during negotiations since they do not have to rely on parliamentary majorities, but they are unable to take decisive actions which may be needed. Once formed, until recently, cabinets have been fairly stable. The stability was based on the alliance of religious parties and Liberals which formed most of the coalitions in the period after 1919 and until the 1970s. A long-term decline in the aggregate vote of the religious parties culminated in a major setback in 1971 and then again in November 1972. From 1971 to May 1973 when Dr Joop den Uyl, Labour Party leader, formed a government there was a near-continuous crisis of government. It was during this time of weakness that a high level of inflation developed without check, the guilder weakened on the international exchanges, and there were other symptoms of 'overheating' of the economy. Un-co-ordinated corporatist decision making thus demonstrated one of its major weaknesses – its lack of overall coherence, and its consequent inability to cope with crises.

Its other weaknesses have also been in evidence. As Nelkin has pointed out, it was in this context that 'a rash of ill feeling against the establishment, particularly among young people and workers, erupted in the late 1960s. The action groups expressing these attitudes argued that the system of institutionalised accommodation of plural interests had calcified; that certain groups lacked representation; and that new problems of rapidly changing society were neglected . . . Quite diverse action groups . . . shared a common theme – the declining influence of the citizen. This sentiment assumed increased importance in the early 1970s.'[3]

Parties, outside the multi-polar, multi-party pattern of which Holland provides an example, do mitigate the deficiencies of interest group representation, articulating, but also aggregating interests, not only of the membership of the party, but of elements of the electorate on whom they rely for support. Like government they tend to be responsive to organised groups, particularly where they are major sources of financial support or have affiliated membership, as do British trade unions in the Labour Party. However, recognising that there are large unorganised interests with considerable voting strength, the parties do frequently become spokesmen for them.

A distinction needs to be made, however, between governing party elites, parliamentary parties, and parties outside parliaments. Party leaders in government have an ambiguous relationship with their parliamentary parties and party organisations in the country. In Britain, Clement Attlee is reported to have said that his Labour government was 'not unaware' of the party outside parliament, and there is no question that governments can and do ignore 'official' party programmes on the presumption that they are responsible to a wider constituency, have special knowledge etc. etc. and, in fact, because they are a key element in the decisive pattern of 'concertation' procedures – part of what Galbraith calls the 'planning system' of political elites, bureaucracy, and leaders of large economic organisations like corporations and trade unions.

The parliamentary party on the 'back bench' is likely to be more aware of the party in the country and attentive to opinion in the constituencies. A number of factors, however, modify the effects of this awareness and work in favour of disciplined support for the parliamentary party leaders. These include such things as hope of office, desire to maintain the government and avoid precipitating an election, and conceptions of parliamentary party loyalty in face of opposition parties. The discipline breaks down from time to time, and factional elements emerge, usually a simple left- and right-wing division, but occasionally more diversely articulative of popular opinions. But it is the party in the country which best exhibits pluralist diversity.

No one, carefully observing and considering mass political parties outside parliaments, whether in two-party or multi-party bi-polar systems, could sustain very long the impression, which parliamentary behaviour might well give, that there is a definable majority view on most issues of policy, opposed by a substantial minority. Parties instead are seen to be loose coalitions of views and interests. Their internal unity is strained, and the divisions between them are blurred by the non-congruency of opinion cleavages. This, the accepted view of the great American parties, is true of all the major parties of Western Europe also, the surviving communist parties being a possible exception. It is a virtue of the American constitution that it succeeds in attaining in the formal institutional setting of Congress itself, continuing, professional articulation of this diversity, without serious detraction from responsible government, since this is effected through the elected Presidency upon whom devolves much of the aggregative burden.

European political parties are forums, outside the parliamentary arena particularly, for the articulation of the diverse interests they embrace. They also do perform, nevertheless, an essential part of the aggregative function, not so much in defining a compromise view on specific issues, or in drawing up a more general party programme, but in holding together under one political roof disparate individual and group elements, and stimulating among them a degree of regularity and commonality of political behaviour. Parties are, in fact, instruments of political socialisation.

It is the party worker who is most effectively socialised. Through mass membership recruitment, through fund-raising activities and social events which reach a wider public, through election campaigning and canvassing, the party's socialisation role is extended to a wider public. Party campaigning activities engender, first of all, a commitment to the party. In all the democratic countries it is clear that the majority of voters adheres to the same party in election after election. Party activities help to, and in part are designed to, reinforce that commitment. Thus, throughout the party, excepting perhaps the alternative system party, the commitment is extended to the political system itself. Even the alternative system party, to the degree that it works within the framework and rules of the existing system, helps, ironically, to legitimise it. The act of voting for a party at an election is both a reaffirmation of commitment to a party and a reaffirmation of commitment to the procedures of the political system. All the Western democracies have a high voting turn-out in spite of a wide variety of voting systems, so that voting, as a socialising activity in itself, 'catches' a large proportion of the electorate.[4]

Political socialisation by the established major parties is an activity supporting and strengthening consensus on constitutional procedures, creating a better climate for interest aggregation and simplifying the task by reducing the range of difference of opinion.

EVALUATION

It is possible to offer some tentative hypotheses about the relative strengths of different kinds of party system. The aggregative and articulative functions, I have suggested, are opposed functions between which, because they are both necessary, a mean must be struck. The aggregative function is necessary to policy making, but if it is performed very effectively, so that policy emerges from the consideration of two simple alternatives – parts of two detailed but only marginally different 'catch-all' party programmes, put before an electorate and considered as a mandate for disciplined party-voting – then the possibility exists that minority views, eliminated or very much compromised at an early stage in a hierarchical pattern of consensus formation within the parties, will be unnecessarily frustrated. Those who hold them will be alienated from the system because they find no effective expression at the level of national decision making. If, on the other hand, the articulative function is performed very effectively at the highest level, the multitude of uncompromised views may well hinder effective decision making and lead to policy stalemate and governmental instability, particularly in times of economic difficulty or international stress.

The British two-party system has come closest to the aggregative extreme. When the country was relatively strong and prosperous and the economy growing, the simple division on most issues between the parties was sharper and it seemed to correspond to the primary division in an otherwise apparently homogeneous population: the class division. The system was therefore tolerable. As class divisions have become less sharp, and complicated by the emergence of an amorphous enlarged middle class, swelled by the growth of the service sector, the parties have become less sharply differentiated on issues, and an emergent range of interests, regional/nationality, ethnic/colour, vocational, sexual and generational, finds inadequate articulation through them. The result of this, in conjunction with the considerable development of corporatist elements in interest intermediation, has been disillusion with politics and a decline of commitment to constitutional procedures and a general loss of confidence and morale.

The articulative extreme is now found in Italy with its multi-polar, multi-party pattern, with no constitutional compensation to strengthen government or facilitate aggregation at the highest level, and with the ultimate debilitating factor of party control outside the parliamentary arena in which decisions have to be made and governments sustained. The Italian case comes close to Sartori's summary of the distinctive characteristics of a multi-party system: that is, centrifugality, ideological rigidity, elite cleavage deepening the fragmentation of basic consensus, absence of real alternative government, growth of irresponsible opposition and, thereby, the politics of outbidding or unfair competition.[5]

Germany and France with their bi-polar systems of multi-party representation come closer to the mean. France has the constitutional advantage of its powerful elective Presidency with its aggregative role. The parties provide an articulation within the Assembly, and at elections, of a variety of views, from the extremes of left to right; but they respond in parliamentary voting and in electoral pacts to the incentives in the constitution for the provision of effective government. A minor weakness in the Fifth Republican constitution, however, is that this has not been achieved without some lowering of the esteem in which parliament is held, because of the reduction in its powers. But it is difficult to see how parliamentary powers could be increased (except perhaps by reducing the scope of the government's regulatory power) without disturbing the whole delicate balance established by the constitution.

Only the American system comes closer to the golden mean than the French. It is nominally a two-party system but in practice comes closer to the multi-party bi-polar conception. The elective Presidency ensures government stability and takes up the aggregative burden, via the Presidential convention and the presentation of specific Presidential programmes to Congress. The confederal nature of the parties is apparent in Congress where a satisfying range of minority views is articulated. There is party voting cohesion, but it is far from absolute, and a view opposed to that of the official position of the majority party is not only articulated but stands some chance of being voted into policy. The two major American parties have been 'open' to new ideas and leadership to a much greater degree than is true of any European party. The federal system, the separation of powers, the Presidential nominating convention and the primary election are all contributory factors. The parties have been able to embrace new political movements, including socialism,[6] as they have arisen and to the extent that they have won popular support.

Though there are, then, differences between party systems in these respects – differences which are partly dependent on manipulable factors like electoral systems, legislative–executive relations and other constitutional prescriptions – we would argue, generally, that excepting their vague campaign programmes and 'official' policy statements, parties are relatively sensitive instruments for the expression of a very wide range of views and opinions and are, therefore, a line of defence of democratic values against corporatist elements in modern government. Though they may exhibit the oligarchical tendencies of large organisations, a mass membership and a larger clientele of sympathisers and voting adherents is wooed and propitiated by a political leadership. Equally important from the democratic against the corporatist viewpoint is the fact that party bureaucracies – the often slender, non-elective, paid expert staff of the parties – do not play an influential policy role. They are not part of the governmental and interest group bureaucratic 'concert' in corporatist policy making which reverses the classical democratic ideal of the bureaucratic role. This aspect of corporatism is the subject of the next chapter.

NOTES

1 In J. La Palombara and M. Weiner, *Political Parties and Political Development* (Princeton: Princeton University Press, 1966), p. 147. Italy has come very near to the point where this paralysis could result in Communist electoral victory. The fall of M. Moro's government in January 1976 was occasioned by the withdrawal of Socialist voting support for the two-party coalition of Christian Democrats and Republicans. One reason for the Socialist action was its concern over the attempts by Signor Moro to come to an agreement with the Communists, the Christian Democrats having only a marginal lead of 2 per cent over its nearest rival. Success of these efforts would have reduced the influence of the Socialists as a potential government party.

2 F. Roy Willis, *Italy Chooses Europe* (London: OUP, 1971), p. 47.

3 D. Nelkin, *Technological Decisions and Democracy* (Beverly Hills: Sage, 1977), p. 26.

4 See D. Urwin (ed.), *Election in Western Nations 1945–1968*, Occasional Papers 4 and 5 (Survey Research Centre, University of Strathclyde, 1968). The figures on voting turn-out suggest that proportional representation is favourable to high turn-out, possibly because the phenomenon of the safe seat and the reduction of interest which it entails is less likely. On this see D. T. Denver and H. T. G. Hands, 'Marginality and turn out in British general elections', *British Journal of Political Science*, October 1972, p. 34, and cf A. S. Cohan, R. D. McKinlay and A. Mughan, 'The used vote and electoral outcomes: the Irish general election of 1973', *British Journal of Political Science*, July 1975, pp. 363–83. The US is sometimes cited for its low turn-out in comparison with the Western European democracies, though when the effect of voting, qualifications (particularly state residence requirements) is taken

into account the comparison is less marked. However, in comparison with European voting requirements, the effects of two American institutions–the long ballot (a consequence of federalism and of the enlarged conception of offices appropriately elected rather than appointed) and the primary system–work to enhance the possibilities for meaningful political participation. Rare, relatively, is the US citizen who does not personally know some person who has been a candidate for public office; who does not know, in other words, a political animal with whom he may air his views and grievances.

5   In La Palombara and Weiner, op. cit., pp. 159–60.
6   On this see S. M. Lipset, 'Socialism in America', *Dialogue*, vol. 10, no. 4 (1977), pp. 3–12.

7

Bureaucracy

The purpose of this chapter is to examine the bureaucratic phenomenon as it occurs in advanced industrial societies, and to consider how its development has affected the democratic accountability of government.

The basic democratic theory about the place of the administration, and the conception of a virtuous bureaucracy, is fairly clear: in the utilitarian-liberal tradition the recognised constitutional objective is to devise techniques which will ensure that the interest of the community, in which every individual has an equal share and equal rights, is secured by legislation. For this purpose there must be created an identity of interest between the legislators and those for whom they legislate. In so far as this *can* be secured, it is through elections, and through the absolute supremacy of the elected assembly in law making. It follows that the bureaucracy must be:

subordinate
malleable
politically neutral
subject to ministerial control through clear lines of responsibility
anonymous (so that the responsibility of the politician is absolute).

The sum of these qualities would seem to make the bureaucracy, as in Weber's conception, the one perfectly rational instrument of government – for him, the defining essence of modernity. The composition of legislatures may change, and with it governments and government policy, but the bureaucracy remains, ready to serve faithfully whatever party may be in power.

There are, though, certain long-standing and growing problems of bureaucracy in the practice of democratic societies. The role foisted on the bureaucracy has grown with the increased role of the state, and of course, the bureaucracy favours tendencies which promote its own expansion. As a particular consequence of this increased state role the burden of legislation by parliaments has increased and the tendency to devolve major rule-making powers upon ministers to fill out the details of legislation has grown with it. The power, in practice, devolves upon the bureaucracy and it is, according to Hewart, the source of a *New Despotism*.[1] It is theoretically subject to parliamentary supervision but this can only be haphazard.

Then, the very requirements of the 'good bureaucracy' – its neutrality, secured by impersonal rules, the hierarchical organisation which preserves clear responsibility, its obedience, its anonymity and secrecy – create problems in themselves – the so-called 'bureaucratic dysfunctions'.[2] These are cumbrousness, the frustration of red tape, jurisdictional disputes, timidity or 'buck passing', and extreme conservatism in organisational matters and to a lesser extent in policy direction.

The apparent fundamental purpose of the traditional bureaucracy has been, it sometimes seems, to back into the future unrolling the map of the past – and trying to make the future look as much like it as possible. It has 'control of the files' and the relatively safe guidance of the precedents it can find in them. It preserves some continuity of policy, but, by the same token, makes it very difficult to change it.

We have become, also, increasingly aware of the *political* role of the bureaucracy: that is, as initiator of legislation, and consequently as an object of pressure group activity. The bureaucracy has many assets which foster this role, going well beyond the obvious asset of well-developed organisation. In the European democracies, where competitive examinations to recruit people who are intellectually well-equipped for demanding work have become the rule, the civil services have consistently attracted the best-educated people. Highly developed methods of post-entry education, both general courses and specialised training, strengthen this advantage. The curricula tested by competitive entry examinations tend to ensure that the bureaucracy also has the asset of class status behind it. The environmental advantages of the middle and upper classes in educational attainment continue to assert themselves – a natural barrier to quite deliberate 'democratising' reforms. The bureaucracy derives authority from its strong connections with the class from which it is recruited. This is frequently supplemented (for example in England, Germany and France, where a reputation for efficiency, impartiality and incorruptibility has been maintained) by a popular conception of its legitimacy.

It is evident too that those who have to implement policy are in a particularly good position to evaluate it, even if only as an instrument for given political ends, and to see how it might be improved. Developed expertise and superior access to politically relevant information, enhance still more the influence of bureaucrats in relation to their political masters. At the same time, pressure group leaders come to value the stable relations they can establish with permanent civil servants in the department – while ministers and their political deputies come and go. Group leaders, therefore, may often act as supports to bureaucratic influence and vice versa. Finally, the practice of appointing civil servants to ministerial office – for example, in France and Holland – adds further to the representation of civil service views at the highest political level. This fits very uncomfortably, or not at all, into the conception we have of democratic politics through representative assemblies.

Nicholas Ridley and Wedgwood-Benn, both with ministerial experience in the UK, are among the many who have attested to this political role and the problems it poses for the political executive. According to Ridley,

> The everyday work and attitude of a Government Department is often more responsive to its Permanent Secretary than to its Ministers. In some Departments it is impossible for all decisions to be referred to Ministers, the work load is so heavy. What is worrying, is the selection of which decisions (and sometimes of which information) should be put before Ministers. It requires good judgement to know when a Minister should be brought in and when not: It is also an opportunity to short-circuit him deliberately.
>
> A good Under Secretary can persist unobtrusively but firmly with policies his political masters may wish to change. He can stonewall initiatives he does not like. Even when it is conceded that a policy or an attitude might be altered, the advisers retire for several weeks to 'review' it, a process which often results in changes more in accordance with their own views than with those of the Minister.
>
> Ministers may neither sack nor change their advisers, even if they are antipathetic personally or politically. It follows from this that often the alternatives are to go along with the official advice, or fight a pitched battle. Shortage of time and energy make it extremely unlikely that the battle will be won. Indeed the whole machine is alerted to thwart Ministers who resist official advice: other Departments mysteriously brief their Ministers to oppose. Civil servants can probably change their political masters more easily than the masters can change their servants.[3]

When the Heath administration attempted to reduce the size of the service and improve efficiency,

> Very strong pressure was brought to bear in the Department of Trade and Industry not to change from investment grants to allowances because the switch threatened several hundreds of Civil Service jobs. Equally plans for reducing expenditure by cutting the

Research Establishments, particularly the Atomic Energy Authority, came up against very strong opposition, because of redundancy prospects rather than for any policy reasons. Invariably the 'advice' sides with the threatened colleagues. Civil servants are obviously not the best people to cut civil servant numbers. The resistance to changes which threaten the jobs or the work pattern of the Civil Service is as strong as in any other profession. Ministers have neither the time nor the power to do it, and a handful of business advisers were not enough to turn the scales . . .[4]

In other words I suspect that the Civil Service is a political party of monolithic view, which believes in a whole series of policies because it thinks they are in the 'national interest'. It has its own incubus, its own political dynamism, its own colossal research department. It thinks it has the solutions that are most nearly perfect.

It realises that it is necessary to make concessions both to the opinions of the governing political party, and to the clamour of the people. But it views concessions as diversions into politics and acknowledges that this is properly the domain of the politicians. It is important to get back to the 'right' road as soon as the political situation permits.

This philosophy explains the Whitehall attitude towards Parliament. Parliament is slightly frightening and unpredictable. A debate in Parliament is a sort of obstacle race which a Minister has to run. They are genuinely sorry for him in this ordeal. They write impeccable draft speeches. The briefing is superb. But Parliament is something to be survived, weathered, rather than listened to or placated. Rather than the elected assembly of the nation, whose views and anxieties they want to accept, Parliament is a hostile ordeal which can occasionally mar their plans.[5]

Benn:

Ministers have no staff specifically charged with the development and maintenance of the political links they need to have with those who work outside Whitehall, or even their own ministerial colleagues. The network of ministerial and official committees under the Cabinet Office, which is supposed to facilitate the smooth running of government business, also acts in such a way as to hinder the political, and strengthen the departmental view at every stage.

What is required is the open acceptance – with proper safeguards – of a new category of political advisers who would be appointed to serve an incoming government, and each of the departmental ministers, and would go out of office with them. Such advisers would have no executive power within the department and no civil servant would be expected to take orders from them.[6]

The difficulty for ministers in Germany is at least as great. The traditional, anonymous, non-political conception of role for the bureaucracy is guaranteed in the constitution itself. Paradoxically, the self-perception of the service, thus strengthened, as guardian of the public welfare, produces a somewhat jaundiced view of the political process. Consequently, 'the tendency of the administration to be autonomous towards the political decision-makers by referring to a pressure exerted by the logic of facts has made the problem of the technocracy acute in the Federal Republic'.[7]

In France the same problems and tensions are exacerbated by the traditional regard of the numerous *corps* for the defence of their own special professional interests and functional monopoly. M. Pisani, as Minister of Agriculture from 1961 to 1966, sought to make far-reaching reforms but found himself persistently thwarted. Unusually determined to impose his views 'despite the vigorous opposition of the ministry's civil servants, Pisani succeeded in his aims, partly because of dogged persistence and partly because of his particular political and administrative skills . . . [and] the backing he received from Matignon and the Elysee'.[8] Another French minister, Albin Chalandon, Minister of Equipment and Housing, 1967–72, involved in a battle with his ministry which became widely publicised, noted 'that the administration possessed power and responsibility without sanctions, since the tenure of civil servants was not related to their efficiency, that it was therefore basically conservative, that it was concerned solely with its own interests, and that it had a privileged position because it escaped political control'.[9]

The problem of bureaucratic influence is worsened as the element of *expertise* in government grows, so that politicians are hostages to their own ignorance. Experts, therefore, acquire their own powers, independent of both government and public. They tend to assert what they regard as professional standards and discretion. But an assertive professionalism in comparison with the generalists' *service* orientation, or even a legalistic orientation, is an additional force to be contended with by the politician. The more that people with professional expertise come to dominate an agency of government, the more likely it is that the agency will not be simply a compliant instrument of political masters, but will be self-assertive.

All agencies of government tend to develop a 'character' of their own into which recruits are socialised. There is a departmental spirit (or *esprit de corps*) and a departmental view on certain policies. A specialist, professional team will tend, still more, to be dedicated to professional goals. A health service with doctors at the head (as in the USA and NZ, for example) or a medical council of some sort, with executive functions, will tend *to reflect the goals and values of the profession* to the neglect of social and even other professional goals in interpreting its role. So, in France, in urban planning, as Self points out,[10] the entrenched position of engineers in government (one of the Grand Corps) has inhibited the contributions of architects and town planners.

Add to these considerations the danger that it is the second-rate specialist who enters administration (where the financial reward is lower), and also that the specialist who turns controller finds that he has little time to keep up with his subject (so that his stock of specialist knowledge becomes obsolete), and a formidable set of problems deriving from expertise becomes evident.[11]

Broadly speaking, there are three kinds of answer proposed to these problems in modern political and administrative theory and administrative practice.

(1) There are proposals for *administrative reform.*
(2) There is the thesis, of which Lindblom is the leading protagonist, that what is needed is not administrative reform but simply *less administration.*
(3) There is the suggested need for a revision of our concept of a legitimate *political role* for the administrator.

1.   Administrative reform: physiological and sociological alternatives.

(a) The first proposals on administrative reform were directed against the cumbrousness of the machinery of government and the wasteful duplication of functions. What was proposed was 'scientific administration'. This was a concept which owed some of its inspiration to Taylorism – the writings of Frederick Taylor in the US, on industrial management. He popularised the techniques of time and motion studies, production control and office organisation and methods – generally, the best ways to organise workers physically for given routine tasks and operations. Henry Fayol in France was one of the first to see the possibilities of this kind of approach to public services: that is, a search for efficiency by a more scientific 'problem-solving' approach to administration. A number of American writers followed the same line, and the 1937 President's Committee on Administrative Management plus the two Hoover Commissions after the Second World War (1949 and 1955) developed it further. Briefly it was thought that the slowness, cumbrousness, duplication of bureaucratic control could be reduced by:

(i)   more and better developed specialisation;
(ii) precise definition of jurisdictions;
(iii) and *staff service bodies*: these were to be secretarial and reporting staffs to ensure that at *the points of responsibility in the*

hierarchy, full information would ensure proper co-ordination with other agencies and departments and more effective supervision to see that decisions were carried out and did not just get stuck in the pipeline. It was a quasi-military approach in that it involved more hierarchy, more specialisation, tighter controls – a stronger prescription to eliminate unwanted reactions.

(b) The weakness in this first 'physiological' approach to administrative reform was rapidly pointed out by social scientists, notably in 1945 by Herbert Simon in his book *Administrative Behaviour*. It is clear that other factors beside formal structure hold an organisation together and determine how it operates. Simon, therefore, took the emphasis off organisation and put it on to codes and modes of behaviour – not rules, that is, but guiding principles and 'mores'. His behavioural model requires that in any situation the administrator – at any level – should examine all possible courses of action open to him, trace the alternative consequences of each course, and then evaluate the benefits and losses of each alternative.

This model is one which stands opposed to the rigidities of officialdom and against taking refuge in impersonal rules or adhering to official single goals without consideration of the harsh effects of the *means* in particular cases.

It puts more of an emphasis on the individual responsibility of officials as opposed to the hierarchical principle. At the highest level, this is very like the rationale for the more recent development of 'PPBS' (planning, programming budgeting systems), an operation which involves different goals and appropriate resources being set out for review, as a basis for policy decisions. This has been very influential in practice, for example in the USA and Sweden, and does provide a practical guide to administrators; but it leaves most of the political difficulties unsolved. Both of these two administrative reforms depend upon a very incomplete, or rather, superficial concept of efficiency – a kind of product/cost calculation. But efficiency is not a concept which stands by itself – it must be related to goals. So there remains the problem of ensuring that bureaucracy works to goals *specified for it* by a democratic process and of ensuring that it does not exercise an *undue influence* on democratic policy makers.

(c) One answer to *the* problem of undue influence is the *competitive solution* – a more or less deliberate overlapping of functions. This conception may be found in Anthony Downs's book *Inside Bureaucracy* (1967). Another account of it is in David Truman, *The Governmental Process* (1951). The thesis is that politicians may be able to stay 'on top' by acting as *mediators* between competing, conflicting agencies and departments. The agencies compete for resources to pursue their goals, they compete to enlarge their own special clientele, and they compete for political support. According to Anthony Downs there is a kind of function and client heartland for each department – an interior zone, a peripheral zone for which other agencies are competing, and a no man's land, where agencies compete on equal terms.

This is an idea viewed with favour in the United States because it is in tune with the theory of the pluralist society. Administrative conflict parallels the conflict between groups – the countervailing pressures which are supposed to be a guarantee against majority tyranny. *And* it is seen as a sign of administrative vitality. The analogy is drawn with healthy competition between firms in the capitalist economy. Administrative conflict of this kind can be seen, for example, in the development of the Central Valley in California. Interested claimants in 1940 were the Bureau of Reclamation – whose interest was in developing the irrigation of the area and in the provision of hydro-electric power, and the Army corps of Engineers – well protected in Congress as a generally useful, 'pork barrel' agency, and primarily interested in flood control aspects.

These agencies were in competition to undertake this project. Eventually it was undertaken by the Engineers, though at one point the President had asked the Secretary of War to call them off.[12] Other examples are multifold. There are, for example, many choices of federal grants-in-aid from different agencies from which a town can select in deciding on a municipal sewage scheme – a very wide range of choice for the politician, resulting from administrative duplication and competition.

At the local government level itself, as Michel Crozier points out, 'there are multiple decision centres. Each of them has autonomous legal prerogatives and extremely confused and intricate duties: school boards, tax assessors, municipal councils, county officials, sheriffs etc. – altogether dozens of autonomous decision units, without even mentioning the local offices of state and federal authorities. The complexity of relationships between all these units is tremendous, and jurisdictional problems are numerous. This system has great advantages. It makes it possible to tap many kinds of human resources which would otherwise remain indifferent or hostile. Very diverse kinds of initiatives flourish, and citizens participate at all levels of the decision-making machinery. No one is kept at a distance by central authorities because there is no other way of preserving their working efficiency. The whole system is more open; vicious circles of routine and apathy do not last so long'.[13]

In the rather different cultural environment of Britain and most other European countries, this theory does not enjoy the same prestige. First, the idea of agencies or departments of government captured by an interest group is unpalatable, conflicting as it does with the conception of government responsibility to pursue a community interest.

Second, it ignores the problem of unorganised interests and under-privileged sectors of society who cannot act as effective supports for the departments which are concerned with their affairs. Of course, in practice government departments everywhere do have very close relationships with interest groups in their functional sectors and the problem of unorganised interests is pervasive: but the ideal of government accountability still lends force to these arguments in the present context.

It is the high economic cost, in certain functional areas, of this kind of competition – which Europeans can hardly afford – which does directly affect bureaucratic organisation. For example, inter-service rivalry in the promotion of military technology in the US is seen as having the advantage of maximising the eventual choices available. It is very difficult to come to discussions about complex technological projects while they are still on the drawing board. It is much easier when they come into operation. The British services cannot afford this luxury of choice – hence the services are integrated in the Ministry of Defence.

A similar integration of procurement has been in existence in France since 1961 when the DMA (la Délégation Ministérielle pour l'Armement) was created. Until that time, except occasionally in war or crisis, responsibility for armament procurement was divided and dependent on different authorities for land, sea and air services and, also, separately for explosives. The rationalisation of 1961 reflected the increasing cost of weapons development and the consequent need to avoid duplication of financial effort and resource application. There is, of course, still rivalry between the services and it is some-times suggested that the decision to equip the army with the Pluton tactical nuclear weapon system is an example of its continued effect on policy – a sop to army jealousy; nevertheless, even in this area, weapons systems and their procurement are clearly complementary across the services, with tactical nuclear weapons for the army and strategic weapons for the other two services complementing each other in the sense that the naval weapon, mobile but vulnerable to attack because it is not on sovereign territory, is supplemented by the territorially based weaponry of the air force.[14]

Even in West Germany where the ideology of the competitive economy might have been expected to carry over into defence pro-curement, the definition of military technological objectives, the development phase of systems, projects and equipment, and the actual procurement phase is dominated by the Federal Office of Military Technology and Procurement (BWB).

In a more general comparison of practice in America and France, Crozier, whose comments on American bureaucracy are generally more favourable, because it is 'less entrenched and somewhat more open to change than the French', points out that 'the detours imposed by the mere existence of all these different authorities, the difficulty of co-ordinating them and of harmonizing possible conflicting decisions, call for an extremely complex strategy of procedures that is the focal point of American administrative dysfunctions'.[15]

This is not to say that there is *no* duplication among government departments in Britain and the Continent or that the duplication does not sometimes fragment the power of the bureaucracy both in policy influence and rule making. There is, for example, in all departments a critical conflict with the Treasury in Britain over costs. While most departments have recruited economists for their own internal needs, there is no doubt that part of the rationale of this recruitment is the need to be able to hold their own against the Treasury experts. Similarly, the long-standing use of civilians in the administration of the Service departments has helped provide continuity and stability in the techniques and tactics of interdepartmental negotiation.

Again, though the Department of Scientific and Industrial Research, established in 1916, was, for the next fifty years, the main vehicle for the direction of science policy, other departments with competing interests and jurisdiction have recruited scientists; and bodies like the Medical Research Council and the Agricultural Research Council have performed similar functions. Efforts were made from time to time to co-ordinate such work, but though expenditure quadrupled between 1920 and 1939, the separate establishments retained their autonomy and competed for allocations. Charles Carter reported, as late as 1959 (as Chairman of the Economics Committee), 'we doubt if it can be said that a Government policy on the application of Science really exists'. There were competing policies. Thus, in the absence of political direction, competitive administration has left a clutter which conforms to a fairly undemanding corporatist conception of government, but not with the prevailing European conception of *responsible* democratic government. It is in the area of defence, then, where the costs of the advanced technological requirements are so high, that the European rejection of the competitive solution to administrative dominance is most unambiguous.

(d) The generally favoured European solution to the problem of linking politics and administration in order to secure responsible government is to have a top managerial class of general administrators. In Britain this is a class of the career civil service – the administrative class – without special training. In France it comprises both career officials, trained for their tasks at the Ecole National d'Administration (ENA), plus a quasi-political class in the ministerial 'Cabinets'. In Germany this class is recruited mainly from the faculties of *law* of the universities. In America it is politically recruited. In the UK the general administrator plays an integrative role – he is a co-ordinator and arbitrator between the specialist claims, opinions and viewpoints within his department. The permanent secretary has a very close relationship with his minister. According to Redcliffe-Maud, 'The heart of the job is to have a common mind with his Minister.' He must have imbibed, in the British civil service, 'a potent tradition of common belief, attitudes and ethics'. His only specialism is his understanding of the machinery of government and his 'awareness of ministerial responsibility'.[16] The French generalist, highly trained for his administrative task, tends to be more assertive in the career service, but the minister's personal 'cabinet' of trusted advisers is some protection from his powerful influence. The German law-trained administrator, according to Sontheimer, tends to see himself as not just the loyal administrator of political decisions, but the real authority on these decisions, by virtue of his training.[17] In the United States the comparable thing is the open patronage system, which depends for its working to a considerable extent on personal loyalties. This provides most of the protective advantage of the personal 'cabinet' system but there are some dangers (if responsibility is to be the criterion) in having, occasionally, politicians with careers to make in administrative positions below the Cabinet level. There is some difficulty too in finding enough people of really high calibre to fill all the posts that customarily change hands at fairly short notice when a new administration comes in. (There are still approximately 1,200 political appointments at the top of the Federal Service – about one-sixth of the key posts.)

None of these administrative reform solutions entirely solves any one of the traditional problems of bureaucracies. They are still cumbrous, impersonal, prone to self-expansion, yet conservative and cautious in their approach to structural change – and at the top, the generalist career officials exhibit a degree of administrative egoism. In spite of 'the code' – they know best and may well try to dominate their ministers, depriving support for their autonomy from their bureaucratic counterparts in the interest organisations in their functional area.

2. In face of these disadvantages, Lindblom, Hirschman, Braybrooke and others argue, quite simply, for *less administration*.[18]

The thesis is that policies should be made within a narrow range of alternatives. Policy change *should* be incremental and marginal rather than radical and dislocatory. They contend that any actor can, at best, achieve no more than a very limited change of policy. Their preferred solution by what they call 'partisan mutual adjustment' assumes that the various interests which ought to be considered in democratic decision making will be better served through a bargaining process between them rather than through the decisions of some supposedly objective official.

The thesis, which comes very close to being an apologia for corporatism, evidently depends on a peculiar conception of the democratic ideal. It draws on economists' insights into the working of the market system for the allocation of values. This is seen as accomplishing a co-ordination beyond the competence of central co-ordinators. And it argues that there is a general capacity for mutual adjustment among human beings – more than is generally recognised or admitted. It is seen in the use of language itself: a complex, uncontrolled, but effectively self-co-ordinated system of communication. It can be seen on pedestrian crossings in the way people and vehicles easily resolve their competitive goals. It is evident in the development of common law, and it is beautifully demonstrated in traffic control, in the way the decisions of one policeman on point duty are co-ordinated with those of his colleagues on the next crossing.

There are, however, a number of problems inherent in the extension of the functional area of *laissez-faire* mutual adjustment in society. One is that it may require sacrifice of desirable social ends. In a prison, for example, the provision of food and clothing, accommodation, and work with training relevance may be readily acknowledged as necessary and desirable activities, since they can be related to values like health, discipline and rehabilitation. They are normally centrally scheduled and administered activities. Other activities equally related to these values like games, and various recreational and cultural activities, are normally regarded as proper spheres for greater autonomy or 'mutual adjustment'. In practice, out of this area of activity there does tend to grow up a set of 'prisoner-regulated' norms and social stratification which is found to be, almost invariably, hostile to the overall societal values for which the prison is responsible – particularly rehabilitation.

A more general example is in the area of wage bargaining, still very much an area of *laissez-faire* in the UK. Until trade unions gained their present legal status and protection, *laissez-faire* bargaining or mutual adjustment was a very unequal process, as it is for example still in Scotland in private contracting for construction and agricultural work. Here a system of something close to slave labour has evolved, perfectly well integrated into the overall social activity in economic terms, but disastrously foreign and hostile to accepted norms of human relations in the United Kingdom. Even where strong unionism has been achieved under legal protection in other sectors of British industry, however, the degree of legal regulation of the bargaining activity itself is very slight, and the result is a very costly process of negotiation in which strikes, walk-outs, lock-outs, picketing, go-slows, working to rule are everyday instruments.

More generally, functional relationships in society often produce patterns of control and subordinacy. There are buyers' markets and sellers' markets. The legal environment is inevitably one of the factors which determines supremacy or equality. These latter are fundamental societal questions which, it might well be argued, cannot be self-regulated through mutual adjustment.

Etzioni has offered a distinction between the 'passive' and 'active' society which is relevant in this context.[19] The 'passive' model is in essence the mutual adjustment model, and Etzioni's critique is, therefore, pertinent. The passive society is unable to choose its goals. It changes, but change is environmentally triggered and not necessarily in tune with conceptions of progress and social justice. The contrasting 'active society' is one in which the attempt is made to achieve an overview – not in terms of an ideology but of a continuing effort at macro-comprehension. This can become the basis of intelligent social engineering. This could well be piecemeal engineering, but not in the sense of a merely pragmatic, immediate situational response. Rather, it is active piecemeal interference with the working of society, each case interrelated and based on an overall, coherent and evolving conception of what is happening to the society.

These are comments which are relevant also to Alvin Toffler's thesis on bureaucratic developments in *Future Shock*. He stresses the likelihood, and even desirability, of some breakdown of traditional bureaucratic patterns, including central, politically directed co-ordination.

One of the most persistent myths about the future envisions man as a helpless cog in some vast organizational machine. In this nightmarish projection, each man is frozen into a narrow, unchanging niche in a rabbit-warren bureaucracy. The walls of this niche squeeze the individuality out of him, smash his personality, and compel him, in effect, to conform or die. Since organisations appear to be growing larger and more powerful all the time, the future, according to this view, threatens to turn us all into that most contemptible of creatures, spineless and faceless, the organization man . . .

The kinds of organizations these critics project unthinkingly into the future are precisely those least likely to dominate tomorrow. For we are witnessing not the triumph, but the breakdown of bureaucracy. We are, in fact, witnessing the arrival of a new organizational system that will increasingly challenge, and ultimately supplant bureaucracy. This is the organization of the future. I call it 'Ad-hocracy' . . .

Man's organizational relationships today tend to change at a faster pace than ever before. The average relationship is less permanent, more temporary, than ever before.

The high rate of turnover is most dramatically symbolized by the rapid rise of what executives call 'project' or 'task-force' management. Here teams are assembled to solve specific short-term problems. Then, exactly like the mobile playgrounds, they are disassembled and their human components reassigned. Sometimes these teams are thrown together to serve only for a few days. Sometimes they are intended to last a few years. But unlike the functional departments or divisions of a traditional bureaucratic organization, which are presumed to be permanent, the project or task-force team is temporary by design.

On the surface, the rise of temporary organization may seem insignificant. Yet this mode of operation plays havoc with the traditional conception of organization as consisting of more or less permanent structures. Throw-away organizations, ad hoc teams or committees, do not necessarily replace permanent functional structures, but they change them beyond recognition, draining them of both people and power. Today while functional divisions continue to exist, more and more project teams, task forces and similar organizational structures spring up in their midst, then disappear. And people, instead of filling fixed slots in the functional organization, move back and forth at a high rate of speed. They often retain their functional 'home base' but are detached repeatedly to serve as temporary team members.[20]

Tendencies of this kind may indeed be observed in government: national planning structures, for example, make use of para-bureaucratic entities, like the French Modernisation Commissions. Then, there are various agencies attached to the Premier's office in France, under the direction of high civil servants, because their task does not fall clearly within the area of any single department.[21] These have *permanence*, but the other qualities are there – no departmental boundaries; gatherings of interests and experts, politicians and administrators. There is the increasing use of interministerial/private advisory bodies. The use of the 'think tank', either government sponsored or, though private, drawing government financial support, or supported by large foundations, is a source of expertise supplementing, or competing with, that of the bureaucracy. In the US, RAND, Brookings, the Institute for Defence Analysis, the Hudson Institute, or in France, SEDEIS (Société d'Etudes et de Documentation Economiques, Industrielles et Sociales) are examples. Similar functions are served by Special Commissions in the UK or in Bonn, councils of advisers like the German Advisory Council on Social Policy, or the Expert Council for Giving Opinions on Overall Economic Development. There is a trend in administration – to be seen especially in the EEC – of bypassing vertical channels of information and control as speed of decision assumes higher priority than overall co-ordination and 'dealing with like cases in a like manner'. Instead there is direct horizontal communication between officials working at the same level, without reference to actual superiors. There are indeed *signs* that the old ideal of a stable bureaucracy, functionally differentiated and centrally co-ordinated, to which functions are accreted as new problems arise in the context of a coherent pattern of social goals, is being eroded, *with some possible threat to the values which have hitherto motivated central co-ordination.*

3. Finally, there is the notion that we must revise our traditional concept of a legitimate public role for the administrator. It can be argued that the whole debate is to some extent a result of failure to come to grips with this. The potential of the politician – whether minister or ordinary member of parliament – is for 'climate setting' rather than detailed policy making, and for brokerage between conflicting interests rather than detailed planning. It is for political discrimination between classes as electoral fortunes dictate, and for championing individual claims and local claims as opposed to the establishment and guardianship of impersonal rules. A permanent administration, whether large or much reduced, competitive and overlapping, or highly co-ordinated, is in the most favourable position to set out detailed policy alternatives, their costs and their incidence of benefit. Its association with interest group bureaucracies within its functional sector in advisory committees and other organs of institutionalised consultation enhances that position further. But this policy influential role, clearly, should not be performed in conditions of secrecy and anonymity and without accountability. This is the dangerous path to corporatism. The expertise of administrators, as Shonfield argues, should be introduced into public debate, confronted with private expertise in the same functional areas, in the press, on radio, and television. Here lies some promise of extending the limits of public accountability.[22]

This would of course place a strain on existing constitutional conventions in some countries. The notion of the minister's responsibility for all activities within his department is taken to imply that all departmental officials are his agents – anonymous instruments of his will. This implication bears little comparison with the realities of modern government. No minister can possibly be cognizant of everything which goes on in his department. The doctrine of ministerial responsibility itself, consequently, often no longer bears very heavily on ministers themselves. In Britain, for example, where the doctrines of collective and individual ministerial responsibility have long been regarded as basic constitutional principles, the present practice of ministers, and the tone of their explanations of administrative actions before parliament, is to accept, formally, *responsibility*, but not *blame.* Their responsibility, and indeed that of the Cabinet, collectively, applies without any question, to the law under which public servants operate, but there is a marked tendency not to accept it for their individual decisions. The minister's resignation, in the event of some major departmental blunder, is no longer considered necessary. Ministers, furthermore, have actually blamed officials.

There has not been, however, at least in the UK, any parallel modification of bureaucratic practice, piercing the veil of anonymity. The extreme possibility that disputes between ministers and permanent officials might become known, and publicised so widely that effective political control might be jeopardised (because of the public commitment of the bureaucrat), remains the governing factor, and is allowed to negate the powerful arguments which would make public statements a critical part of the responsibility of senior civil servants.

Swedish practice and thinking is in profound contrast. There, administrative agencies are separated from the small departments headed by ministers. Individual ministers do not take responsibility for the work of the agencies, which are headed by directors. The Cabinet as a whole supervises and co-ordinates their activities, assisted by numerous commissions of inquiry and an elaborate system of internal and external controls over the agencies, including the ombudsman and administrative appeals courts. Official documents are open to public scrutiny. The individual civil servant is held responsible for his actions. In turn, the civil servant is free to play a much more public role. He can make public, political statements. He may, like the French public functionary, stand for parliament in the name of one of the political parties, and if elected he may either be granted leave of absence or, going well beyond French practice, continue in his bureaucratic role, combining it with the parliamentary. As with any system there are problems, not the least being the problems of co-ordinating the agencies through the Cabinet, but the system does provide direct public administrative responsibility without any serious detraction from the political responsibility of the Cabinet. Furthermore, 'the convention is now firmly established that any political differences with the government of the day shall not be carried over into the job, where loyal service is required irrespective of political affiliation'.[23]

Few modern societies seem likely to carry open administration as far as Sweden but if, more generally, it were accepted that departmental officers could contribute papers to academic groups and institutions, or to societies and institutes which discuss public affairs on a non-partisan basis, or could contribute to balanced debate in the press and on radio and television – if they were encouraged to do so, and partly judged on their abilities in this sphere – there is little doubt that, though it is impossible to lay down precise rules as to what an official should or should not say, practice, and increased knowledge and understanding of the problems, would, as the Swedish case suggests, develop appropriate conventions for avoiding embarrassment of the government. The material contribution which the public servant has to offer to policy debate, and occasionally, his explanation or defence of apparent failure, would be a significant extension of public accountability, and some alleviation of the threat of corporatism.

To the old question 'Quis custodiet ipsos custodes?' (Who guards the guardians?) Sweden, in effect, answers 'the public at large', in the spirit of participatory democracy. In the advanced societies, the existence of highly developed media of mass communication – radio, television and newspapers – offers an increasing possibility of this kind of public, bureaucratic accountability. It is capable of supplementing the constitutional instruments which have served in the past but have become less adequate. We must, nevertheless, examine the constitutional options, since parliamentary powers, parliamentary organisation and procedure and relations with the executive, electoral systems, and the 'guardianship' roles of judicial and administrative courts and tribunals are all capable of affecting the openness, accessibility, responsiveness and responsibility of government. These, therefore, are our concern in the next chapter.

NOTES

1 G. H. Hewart, *The New Despotism* (London: Benn, 1929).
2 See M. Crozier, *The Bureaucratic Phenomenon* (Chicago: University of Chicago Press, Phoenix Books, 1967), pp. 178–208.
3 Nicholas Ridley, MP, 'Industry and the civil service' (pamphlet, London: AIMS publication, 1973), p. 2.
4 ibid., p. 6.
5 ibid., p. 4.
6 Anthony Wedgwood Benn, 'A little light in dark corners', *The Times*, 11 July 1973.
7 K. Sontheimer, *The Government and Politics of West Germany* (London: Hutchinson, 1972), p. 146.
8 E. N. Suleiman, *Politics, Power and Bureaucracy in France* (Princeton: Princeton University Press, 1974), p. 172.
9 ibid., p. 174.
10 P. Self, *Administrative Theories and Politics* (London: Allen & Unwin, 1972), p. 198.
11 These problems are discussed at length in G. Benveniste, *The Politics of Expertise* (London: Croom Helm, 1973).
12 See the study of the episode in Arthur Maas, *Muddy Waters* (Cambridge, Mass.: Harvard University Press, 1951), especially pp. 208–59.
13 Crozier, op. cit., pp. 235–6.
14 See the article 'La délégation ministérielle pour l'armement' in *Forces Armées Françaises* (no. special), May 1974 (Services informations et relations publiques des armées), pp. 69–78.

15 Crozier, op. cit., p. 236.
16 Cited by Self, op. cit., pp. 163–5.
17 Sontheimer, op. cit., p. 145.
18 See especially Charles Lindblom, *The Intelligence of Democracy* (New York: Free Press, 1965), and D. Braybrooke and C. Lindblom, *A Strategy for Decision: Policy Evaluation as a Social Process* (New York: Free Press, 1963).
19 A. Etzioni, *The Active Society* (New York: Free Press, 1968).
20 Alvin Teffler, *Future Shock* (London: Bodley Head, 1970), pp. 112–21.
21 See F. Ridley and J. Blondel, *Public Administration in France* (London: Routledge & Kegan Paul, 1964), pp. 75–80.
22 Andrew Shonfield, *Modern Capitalism* (London: R11A/Oxford University Press, 1969), pp. 404–410.
23 Neil Elder, *Government in Sweden: The Executive At Work* (Oxford: Pergamon, 1970), p. 102.

8

Constitutions and Rules

The 1950s saw the beginning of a revolt against what had been the traditional approach to comparative government. This was, in the words of one of the 'Young Turks' of that time, 'the study of foreign governments, in which the governmental structures and the formal organisation of state institutions were treated in a descriptive, historical, or legalistic manner'.[1] Against this preoccupation was urged the desirability of paying attention to political behaviour and attempting to arrive at explanatory generalisations based on comparisons between political systems. Various ways of undertaking the comparative task were elaborated. Easton,[2] for example, suggested the use of the systemic analogy – political life might be viewed in any state and compared with any others by reference to societal inputs or demands, their conversion through governmental processes into outputs or policy, and the 'feedback' process through which outputs affect society and partially determine further inputs or demands. Any political system could be analysed on this basis, so comparisons across political systems could be ordered in such terms. Structural-functionalism was a development of this idea. It required investigation of the structures, in any political system, which fulfil the various functions which may be ascribed to all political or demand-processing systems.[3]

There is no doubt that these suggestions have proved very fruitful in political studies. To a degree, however, behavioural analysis is subject to the criticism of having gone too far in reaction against institutional studies and, therefore, of tending to neglect the importance of *constitutional arrangements as a systemic variable affecting behaviour*. This is a subject rich in its possibilities of generalisation to which relatively little attention has been given. There are a number of studies of 'federalism' in this vein.[4] And European students of politics continue to ignore the behavioural revolution in the United States and produce works of primarily descriptive, historical and legalistic value which, like some of the studies criticised by Macridis, do in fact incorporate valuable behavioural observations. There are, too, isolated works like K. C. Wheare's[5] study of legislatures as a political variable. With some difference in emphasis Robert C. Fried[6] does the same for executives, legislatures, courts, bureaucracies, the military, parties and electorates. Then, the constitutional change in France in 1958 has stimulated numerous reflections on the relationship between changes in the rules and the observable political developments since then. There are other examples. Herbert J. Spiro[7] sets out to answer the question whether constitutional forms and practices can be evaluated in terms of their political results, both in conforming to the goals of constitution makers and also, more generally, by reference to the values of stability, adaptability, efficiency in dealing with basic social problems, and, finally, in achieving popular acceptance for policies. As he examines functional structures comparatively he formulates what he calls 'guidelines for constitution makers' in each functional category. These are readily translated into general propositions. The outstanding recent contribution to the analysis of rules and political behaviour, however, is that of Ivo Duchacek[8] who sets out directly and explicitly to study 'constitutions as blueprints for functional and territorial organisation, uses and restraints of public power and . . . the role of constitutions as an instrument of socialisation in various political cultures'.[9] One other interesting contribution has come from outside the ranks of political studies. The social anthropologist F. G. Bailey has explored the rules of the political arena on a very general comparative basis in an attempt to discover general principles of rule-related political manoeuvre which hold good in any culture and any context. His survey contemplates village politics and extends to contemporary British and American national politics.[10]

Consequently, though such studies are rare, there are a number of propositions about the constitutional variable which would find ready acceptance: for example, we know that popular election, or majority support in elected representative assemblies, tends to enhance the authority of political leaders; that, in interaction with political cultural factors and immediate environmental conditions which help to shape the demands of groups and parties, and determine which assets are available to them, the organisation of interests tends to follow the dictates of electoral requirements, distribution of decision-making powers, and the necessities of procedure; that the power to tax and spend can be utilised to assert a dominant influence in decision making; that the ultimate constitutional supremacy of a legislature or other popularly based leadership tends to give ground in the day-to-day business of detailed legislative drafting to the competence and information resources of the administrative bureaucracy; that bureaucratic competence without strong political leadership support on an established constitutional base lacks co-ordination and is incapable of tackling a range of problems in different sectors and giving direction and unity of purpose to their solution. These random observations are part of the conventional wisdom of political studies, but still, it cannot be said that the search for a comprehensive, coherent and substantiated body of qualified propositions about the relationship between different democratic constitutional arrangements and political behaviour is a preoccupation of many scholars. It is true, of course, that constitutions may be regarded as effects rather than causes. They are products of traditions. They reflect values; their authority is based on consent. This does not mean, however, that the dimension which law adds to the values it expresses does not have behavioural significance, sometimes helping to preserve, sometimes modifying, values and behaviour.

A '*constitution*' *is the set of rules, written and unwritten, which govern the exercise of the authority of the state.* It creates 'offices' with functional responsibilities. It specifies how office is attained, and the jurisdictions and relations between offices. Some of the rules in question may be embodied in a written document, the amendment of which may be different from the ordinary legal process. Other organic rules may be incorporated in ordinary laws and courts' interpretations of them, in custom and convention, or in the rules and working conventions of 'private' bodies like political parties or business corporations, trade unions and other pressure groups. Though the last category goes beyond what is ordinarily regarded as constitutional, such rules may very well have organic significance for a whole society.

Human behaviour is very generally affected by rules, convention and customs, so there are difficulties about assigning 'constitutional' or organic status exclusively to any part of them. *Certain kinds of rules*, however, are of immediate constitutional significance, (a) in that they *clearly help to determine the consensual structure of a society*, or (b) in that they *determine the value of the different assets of different groups* in the struggle for office and influence on office holders, reflecting and protecting a particular set of values. This chapter will examine in turn these two kinds of effects.

A. CONSENSUAL STRUCTURE

Constitutional effects on consensual activity are important because any society has to depend on two factors for the resolution of conflicts of interest. These are mechanisms of control in general, and, second, mechanisms of consensus formation. Controls and consensus are alternative supports of the government writ. The building of consensus depends on institutions which bring different interests together and provide accepted procedures for creating compromises to which all the parties to them will adhere. The process does not necessarily or even normally entail a change of view on the part of the competing interests. Minimally a 'consensus' may be one in which some powerful interests have been defeated or have conceded – a reluctant permissive consensus – but whether of this minimal kind or whether it represents a view to which all the interests have been fully persuaded, it has the essential quality of committing them not to express their dissent by calculated disobedience of the law. Party structures, pressure groups, elected assemblies, both local and national, all perform such functions. The consensual structure of a society is the totality of such mechanisms. They provide the consensual environment for government policy.

Where consensus does not provide an adequate support for policy, controls may be used to support a particular resolution of conflict. With consensus, reliance on controls is diminished. The nature of available controls and consensual mechanisms in different societies helps to explain why one society is more capable than another of resolving conflicts decisively in defining, revising and achieving goals.

The democratic form of government relies primarily on consensus rather than controls. A 'free' speech and press, and freedom of association are working constitutional requirements, in the absence of which institutions like elections and parliament lose most of their relevance in the liberal-democratic tradition. In democratic societies, consensus is a prelude to decision, and the more inefficient the consensual structure the more such societies will be subject to unstable leadership and indecision. A number of virtually self-evident propositions about consensual structural requirements conducive to efficient conflict resolution in the democratic advanced industrial society may be offered.[11]

We may say that a consensual structure is more efficient if it is (1) socially comprehensive, (2) specialised, (3) multi-tiered hierarchical, (4) balanced.

1. The more numerous the societal bonds and links between members of a society the greater are the prospects for achieving effective consensus. Such bonds or links, when expressed through organisations, are instruments whereby the goals of actors are established as complementary or re-specified through interaction. Initially, as Etzioni points out, goals are likely to be vague and fluid, but 'if consensus building is effective they become specified in a congruent direction'.[12]

2. Consensus building should be specialised to some degree, taking place in political units such as parties and legislatures in which the numerous interest-based collectivities are proportionately represented and in which partial processing of divergent views is effected.[13]

3. A multi-tier structure of consensus building enables a successive levelling of divergent views. Its utility depends on representatives at higher levels acting within the consensus reached at lower levels. As 'perspectives are transferred upward in the conversion process',

Etzioni observes, 'they are altered; the tendency is to bring them closer together and to reduce their number'.[14] The reverse is also true. In the downward transfer 'the tendency is to relate the general society perspective to the specific ones of the member units'[15] Thus, the leaders of groups who take part in a collective decision at a general conference or at executive committee level tend to accept its consequences, including a responsibility to persuade their local organisation of the desirability of the line of action agreed upon.

4. A spread of activity through the lower and upper tiers of consensus formation is desirable and, further, the process ideally encompasses all collectivities. The more balanced the spread of activity and the more encompassing the process of consensus building, the wider the range of alternatives which is likely to be considered and processed, the greater the relevant information scanned and the more general the commitment is likely to be. In a bottom-heavy formation there is the advantage, Etzioni has argued, that an alternative tends to be widely supported once it reaches the higher levels – a tendency which favours decisive action. But in such a system, many alternatives never get beyond the lower tiers as too much processing and hence elimination occurs within them. Where, on the other hand, much of the processing is left to the higher, more formal levels, too wide and divergent a range of perspectives makes itself felt. This limits the potential for decisive action, and the more limited lower-level participation reduces the generality of the commitment. Limited base-level participation is one of the most common weaknesses in the consensual structures of advanced industrial societies.

But in these respects, *a consensual structure is strongly affected by the constitutional control structure*, the parts of which it seeks to capture or influence.

The very wide functional range of state control in the advanced industrial society is itself conducive to group formation and activity. Wherever the state exercises its power there is an incentive to organise affected interests to exert pressure. In addition, the 'constitutional' rules may directly encourage the development of specialised groups and enhance the value of association. They may accord rights of free speech and freedom of the press and of association, providing the moral as well as the legal sanctions for consensual activity.

The setting up by the state of consultative institutions with group representation for various functional purposes is a 'constitutional' act of some importance since groups will tend to come into existence to supply the necessary interest representation at this official level. Institutions like the regional councils in France and the Economic and Social Councils in France and Holland are constitutional incentives to association.

A highly centralised constitutional decision-making structure, other

things being equal, will result in highly centralised consensual structures. If there are, within a centralised control structure, intermediary
levels of delegated powers the specialised consensual structure is likely
to be tiered accordingly. A decentralised administration will not
necessarily result in decentralisation of consensual structures. It could
in fact lead to a situation where citizens are having to deal with
representatives of central government locally without the support and
intervention of the association bureaucracies. Branches of associations
tend to have parochial concerns and a primarily consensual role
rather than a negotiating role, and may be ill-equipped intellectually
and administratively to deal with the local representatives of central
government.

In so far as power is devolved to regional and local legislatures, the
organisation of parties and pressure groups will respond to the
exigencies of election and representation. Intermediary tiers of decision making will be reflected in a multi-tiered consensual structure.

Finally, *the spread* and *balance* of consensual activity will be largely
determined by controls. Some rules, for example, attempt to define
and limit the boundaries of political community, excluding certain
categories from participation in consensual activity.

In this last respect, certain electoral rules are particularly significant.
Qualifications laid down for voting eligibility define the minimum
requirements for entering the competition for the power and perquisites of public office. Almost everywhere, citizenship is a primary
requirement. This means that though citizenship does not absolutely
define the boundaries of the political community, since some aliens
may well enjoy considerable informal influence on the politics of a
state in which they reside and may, furthermore, be exempt from
some of the duties and restrictions placed on citizens, generally, any
substantial minority of resident aliens is left outside the specialised
consensual apparatus which organises the electorate, namely, the
political parties. The alienating effect of this exclusion, the tendency
it promotes to exclude the interests of aliens from consideration in the
final consensual activity which leads to policy formulation, may well
be adverse to orderly government. The long exclusion of Negroes
from citizenship and voting and, therefore, from office and party
influence in the United States has contributed to the racial problems
which that country has experienced. Violence has provided a means
of expressing interests and exerting pressures denied within the con-
stitution-reflecting consensual apparatus. In Western Europe too,
particularly in the UK and West Germany, non-citizens of alien
stock are relatively easy targets of community violence, first victims
of unemployment and inadequate housing, most likely to be forced
outside the law, which they have not had an opportunity to affect or
consent to.

Besides citizenship, other electoral qualifications may exclude people from opportunity to participate in some aspects of consensual activity. Minors, lunatics and prisoners are often excluded. Residence requirements for registration may exclude others. Varied, often stringent residence requirements in many American states tend to disenfranchise large members of a relatively mobile population. This population has some predominant characteristics. In particular, a high percentage is in the low-income category. This means that a group, already most prone to eschew participation in consensual activity, is affected also by formal requirements about formal voting eligibility. Less stringent requirements in Western Europe have a smaller but similar affect.

Thus, in Italy, registration is automatic, effected by the authorities as soon as records show that a person has come of age. The voter remains on the rolls until his death or until he notifies a change of residence. Certificates are delivered by the municipal authorities to each voter, before an election, if the voter can be found. Certificates not delivered amounted to 5·4 per cent of the total in 1946, 3·5 per cent in 1948, 2·7 per cent in 1953, 2·7 per cent in 1958, 3 per cent in 1963. In regions of heavy emigration the undelivered percentage may be still higher. In 1963, in Molise, it was 14·9 per cent.[16] Since turnout over the whole country is high in Italian elections (over 90 per cent) these undelivered certificates constitute a significant proportion of the non-voters.

Electoral lists are also compiled by the authorities from their records in Belgium. In spite of its being mandatory for changes of address to be notified to the authorities a high level of inaccuracy in electoral lists has been noted in Brussels, where residential mobility is high. Since lists are compiled biennially and eligibility is established six months before publication of lists, new voters may be excluded from voting for as long as two-and-a-half years from their coming of age.[17] In Britain, where electoral rolls are compiled annually based on household returns, some 4 per cent of those who are technically eligible are omitted from the Register. 'This group includes a disproportionate number of persons recently of voting age, those who have moved during the year, lodgers and immigrants.'[18] While not all such disenfranchised categories are excluded from party 'consensual' activity, their position is a disincentive to participation.

B.   ASSETS

We turn now to the second of our two categories: the effects of constitutional rules on assets. Of equal importance to the determination of consensual structure and the overall decision-making efficacy of government is the place of rules in determining the value of the assets of competing groups. Rules may constrain or impede some groups and provide opportunities for others by prohibiting, permitting or requiring.

In democratic, advanced industrial societies the critical rules affecting the assets of participating competing groups are:

(a) rules governing recruitment to public office;
(b) rules defining how the competition for office shall be conducted;
(c) rules defining offices of power and responsibility, the limits upon them and the relations between them;
(d) rules which apply when operating rules are broken.

  (a) In the rules determining eligibility for recruitment to public office in many of the advanced societies there are survivals of early conceptions of political role playing which have been eliminated with regard to voting. Age requirements, for example, differ from those which apply to elections. Thus, in Holland, candidates for the Upper House must be over 25 years of age. For the French Senate, candidates must be 35 or more. The House of Lords, in the UK, in practice conforms to this tendency to enhance the value of the assets of age and experience by the appointment of life peers, predominantly from among those whose main career is over. The Italian Senate is elected on a regional basis but the constitution provides that all former Presidents are members of Senate, and a President is entitled to nominate to the Senate five citizens 'who have brought honour to the nation'.[19]

Though the powers of second chambers are limited, these provisions tend to produce a small, but still disproportionate, conservative influence into the legislative process. They reinforce other factors, formal and informal, which enhance indirectly the assets of the middle and upper socio-economic groups in the political arena. The payment of members of legislatures, for example, in most Western democracies has been recognised as having an important effect on the nature of class representation. Working class recruitment depends to a considerable extent on the degree to which legislative office will provide an adequate career for those who have no other income. Salary is clearly one factor, though the extent to which the legislature is the exclusive recruiting ground for the political executive is another. In many countries, until recently, legislative office was based more on the ideal of public service than on career. A change in attitude took place in the United Kingdom in the decade after the Second World War, and parliamentary salaries now reflect the burden and the full-time professional nature of a parliamentary career. In Holland, until 1958, pay and allowances were very small. Considerable increases have been made subsequently (e.g. 10,000 guilders, 1958, to 40,000 guilders, 1969). Though members are often appointed burgomaster of a town, with good pay, or they attract offers from industry, if a deputy earns more than a relatively small sum outside parliament, half of what he earns is subtracted from his parliamentary salary, though the latter never falls below a specified limit. Young and ambitious people therefore, without private income, are not strongly attracted to parliament, particularly since ministerial jobs do not readily follow, being filled still, to a considerable extent, from outside parliament.

In most constitutions eligibility rules relating to public office differ from point to point in the hierarchy of power, becoming increasingly restrictive. Thus, for the Senate and Congress of the United States there are rules of eligibility for membership, more restrictive for the Senate than for Congress, and within both chambers there are rules like the seniority rule which determine eligibility for committee preferences and committee chairmanships. The seniority rule simply gives preference in committee appointments to those with the longest uninterrupted service. These rules enhance the influence of the politically 'safe' states of stable population (in practice, states with a predominantly rural character) since the legislative influence of committee chairmen, given the standing orders of the House of Representatives and Senate, is very strong.

For the Presidential Cabinet of the United States, as a matter of prudence and convention, there are working rules, loosely adhered to, that there should be some kind of geographic balance in the Cabinet and that sectional interests should be represented in appointments to the offices which are most appropriate. In the United Kingdom, there are rules which effectively specify, though they are not written, that a Prime Minister must be drawn from the House of Commons and that the majority of his ministers should be drawn from the lower house also. There are rules, also loosely adhered to, about the composition of Cabinets – the kinds of geographic and sectional interests that should be represented, and the need to incorporate in the Cabinet leading figures from the various wings of the majority party. Such arrangements inevitably best protect the dominant well-organised groups within sectors, strengthening corporatist tendencies in modern government.

Certain other eligibility rules reflect conceptions of incompatibility between roles. The French constitution gives a very clear expression of this in its so-called incompatibility rule.[20] 'Membership of the government is incompatible with that of Parliament, with the representation of any trade or professional organisation on the national level, with any professional activity or public employment.' The intention and the principal effect of this rule is to detach government from some of the burden of defence against parliamentary criticism, to exclude temporarily from political office Cabinet members who resign, but also to reduce the primacy of parliament, the popularly representative assembly, as a recruitment mechanism for executive office. Unlike provisions in, for example, the British law, which regulates in a restrictive way the candidacy for parliament of civil servants and military, requiring their resignation before standing, the French rule sanctions, by implication, appointment to high political office of men distinguished in varied walks of life outside parliament. Though they have to give up their other careers on accepting appointment, they do so for the certain rewards of high office rather than the uncertainty of parliamentary candidacy. Another conception of incompatibility has affected women's rights. The long ban on women in politics in most of Western Europe implied that a woman's domestic role as a housekeeper and mother unfitted her for a role in public affairs. Though the formal ban has been lifted everywhere there survives an informal discrimination so that the number of women in parliaments, ministerial posts, the higher echelons of the civil service, in the judiciary and in the higher levels of the interest group bureaucracies remains low throughout Western Europe. The contemporary campaign for sexual equality has drawn attention to the consequences of this under-representation in many spheres of social activity where women's equality of treatment has still to be established.

Bureaucracy eligibility rules are also important. The constitutions of most Western democracies draw a distinction between the law-making and the executive or law-implementing functions of government. Montesquieu's thesis on the desirability of separating these powers in the interests of liberty provides one powerful rationale for so doing. But in most constitutions it is also implicit that the two functions require different qualities of their personnel. Implicit in the minimal qualifications for legislative office is the conception of representation of *all* the citizenry. No interest grouping, however peculiar or lowly, it is assumed, should be legally barred from trying to elect one of its own to represent it in the legislative body. Thus, though the principle that anyone eligible to vote should be eligible for legislative office is not fully established in practice, this is the standard to which debate on the subject tends to be related. The exceptions to the rule are minor historical and local anomalies.

The executive bureaucracy, on the other hand, and of course the judiciary, are expected to demonstrate the qualities necessary for administrative or judicial competence. For the bureaucracy a high standard of educational attainment, and increasingly, various kinds of expertise are demanded. These are qualifications which designedly differentiate the executive bureaucracy and the citizen body in general but ensure empathy with bureaucracies in large organisations in the 'private' sector. Inevitably they give a dominance in the bureaucracy to the middle and upper socio-economic groups of society, and, in the case of multi-lingual societies,[21] to the dominant language group. In other words, the assets of the classes who have traditionally dominated the government bureaucracy tend to be maintained by competitive merit-testing systems of civil service entry.

Since the tendency towards the acquisition of powers by legislatures against which Madison warned[22] has been reversed in favour of the bureaucracy, this particular form of asset enhancement has been accentuated. Attempts have been made, consequently, to eradicate the middle and upper class, or linguistic group, dominance of bureaucracies and to 'democratise' them, but these have always been very much reduced in their effect because of their conflict with the perceived need for educational qualifications and expertise.

(b) Rules defining how the competition for office shall be conducted also determine the value of assets in politics. Formal requirements for the nomination of candidates for elective office, party nomination procedures, spending limitations on campaigns, electoral systems, the comparable rules within parties and groups are particularly relevant in this respect.

Procedures governing the nomination of candidates for office are normally designed to exclude frivolous candidacy without presenting too much of an obstacle to individuals who have some minimum of potential electoral support. Rules, therefore, normally require that a nomination be supported by a certain number of signatures and that a money deposit be made, returnable if there is an *ex post facto* indication that the candidate did represent a significant group of voters. Very poor election results lead to the forfeiture of the deposit. Such requirements do, needless to say, favour established parties and they may well, as in the UK, be a serious financial burden even for substantial third parties. Taken in conjunction with the 'first past the post' rule, and a vague perception by voters of the logic of government accountability, the two major parties in the UK are so strongly favoured that their selection procedures for candidates have to be regarded as organic rules of major importance, to be compared with, say, primary elections in the United States. Thus, the selection procedures and conventions of the Conservative Party operated by an inner group in local Conservative associations, composed generally of employers, farmers, middle management, tradesmen, retired military people and 'gentry', favour public school men of 'good family', Anglo-Saxon, in business, farming or the professions. On the Labour side, trade unionists, teachers and employees operate the local selection procedures and these categories tend also to be among those favoured strongly as candidates.

In Germany the nomination of candidates is very strictly regulated and a distinction is drawn deliberately between 'established' parties, other parties and independents. 'Established' are those which already have representation in Bundestag or Landtag of at least five deputies.

The nomination of their candidates needs only the signature of the Land executive committee of the party. Other parties must comply with various clauses to qualify, and having had their status officially certified, must collect 200 signatures in each constituency where they wish to nominate a candidate, and one signature per 1,000 electors in order to nominate a Land list.

An independent candidate also requires 200 signatures. Not surprisingly the number of independent candidates has been negligible. The rules are designed to eliminate small parties, and have helped to do so.

Since parties meeting these requirements enjoy a privileged electoral position the nomination process within parties is also subject to law. A candidate must be selected by a secret ballot either directly, by all the members of the party in the constituency, or indirectly, by an elected selection committee also subject to secret ballot in its final vote. All the preliminary proceedings, including attendance records and adoption meetings, minutes and ballot results, have to be submitted to the returning officers with the nomination papers.

In contrast, the Belgian law makes entry to the lists much easier. Nomination requires 500 signatures in Brussels, 400 in other large towns, and 200 in cantons. No deposit is required. Parties lay down quite stringent conditions for acceptance as a candidate, and, for those who meet the conditions of party service etc., they run, in effect, closed primaries for election in which all party members may vote. Party leaders retain the right, however, to amend the lists. Voting in the elections is by PR using the d'Hondt system.

Election rules are particularly influential, both in affecting consensual activity and as determinants of assets. Electoral systems deliberately contrived to effect accurate proportional representation, like the Dutch national list system, and the Belgian and Danish which comprise sub-national multi-member constituencies using d'Hondt PR with proportionate allocation of remainders on a national list, tend to produce parliaments with several parties, often difficult to bring together for government formation and support, or to combine into an effective opposition. Local–central, town and country, class and religious cleavages have consequently had separate party articulation at the highest level. In the 1967 election in Holland there was a bachelors' party pressing, among other things, the claims of homosexuals. In Belgium, linguistic cleavages have also recently created new party divisions. These three countries have surpassed all others in Western Europe, with the possible exception of Italy, which has a very similar system to the Belgian and Danish, in the difficulties they have experienced in forming governments. The Dutch, since 1917, have tried to meet the serious deficiencies in consensus formation, inhibiting stable government, by 'Verzuiling' – the strict maintenance of proportionality in allocating government services and funds, offices, radio and television licences etc. to each of the main political, sub-cultural tendencies.

It is practical, within the restrictions of a summary discussion, to confine attention to the direct effect of constitutional rules. But like any social act or event, rules have a range of secondary effects which may be profoundly important in themselves. In so far as rules affect assets, their effects may snowball from a marginal political advantage to something much greater. As noted above, the electoral system in the Netherlands favours a multi-party system in which religious as well as socio-economic distinctions have been articulated. In the mid-1920s when regular radio broadcasting started, various amateur groups representing the same distinctions were authorised to broad-cast, and when television began in 1951 the same organisations were licensed to provide programmes. Dutch radio and television was therefore in the hands of five main organisations and stations: AVRO (neutral to Liberal), KRO (Catholic), NCRV (Protestant), VPRO (Latitudinarian Protestant) and VARA (Socialist). These stations and the associations which support them have opposed attempts to intro-duce a general or a commercial service, but though inroads were made into their monopoly by the licensing of new associations in 1967, they continue to dominate the broadcasting media and to support their values in programming.[23]

A broad social consensus in Denmark has made the multi-party system a tolerable luxury. Nevertheless, the parliamentary election of February 1977 was the seventh in only thirteen years and it had become almost impossible to deal with the country's economic diffi-culties in the seventies in the protracted political crisis conditions which, of course, economic problems helped to engender. To look at other examples, a case could be made that Belgian government has suffered from the burden of consensus formation at the highest level, though as a small country, successfully dominated until recently by the French sub-cultural group, its problems have not been as severe, nor its conflicts so difficult to resolve as those of Italy. Weakness has characterised Italian government since the fifties. It has reduced the weight of Italy's voice in international affairs and in the European Community, and has left unresolved Italy's domestic problems of regional imbalance in development, corruption in the bureaucracy, organised crime, disturbed industrial relations and environmental spoliation.

These extremes of proportional representation may be contrasted with the first-past-the-post electoral system of the United Kingdom. The system tends towards two major parties though it does not exclude challenge to their dominance.

The two-party system seems to be most effective as a consensual structure when the main parties are presenting what appear to the electorate to be genuine though not extreme alternatives. There is a tendency, however, for the parties to move towards the centre in programmes and policies, placing more and more emphasis on winning the middle ground rather than on satisfying their core of support at opposite ends of the socio-economic continuum. The effects are complex.

The healthy alternation between reforming government by a party of the relatively underprivileged, responding strongly to environmental changes and new social and economic needs with a coherent and comprehensive programme of reform, and a government of consolidation and minor pragmatic readjustment, by the party of the relatively privileged, is lost. It is replaced by alternation between governmental teams leading parties which preserve the trappings of difference in their programmes and language but which exhibit only minor policy difference in office.

Apathy and alienation are products. The core basis of support for the parties is undermined at least to the degree that participation falls off. Entryism becomes a feature of local organisation, and is met by attempts to strengthen the central oligarchy's controls or by proscription of their challenging ideological tendencies. Weak break-away groups and new parties proliferate, mainly on the left, but not exclusively, and, frustrated by the electoral system, the more militant survive as pressure groups committed to the overthrow of existing institutions.

In a first-past-the-post system, furthermore, the drawing of electoral boundaries is always a critical exercise. There is always some distortion of the relative strength of the two main parties as reflected in popular votes and their gains and losses of parliamentary seats.

The electoral systems of Germany and France are a halfway house between the extremes of proportional representation and the first-past-the-post system. German citizens exercise two votes. One is for a constituency candidate. There are 248 single-member constituencies. Each is won by the candidate with a plurality. Besides the constituency seats there are an equal number of seats to be won on a party and list system of proportional representation. The second vote, for the party lists, is the decisive one, since the constituency seats gained by a party are deducted from the proportion to which the party is entitled on the second vote, on the d'Hondt (greatest average) method. Thus the constituency seats are a part of the proportionality, not distinct from it. They allow for a personal element within the system. If the number of constituency seats won by a party actually exceeds its proportional entitlement, extra seats are added to the Bundestag total to permit proportionality to be restored according to the deserts of the other parties. The system not only allows the personal constituency relationship to be established by some half of the members of the Bundestag, overwhelmingly men who are strong in the local party organisation, but it avoids any unfairness in representation arising out of the way constituency boundaries are drawn, or the size of different constituencies, since proportionality is restored via the list elections. The German system, however, does attempt to avoid the PR tendency towards extreme multiplicity of parties. The electoral law stipulates that to participate in the distribution of list seats a party must have either 5 per cent of the national vote or at least three constituency seats (unless the party can claim exemption on the grounds that it represents a national minority). It is difficult for a small or new party to overcome this hurdle so that, since 1957, only three parties have actually won representation in the Bundestag – the CDU/CSU, FDP and SPD. In addition to the barrier represented by the 5 per cent threshold the Basic Law does not allow parties which are deemed to be working for the overthrow of a 'free and democratic order'. Two parties, the communist KPD and the SRP (neo-Nazi party), have been banned by the Constitutional Court under this proviso.

The French electoral system in the Fifth Republic is basically the same as that operated during the Third Republic when it led to multiplicity of parties. In single-member constituencies any candidate who gains a majority of votes cast on a first ballot wins the seat. If there is no majority a second ballot is held a week later in which a plurality suffices to gain the seat. There is an incentive to combination between parties on candidates and constituencies on the second ballot because it is decisive; but not on the first, to anything like the same extent. The rule that requires 12·5 per cent on first ballot for a place in the second ballot is, however, significant. A number of factors have conspired to make for bi-polarity in the multi-party system which this method helps to sustain. One of these is the requirement since 1962 that the President be elected on a nationwide popular vote. This is a two-ballot system in which, failing a majority on the first vote, only the top two candidates contest the second ballot. The coalitions necessary to win the Presidency by gaining at least one of the top two positions on the first ballot have had their effect on the party system generally, so that, at least partly as a result of this, it is concentrated around two poles and two leaders. The concentration is by no means absolute but it has very much reduced the importance and unpredictability of minor parties in government coalitions which characterised the Third and Fourth Republics. The tiny Radical-Socialist Party in the Fourth Republic achieved its best electoral results in 1951 when it gained 76 of the 627 seats in the Assembly, but 12 of the 29 Prime Ministers of the Fourth Republic were drawn from its ranks. The new system continues to provide a strong base for local notables, either capable of winning a seat for a party on first ballot, or offering a clear marginal advantage to a coalition on second ballot. Indeed, de Gaulle seems to have hoped that the system would prevent a sweeping victory for a party of 'Gaullists' who might tie his hands on Algeria and, therefore, elected for the return to prewar arrangements which so consistently produced parliaments of individualists drawing their strength from their localities. Though, in spite of this choice, a massive Gaullist majority was returned under this system, a locally important candidate remains an asset for any party, or for a coalition whose agreed candidates in several constituencies can exploit local reputation. The continued significance of the 'notable' in French politics continues also to provide a base for the 'cadre' party – the party of leaders without a mass membership, made up largely of notables with their own local electoral and financial support.

(c) *The rules which define and limit offices of power and express relations* between them also play an important part in asset determination. Constitutional government was itself the product of a desire to reduce the power and influence of monarchy and aristocracy in Europe. Constitutional role definition still serves the purpose of curbing the powers of government altogether and of curbing one branch of government at the expense of another. Executive-legislative relations in democracies are either of the Presidential type, each authority being separately elected, or of the parliamentary type where the executive rests on majority support in the legislative body. To the extent that different branches represent different group interests the effect is to determine partially the relative strength of groups in the political arena.

In the United States, the votes of the most populous states are very significant in Presidential elections because of the working of the electoral college system. A slight majority delivers the whole electoral college of any state so that it is possible to win the presidency on a minority vote by barely carrying the populous states with their large quota of electors in the college. The powers of the President, who is, thus, frequently representative of urban industrial America, in comparison with the House of Representatives and Senate, much more strongly rural in their electoral supports, help to define the relative strength of urban and rural interests in American politics.

The President in France, based on nationwide direct election, and the Assembly, based on local representation, are separately elected. They are linked through Cabinet, whose membership is formally incompatible with parliamentary membership and whose leader is appointed by the President, but whose continuance in office is dependent not only on the President but on parliamentary support. The position of the Cabinet in relation to parliament is strengthened by constitutional rules which curb parliament's powers and enhance and enlarge those of government in comparisons with the Third and Fourth Republics. The main rules which determine executive ascendancy are referred to at other points in this chapter, but, in general, these rules specify and, thereby, limit parliamentary powers in the legislative process, and make defeat of the government a formal process requiring organisation and reflection rather than a matter of impulse in the heat of critical debate.[24]

The intention and the actual effect of these provisions is clear. It is to strengthen the President and Cabinet, symbolic and representative of a *national* interest against a parliament which has, in the past, been mainly representative of partial and local interests. The era of parish pump politics has been ushered out by the new constitution.

The relations between executive and legislature in the German Federal Republic give the Bundestag a somewhat more independent and influential role than is enjoyed by the French legislature. At the same time, unfortunately, they strengthen local sectional interest influence in comparison with any national community influence. The Chancellor is formally elected by the Bundestag on the suggestion of the Federal President whose choice is normally dictated by party strength in the house. His Cabinet is, with only occasional exceptions, chosen from the Bundestag. His dismissal is possible only if the Bundestag can, in removing him, agree on a successor. The effect of this rule is that the Chancellor's continuance in office does not depend on his consistently winning majorities for his legislation. So in practice the modification of legislation by parliament is common and may, on some Bills, be quite extensive. The committee phase in the Bundestag is quite important in this respect since the form in which legislation is reported by the permanent and expert committees is the one in which it stands a good chance of being accepted by the house. The committees are influenced to a considerable extent by members who are lobbyists for the organised social and economic interest groups operating in the sector with which any particular committee is concerned – an extension of corporatist structures as in the United States. The effect, as Sontheimer has put it, is that 'the Bundestag has not become a national forum in which the problems of German society are discussed in a representative way. Its members are too occupied in influencing politics with detailed work on legislation to have time and understanding for the educational and informational function which is the real function of parliament as the highest representative body.'[25] It can be argued that to the degree that interest group power and influence within a system approaches the point where any group has a virtual veto on legislation which directly affects its position, a negative aspect of corporatism – a unit-veto system – then to that degree there is a conservative, restraining influence

on government action. G. B. Shaw's comment on the US constitution –
that it was a guarantee to the American people that it never should
be governed at all is an exaggeration drawing attention to the fact
that at any time in such a system the then dominant interests in
society are in a good strategic position to resist any changes in the
status quo which would diminish their dominance.

The strength of representation of local interests in German politics
is increased strongly by the role and composition of the Bundesrat. It
is a relatively powerful upper house having suspensory powers on
some issues and, on others, equal powers with the Bundestag. Its
members are Land ministers, with their retinue of aides from the
Land bureaucracy, defending Land interests.

Evidently, strengthening parliaments as instruments of participatory
democracy and as a counter to corporatism must take account of the
dangers (exhibited in the Bundestag, the powerful assemblies of the
Third and Fourth French Republics and the US Congress) that
parliaments themselves may be partially absorbed in the corporatist
complex. This corporatist potential lends particular interest to questions of parliamentary organisation and procedure, particularly committee systems and the rights of government and opposition to parliamentary time. They have to ensure that the functions of parliament –
to recruit political leaders, to debate and vote on legislation proposed
by the government, to act as watchdog on the administration, and to
lead and represent public opinion – can be fulfilled. The problem is
to give parliament means by which it can demand and ensure government responsibility and not detract from it.

Parliamentary procedural rules, whether enshrined in a written
constitution or having the force of constitutional convention, may
determine legislative–executive relations to a significant degree. The
Standing Orders and Speakers' Rulings of legislative assemblies are
therefore important constitutional rules, though this is not ordinarily
recognised. One important aspect, of which the German situation
referred to above is an illustration, is committee procedure. Select
committees tend to be more effective critical supervisory instruments
over the executive than general committees. They acquire expertise
and they attract experts. They also attract legislators, however, whose
constituency interests are affected by their work or who are spokesmen for interests in the full house. Unless, therefore, the rules require
frequent rotation of membership they enhance the power of the best-
organised interests to affect legislation (particularly when they wish
to exercise a negative influence), especially if they have powers to
amend Bills before they are considered in plenary legislative session
or if the committees can decide for themselves whether to report a
Bill to the house or not. In a multi-party system with loose coalition
government, furthermore, it is hard to avoid a situation in which

committee chairmen are rival 'shadow ministers'. Even though they may be from a party which participates in the current coalition government, they may, quite realistically, have an eye to the possibility of displacing the minister in the functional area in which the committee specialises. This was the case in the French Third and Fourth Republics. In the Fifth Republic, in explicit recognition of the problem, the number of committees and, consequently, their degree of specialisation and of coincidence with a particular interest group, has been much reduced. The committees' powers to amend legislation before plenary consideration have also been taken away.

Rules within parliaments governing the defeat and resignation of governments are important since they determine the costs of confrontation with the government and between interests as they are reflected in parties in parliament. In the Fifth French Republic these rules are embedded in the constitutional document itself. They protect the government to some extent from confrontation, but also, when confrontation does take place, from the costs that were incurred in the Third and Fourth Republics in parliaments that were unable to discipline their own proceedings. These rules, and many others governing Bill procedures – time limits on debate, restrictions on proposing resolutions leading to a vote, particularly if they involve a charge on the revenue – would normally be considered part of the Standing Orders of a house, as in the UK, subject to its own control, but they have been written into the French constitution in a rare and perceptive recognition of their significance. The changes seem to have made the French parliament a more effective consensual mechanism and less of a battleground for uncompromising group conflict.

The Standing Orders of the British House of Commons provide more opportunities for confrontation in a less dangerous party situation than the French, but they too are restraining mechanisms. The preference for standing general committees rather than specialist committees, the embargo on resolutions from ordinary members which would impose a charge on the revenues, and the priorities in agenda are as deeply entrenched as any other constitutional elements in Britain. Reform of the House of Commons procedure and organisation has consequently proved extremely difficult.

The attempt to secure public accountability takes place in an institutional and procedural context which may be quite anachronistic. Parliaments are the traditional institutions within which executive behaviour is scrutinised. There is a kind of pre-audit in the form of debate on proposed legislation, and a continuing audit on the actual performance of governmental functions through questions, opposition motions, investigations and various informal channels through which legislators approach executives to raise the grievances of their constituents. The 'watch-dog' function of parliaments is at least as important as any other function they perform.

The rationale of accountability is as old as the argument for representative government itself. Bureaucracies, both governmental and private, have characteristics and interests which are not identical with those of the public at large. There is a class and educational superiority, an interest in an increased scope of government action, a technocratic bias shared with industrialists but not with employees whose skills are threatened with obsolescence, and there is, of course, a peculiar pecuniary interest in the pay and perquisites of public servants. The supervision of a parliament or representative assembly dependent on constituency electoral sanctions has therefore been traditionally regarded as a safeguard of the larger 'public interest'.

Many developments in governmental activity have tended to reduce the efficiency with which that role is undertaken. The enlarged scope of government activity by itself, not matched in most states by an increase in the number of parliamentarians, clearly adds absolutely to the parliamentary burden. Devolution of power and functions to regional assemblies has been discussed, but the measures which have actually been taken, and those which have attained the status of proposed legislation, cannot be clearly seen to reduce the central government burden. Caution, unwillingness to relinquish power, and competitive interests have often meant that duplication of tasks and complication of the central government's role is the product of such measures.

Devolution aside, the increase in the burden of government has resulted in many instances in attempts to speed up parliamentary processes or, more dangerously, to bypass them. This is particularly clear in France where the constitution has been modified to reduce the undoubtedly dominant and frustrating role of the Assembly as it operated in the Third and Fourth Republics. The domain of parliamentary legislation is specified and limited in the Constitution and the residue of power is with the government to rule by decree, virtually without parliamentary supervision. The power of the government to insist on a vote on its own Bill as a package without amendment, to make legislation a matter of confidence on which no vote takes place unless the procedure is challenged by a vote of censure, and the time limit imposed on the Budget debate, are a few of the constitutional prescriptions for speeding up parliamentary scrutiny of legislation. The Assembly's ability to conduct an ongoing examination of governmental activity has been cut down by eliminating or reducing the efficacy of most of the mechanisms by which the parties of the opposition could initiate an inquiry or a subject for debate.

Some change in the role of parliament was certainly overdue in 1958 since its absolute supremacy over the executive obscured the necessary relationship between the executive and legislature in the initiation and consideration of legislation. The executive is the natural source of a coherent leglislative programme. French executives were too much at the whim of parliament to provide a programme and see it through. That situation has been corrected – to a considerable extent through constitutional means – and the legislature is now probably a more efficient debating chamber for the consideration of government Bills than it was in the past. But as a watchdog on government performance rather than as a consensus mechanism it could be more efficient, and the constitutional changes have been too far-reaching.

Even without such constitutional impediments to administrative accountability through the Assembly, most parliaments have lost ground in their performance of this role. Many activities of government have been placed outside the scope of direct parliamentary supervision by being invested in agencies, boards, corporations, or through the medium of very wide powers of delegated legislation to ministers. The range of expertise required to exercise adequate supervision in many areas is also unlikely to be available in parliaments. Such expertise may be particularly necessary in cases where, because of the enormous sums of money involved, accountability is of paramount importance. In this category falls the promotion of projects of high technology – for example, in aerospace and nuclear power. This is the kind of activity, also, where international co-operation may be a complicating factor. A range of parliamentary supervisory problems occur because the advanced societies are involved in international inter-governmental or supra-national organisations.

Changes in the procedures, powers and resources of parliaments, which might go some way to answering the new needs, are the strengthening, or development where they do not exist, of specialised committees and investigatory committees, of rotating membership, with non-governmental chairmen, able to adjourn from place to place, call witnesses etc., hold proceedings in public, and appoint specialised staff. Parliamentary commissioners may also have a place if their brief is sufficiently wide, and their powers adequate. More members, with better individual accommodation and personal services, would also seem appropriate.

Turning to other aspects of power definition which affect assets, civil liberties – the idea that there are certain areas of individual and social action upon which government should not intrude at all – tend to be threatened everywhere by the enlarged sphere of government action in advanced societies. A number of constitutions, of which the United States is the most notable, spell out 'freedoms' or civil rights. In Britain with its unwritten constitution, the same freedoms, freedom of speech and press, freedom of association, equality before the law, and the rule of law, are generally seen as being constitutional rights. Nowhere, however, are such rights regarded as absolute, and they are generally threatened by the development of corporatism. The degree to which they are limited (or enlarged) by ordinary law and executive action is restricted by their constitutional status, but a historical comparison of the extent to which they are preserved in different societies does not suggest the superior efficacy of either written or unwritten constitutional protection. The political climate, the range, everywhere increasing, of executive discretion, and the efficiency of parliamentary surveillance of the executive, seem to be the determining factors.

Another element of power definition which may be important in determining assets is the constitutional distribution of powers between central and local government. This is essentially the effect of 'federalist' or quasi-federalist arrangements, deconcentrating either policy-making power or administrative powers. While most of the claims of classical federalist theory bear little examination there is no doubt that some elements of political behaviour can be attributed to this source. Many writers have found that there is a coincidence between federalism and the protection and entrenchment of dominant interests. A federalist element in a constitution may be a reason for a tendency to delays or obstruction in the progress of legislation because it introduces a degree of complexity in the legislative process. Then, in a federal system certain functions, though nationally important, may depend on action by many local authorities, not all of whom move at the same pace, not all of whom, too, can afford the same measures because of disparities in wealth between them. Some authorities can be persuaded that inaction may bring advantages, attracting interests and activities which seek to avoid the regulations in other states. Jurisdictional ambiguities can be exploited by affected interests to prevent action by state or federal government. There is little reason for surprise therefore at Riker's conclusion, based on a comparative study of federal institutions, that the main beneficiaries of the admitted limits which federalism imposes on government have been capitalists, landlords, linguistic minorities and racists.[26] Studies of federal systems as diverse as those of the United States, Switzerland and Australia[27] help to confirm this view. In Western Europe, among the advanced industrial societies the strongest example of federalism is the West German constitution which gives Länder government powers, particularly significant administratively; and, in a much more directly delegatory way than through the United States Senate, gives Länder a role in the federal legislative process. The effect of the system in operation is to give the Länder the main administrative role and a highly important review function over legislation emanating from the Bundestag by Länder ministers and officials in the Bundesrat or the upper house. Though there is, normally, no Länder-specific interest since the Länder, with the exception of Bavaria, are not historical entities but constitutional creations and the dominant role in the initiation of policy is that of the federal government to which the Länder have lost some ground, they still constitute a restraining influence on national action. However, it is the fact that approximately 90 per cent of all governmental administrative personnel are Länder or local government officials which is most significant in this system,[28] distributing as it does the recruitment to the bureaucracy, and the financial and cultural advantages of its location, among the states rather than concentrating them in the federal capital, Bonn. Furthermore, the Länder assemblies, like those of the US states, serve as training grounds and stepping stones to service in the federal parliament. A number of important figures in national politics, including two Chancellors, first achieved prominence in their Länder.

The Italian constitution of 1947 provided for extensive regional devolution, but the relevant provisions were not implemented in *all* regions until April 1972 so it is still too early to consider their effects. The regions which had enjoyed autonomy before this time had already shown, however, their potential for breaking the monopoly of power by the Christian Democratic Party.

Decentralisation forcefully demonstrated, also, that the specification of a capital city is perceived as conferring an automatic increase in the value of assets of the citizens in the designated centre. Violent street action in the cities of Pescara and L'Aquila in the Abruzzi region, and in Reggio Calabria against the chosen capital Catanzaro in the region of Calabria, marked the transfer of power and the choice of regional capitals that accompanied it.

In strong contrast to these federalist measures the French pattern of territorial delegation of power to local government indicates the reluctance of central governments to allow local challenge to their power. Louis XIV curbed the independence of the regional nobility by forcing them to dance attendance on his court. Later the revolution made in Paris had to be imposed on the provinces, and the prefectures and police were the instruments. The departments bear little or no correspondence to patterns of provincial territorial identification and, unlike the German Länder, their administrative role has been kept strictly under Paris control, so that they are instruments of central government dominance. Parochial loyalty, however, is still strong and often at odds with central government's interpretation of the national interest. But there are still doubts about the political and administrative competence of rural France, so the pattern of central assertion of authority endures. The effect is to make Paris the focus of political ambition of the gifted, and to make local government, in the larger towns rather than the villages, interesting primarily as a stepping stone to central government office. The villages of France are left to a relatively neglected peasantry and small business class – an entrepreneurial group with a standard of living often below that of the urban proletariat. De Gaulle's referendum proposals in 1969, for regional devolution, which would have given the regions taxation powers and Senate representation, failed in a vote which effectively expressed no confidence in de Gaulle personally. Devolution remains, therefore, rudimentary, and rural interests depend on urban concern.

There is no clear evidence that devolution (or federal institutions) encourages or inhibits corporatist development. It can emerge at any level and, though it is primarily a feature of central government diffusion of responsibility, it is a function of governmental weakness rather than strength. So Shonfield has argued, plausibly, that the highly centralised and efficient machine of administration in France gives that country peculiar advantages, yet to be fully exploited, for coherent government leadership. One might, to put the point in Galbraithian terms, argue that the powers of states in a federal system could (influenced by powerful economic groups as they are in the United States) be something of an impediment to 'emancipation of the state' from the corporatist 'planning system'. It is possible, on the other hand, that a truly 'balkanised' federal system would be an unfavourable environment for corporatist development. This has been suggested, albeit tentatively, as a reason, among others, for the low level of its development in Canada. Evidently no easily defensible hypothesis can be offered.

(d) It remains to consider the importance of rules which apply when operating rules are broken or subverted.

Prolonged 'crisis' conditions – for example, civil revolt, or war with occupation, or severe economic depression with mass unemployment, strikes and demonstrations – when, in fact, the government has partially failed, justifiably or not, to fulfil its necessary functions of guaranteeing security or managing the economy – may result in very important changes in political assets. Depending on the nature of the crisis, army and political elites may enjoy much greater influence, the dominance of major parties may be threatened by new parties of radical or authoritarian stamp, recruitment to the political elite may well extend to different groups and classes (most kinds of prolonged crises tend to enlarge working-class recruitment, for example, resistance leaders in war, and strike leaders at times of industrial difficulty), and the age distribution of the elite may well be altered.[29] There is a very difficult and necessarily imprecise distinction to be made, however, between manageable strain, and, on the other hand, threat to, subversion, or breakdown of constitutional operating rules. Constitutions when they recognise this last possibility attempt to meet the problem mainly by prescribing emergency rules and powers like those afforded the French President under Article 16 of the constitution, or by legal safeguards applied by the judiciary specifically to cope with threat before it becomes a dangerous reality. The impact of such rules is varied, but within the limits of this work it must suffice to generalise that though interest-bias may be seen in practice to affect their operation, favouring some groups and values over others, such rules have apparently served their basic defensive purpose. Action taken in such circumstances may have a lasting impact. President de Gaulle, for example, in settling the Algerian dispute, used Article 16 to purge the army and discipline the police and public service.

The role of a judiciary in interpreting rules and deciding when they have been broken or subverted may also be of lasting importance, affecting both consensual activity and the assets of groups. First, the process of interpretation may, in fact, be rule creation. All judiciaries, in a more or less limited way, legislate. Their interpretations add to ordinary law or detract from it in every sphere of social activity. They exercise an office of power in which methods of recruitment, tenure, and relations with other offices are as significant as they are in other constitutional branches. When, furthermore, they are the inter-preters of constitutional law, as they are, for example, in the United States and West Germany, their influence can be profound indeed. Thus, the Supreme Court of the United States has attracted group interests and pressures, particularly in the fight for civil rights, and the Court has challenged and checked the activities of Congress and the Presidency, sometimes to preserve the values and assets of the business community against state intervention for welfare ends and at the same time to preserve the power of the states against central government; sometimes to afford or deny civil rights to religious or ethnic groups.

In Germany, the Third Reich made clear the danger that basic social values could be subverted within the formal framework of law. The experience suggested the desirability of a special category of rules enshrining values, as well as defining constitutional practices, procedures and power relationships between organs of government. The Basic Law, therefore, includes a general definition of a social constitutional state (Sozialer Rechsstaat) to be interpreted and pro-tected by an independent judiciary. A complex court system, with many specialised branches, including one which deals with claims by citizens against the bureaucracy, is the guardian of the constitu-tion. Ultimately constitutional questions are determined by a Con-stitutional Court to whose jurisdiction even parliament itself, in its legislative role, is subject, since the Court may consider the compati-bility of federal and Land laws with the constitution.

The Court has readily seen itself, in the words of one of its

members, as 'above all the "Supreme Guardian of the Constitution",
inasmuch as it interprets the Constitution in a binding fashion, keeps
watch over the constitutional interplay between the constitutional
organs of the Federal Republic and its "Länder", takes care that the
State functionaries respect the fundamental rights of man, and safeguards the existence of the free democratic Legal Order'.[30]

Clearly, basic social values can also be subverted within a system
which embodies constitutional judicial review, for a court itself may
be a compliant instrument of tyranny. In Germany, nevertheless,
following the Nazi era, the constitution attempts to defend against
that possibility by identifying the nature of the threat and providing
procedures to limit it. In particular, the definition and proscription of
unconstitutional political parties, interpreted by the Constitutional
Court, has proved an important weapon against parties subscribing
to illiberal doctrines and methods which provoke intolerance and
violence, like those of the National Front in the United Kingdom.

Breakdown rules then may, specifically or coincidentally, discrimin-
ate against some groups and favour others, and like all other forms of
constitutional rule they may enhance or diminish the value of assets
and, thereby, affect the competition between groups, as well as determine patterns of consensual activity.

The constitutional rules with which we have been concerned in this
chapter are manipulable features of man's environment, and comparative study of their effects on political behaviour has suggested ways
in which corporatism might deliberately be checked and democratic
accountability strengthened. States, however, though legally sovereign,
are not completely independent and the potential for self-control
through manipulation of constitutional rules is limited, like most
other aspects of governmental performance, by the international
environment. The dimensions of this problem are our concern in the
next chapter.

NOTES

1 R. C. Macridis, *The Study of Comparative Government* (New York:
   Random House, 1955), p. 7.
2 D. Easton, 'An approach to the analysis of political systems', *World
   Politics*, April 1957, pp. 383–408.
3 G. A. Almond and J. S. Coleman, *Politics of the Developing Areas*
   (Princeton: Princeton University Press, 1960) provided the model.
   The theory of systemic functional requirements was based on the work
   of the sociologist Talcott Parsons.
4 See especially Ivo D. Duchacek, *Comparative Federalism* (New York:
   Holt Rinehart & Winston, 1970).
5 K. C. Wheare, *Legislatures* (London: OUP, 1963).

6 Robert C. Fried, *Comparative Political Institutions* (London: Macmillan, 1966).
7 Herbert J. Spiro, in his *Government by Constitution* (New York: Random House, 1959).
8 See e.g. Ivo D. Duchacek, *Power Maps: Comparative Politics of Constitutions* (Santa Barbara: Clio Press, 1973), and see, however, Spiro, op. cit.
9 Duchacek, *Power Maps*, p. xiii.
10 See F. G. Bailey, *Stratagems and Spoils* (Oxford: Blackwell, 1969).
11 These propositions or hypotheses assume a distribution in any society between left and right political values in which the main body of opinion tends towards the centre of the spectrum, while extreme left and right positions are held by only small minorities. Of a deeply divided society, which might be represented by a value distribution curve highest at the extremes, it might be argued that democratic institutions with somewhat indecisive government could possibly survive, provided that efficient mechanisms were *not* available for achieving consensus on, and active commitment to, the two clearly defined but irreconcilable views.

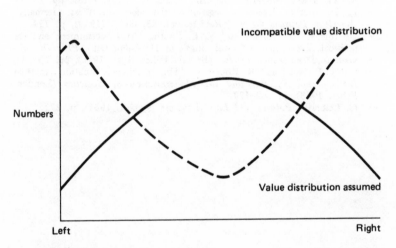

I have related the same propositions to theories of regional international integration in my *Europe in Question* (London: Allen & Unwin, 1974), pp. 118–27.
12 For the data and analysis on which these assumptions rest see A. Etzioni, *The Active Society* (New York: Free Press, 1968), pp. 466–94; Herbert McClosky, 'Consensus and ideology in American politics', Paper A22, Berkeley, University of California, Survey Research Centre, revised and reprinted in J. R. Fiszman (ed.), *The American Political Arena* (Boston, Mass.: Little, Brown, 1966), pp. 39–70, especially p. 41; S. J. Eldersveld, 'Parties and the foundations of political consensus' and Heinz Eulau, 'Groups: the vertical dimension', both in Fiszman, op. cit., pp. 349–56 and 357–63; R. J. Monsen and M. W. Cannon, *The Makers of Public Policy* (New York: McGraw Hill, 1965).
13 Etzioni, op. cit., p. 476.

14   ibid.
15   ibid.
16   Samuel H. Barnes, 'Italy', in R. Rose (ed.), *Electoral Behaviour, A Comparative Handbook* (New York': Free Press, 1974), pp. 177–8.
17   Keith Hill, 'Belgium', in ibid., p. 69.
18   Richard Rose, 'Britain', in ibid., p. 493.
19   Article 59.
20   Article 23.
21   Compare Canada, Belgium and Holland.
22   *The Federalist*, No. 48.
23   See F. E. Huggett, *The Modern Netherlands* (London: Pall Mall, 1971).
24   The Presidency itself is as much a function of personality and party as new power. Election attracts the big personalities, leaders of the major parties.
25   K. Sontheimer, *The Government and Politics of West Germany* (London: Hutchinson, 1972), p. 122.
26   William H. Riker, *Federalism: Origin, Operation, Significance* (Boston: Little, Brown, 1964), p. 155.
27   See G. Sawer, *Modern Federalism* (London: Watts, 1969), pp. 183–4.
28   P. H. Merkl, 'Executive legislative federalism in West Germany', *American Political Science Review*, vol. 53, no. 3 (1959), p. 734.
29   On this see S. Tarrow and V. L. Smith, 'Crisis recruitment and the political involvement of local elites', in H. Eulau (ed.), *Elite Recruitment in Democratic Societies* (Beverly Hills: Sage, 1976), pp. 205–37, and J. P. Nettl and R. Robertson, 'The inheritance situation', in their *International Systems and the Modernisation of Societies* (London: Faber, 1968), pp. 63–127.
30   G. Leibholz, *Politics and Law* (Leyden: Sythoff, 1965), p. 272.

9
Interdependence

The starting point of this chapter is that, in trying to understand the contemporary political problems of the advanced industrial societies, it is dangerous to ignore the fact that each and every one of the states in this category exists in an environment which profoundly affects its behaviour. It favours or creates opportunities or motives for some actions (including government action) and it inhibits or prevents others.

For a preliminary example, one of the motivating factors in the events of May 1968 in France was a war in which France had no part; which the government, in fact, condemned – the Vietnam war. Another motivating and mobilising factor in the movement of student protest was a variety of radical doctrines, most of which originated outside France, but which had become the unifying ideologies of international student formations. Not insignificantly, the most well-known leader in May 1968 was a foreign student, Danny Cohn Bendit. One could go on to argue that the crisis, when it came, might have been managed by the government better if its head, and best tried crisis manager, General de Gaulle, had not been off in Romania, pursuing his conception of the international interests of France.

That example is illustrative of a proposition that is common to all states, not just the advanced industrial societies; namely, that there are what Rosenau has, quite literally, labelled 'linkages'[1] between domestic and international events. There are virtually no purely domestic-regarding actions. The domestic politics of any state may profoundly influence domestic politics in another.

The linkages which can be traced tend to illustrate the extent to which any national society, far from being self-contained, is part of a global society. Its cultural, economic and political activities are part of a pattern of interwoven activity of many kinds and levels and of varying scope. One approach to the study of international relations, the 'world society' school,[2] goes as far as to suggest that we are too much preoccupied with states as political actors and that, as a result, contemporary international studies ignore such things as animal aspects of human behaviour, and cultural, economic and political forces which transcend national political boundaries. Whether this is true or not of international political studies, our present purpose is to examine how far forces of all such kinds, emanating from the global environment, do affect the politics of the advanced industrial societies.

We may, however, limit our task. First, we may recognise and merely record the fact that many of the politically significant sub-systems of national politics are linked with others across national boundaries. Education, for example, is international in many of its aspects. Thus, the science curriculum develops internationally rather than nationally. Demands for communication skills help to determine the provision of language courses in curricula. The power and influence of states in the international system is roughly reflected in marginal changes of emphasis internationally on one language rather than another in school curricula. The student body in most tertiary educational establishments is international. Issues like foreign students' fees, provision for exchanges of students and teachers, may well become issues in domestic politics, as well as matters of concern for other governments, for intergovernmental organisations, and for private national and international organisations throughout the world.

One other example will suffice to illustrate the point – an aspect of the environmental control function. The once lowly oil tanker has become, in the past two decades, the most vital, the largest and, for governments, the most formidable vessel on the high seas. It carries the arterial blood of the advanced industrial societies – their principal energy source. In 1951, approximately 5 per cent of Europe's energy requirements were met by oil, and the creation of the European Coal and Steel Community was seen as an enormous step in the interests of peace because coal supplied 60–70 per cent of fuel requirements. By 1968, oil accounted for 56 per cent and the proportion was rising by about 8 per cent per annum. About half the oil came from one area, the Middle East, by tanker. Fleets of ships were necessary and the size of ships grew with the need. By 1973, half the tonnage of ships afloat was in oil tankers. Tankers under construction in 1974 equalled the entire tanker fleet of 1957. Most of the new vessels are much bigger than the 'giants' of the fifties, the *Queen Elizabeth* and the *Queen Mary*. The *Queen Elizabeth* was 83,673 tons. The *Torrey Canyon*, which achieved some notoriety when it was wrecked off the Scilly Isles in early 1967, was 120,000 tons. The vessels of the seventies are more than three times larger than this. The two *Globtiks* are 476,000 tons. They are 1,243 feet long and have a draught of 91 feet 11 inches. Each tank in such a vessel is the size of an office block. They are so big that in waters like the English Channel, they cannot obey the rules of the road or they would run aground. They have run over other ships without being aware of having hit anything. Smaller ships at night have attempted to steer between their forward and aft lights because they appear to belong to two vessels.

There are very few dry docks or even ports which can receive these vessels. They lie at special terminals offshore to discharge their cargo in deep water. They represent a gross and imminent threat to the environment because if they founder they can spill up to half a million tons of crude oil into the water.

In many coastal areas they sail with a clearance in draught of 2 to 3 feet, vulnerable to shifts of sand on the bottom and to wrecks. They have a demonstrably much reduced manoeuvrability once they are within 40 feet of their draught.

The cargo of these vessels represents an environmental threat not merely when it is spilt in large quantities but also when small quantities are regularly dumped. The Swiss oceanographer M. Jacques Picard, speaking on behalf of the Secretariat on the eve of the United Nations conference on the environment at Stockholm in 1972, said that many experts believe that, at the present rate of pollution from all sources, life in the seas could be extinguished within the next twenty-five years. Oil is the single largest pollutant of the sea. The vessels which carry it are the most unsafe and ill-manned vessels afloat. Empty tank inspection and clearing has a dangerous risk of explosion and fire, and few, if any, of the mechanical or electronic systems on board have the emergency backing available on orthodox ships. A minor fault anywhere on a computer-directed complex may well leave a vessel helpless.

The conning problems of such vessels are so different from those of orthodox ships that the Esso oil company has a special training programme for its masters in simulated conditions. Another simulator programme is run in Holland at Delft, but most vessels are charter vessels of Liberian or Panamanian registration and their masters, officers and crews learn on the job, and their qualifications for their responsibility are dubious. Expressing French opposition to the use of flags of convenience when the Liberian-registered supertanker *Olympic Bravery* (275,000 tons), owned by the Onassis shipping company, went aground off Ushant in 1976, M. Jean Chapon, Secretary-General of the French Merchant Marine, said: 'Experience showed that it was through doubtfully skilled crews and doubtful respect for international safety regulations that such companies were able to offer serious competition to national lines.'[3]

Only a few months earlier, in November 1975, the *Olympic Alliance* in a collision with a Royal Navy frigate *Achilles* discharged 2,000 tonnes of crude oil into the Channel causing widespread coastal pollution in addition to sea pollution. In spite of Board of Trade spraying of dispersants, 300 tonnes of oil polluted beaches between Sandstone and Folkestone. Though there is consultation on this problem, particularly between Britain, France and Norway and, on a multilateral basis, within IMCO – Intergovernmental Marine Consultative Organization – the only action that has proved possible is national and *ex post facto*. No means have been found to tackle the basic problem of flags of convenience.

Thus, in a functional area of great importance, individual states can do virtually nothing to protect themselves, dependent as they are on the actions of the 'flags of convenience' states. And the interdependence is so widely diffused and complex that concerted action has so far proved beyond the grasp of the states concerned.

Education and environmental control, then, are just two examples of functional areas in which activity is constrained or enlarged by international factors. Agriculture, transport, labour, energy production and consumption, maritime activity, post, telephone, radio and television services, police, prison, health services, security, social security, and management of the economy, all have their international dimensions. A range of international functional agencies, most of them with state-maintaining rather than transforming objectives on the part of their members, bear witness to interdependency in these areas.

The term interdependency covers a range of relationships between states. It refers to both egalitarian and mutual dependency as well as to relationships in which one or some actors are subordinate. It includes both bilateral and multilateral relationships which any government may have to take account of in policy making. As was suggested by the opening statement of the chapter, interdependency is visualised, as in popular usage, as having both positive and negative aspects, enlarging as well as constraining the scope of possible activity. Thus, international imitative behaviour is an important positive aspect of both domestic and foreign policy of states. The wildfire spread of the regional common market and community idea is one obvious example. Alliance matching and arms racing are others.

It is possible however, to single out two areas in which, for the advanced industrial societies, the term interdependence has a particular significance: economic interdependence and security interdependence.

ECONOMIC INTERDEPENDENCE

While virtually every functional area of government has its economic aspect, the concept of economic management, as such, does have a distinct connotation. It refers to government's overall role in attempting to regulate the long-term rate of growth of, and cyclical fluctuations in, business activity, through such instruments as variations in public spending, taxation, tariffs and other aspects of foreign trade regulation, direct or indirect control of the money supply, and selective encouragement or discouragement of investment in particular regions or in particular sectors.

Two factors, international in their effects, have complicated this task. The first is the level (with other transactions like loans, aid and investment) of trade, particularly with and among the advanced industrial societies. The proportion which trade represents of their total national income is high enough to create mutual vulnerability.[4] Of course, the continental-scale United States of America is not as highly vulnerable in this respect as the relatively small nation-states of Western Europe or Japan, but the part that American trade plays in their total[5] is significant and makes United States economic management of vital concern to them.

Trade on this scale means that, to a considerable extent, prices on the domestic market for raw materials, and consumption goods and services of all kinds, are influenced by international conditions of demand and supply. International trade constitutes a transmission mechanism by means of which a decline or upsurge of economic activity in one country, reflected in falling or rising demand for imports, makes itself felt in other countries. The virtue of international trade is, of course, that supply fluctuations in different countries may cancel themselves out. For example, a glut in cereals can be disposed of to a country which has experienced harvest failure. Material advantages and specialised skills, in the classical free trade conception, are exploited through trade to mutual advantage. This argument has provided a powerful incentive to trading agreements, including customs unions like the EEC (the members of which are each others' best customers), and to a whole range of international organisations like GATT, the IMF or the Rome Convention, which are designed to maintain and increase trade by removing or inhibiting the imposition of tariffs and quotas and temporarily cushioning the monetary effects of an imbalance of trade.

Through international arrangements of this kind, it can be argued, states have reduced their ability to regulate economic behaviour. The traditional instruments for correcting an adverse balance of payments – tariffs and quotas against imports, exchange controls, and export subsidies – have often been removed from their competence by international agreement. Even devaluation of currencies, the weapon of last resort, is inhibited to some degree by international monetary strategies like the European 'snake-in-the-tunnel' objective. It can quite properly be argued that such agreements and arrangements are, in fact, devices for maintaining independence – that is, the ultimate independence of the nation-state to operate a chosen form of government and, within the constraints imposed by the environment, determine its own destiny. The EEC is a possible exception since at least lip-service is paid by some members to the notion that it has a transformation goal – political unity. Most intergovernmental arrangements and organisations and, in its present style of development, the EEC, are, however, maintaining devices. But they are responses to an international environment of increased interdependence, of more numerous linkages between foreign affairs and domestic affairs, which reduce the independent range of action of governments. The international agreements do not entirely restore this lost capacity for action. They may merely make it less damaging or give it some more acceptable form.

International trade, however, not only creates mutual and more or less general dependence, but also particular dependent relationships. 'Developing', low-income countries and low-income primary producers, for example, are as vulnerable as the advanced societies to the vagaries of international commerce (in so far as vulnerability can be measured by trade as a proportion of GNP). And since they tend to rely on one or two commodities for exports they may well be adversely affected by short-term variations in demand and supply in the world market for their product when there is no general cyclical problem.

One way of avoiding these vagaries is to enter into a long-term trade agreement with one major customer to provide a guaranteed market and price, in return, normally, for preferential tariff treatment or a more or less exclusive market for a range of industrial products. This, however, creates a particular dependent relationship. The arrangements between the UK and New Zealand prior to British entry into the European Economic Community had this character.[6]

The particular problem for the advanced industrial societies is that with their large industrial and service sectors they are much further away from the position of being able to 'fall back' on a self-contained subsistence economy. To take just one aspect, agriculture – even those advanced societies which are net food exporters, like France, Denmark or Holland, rely on methods of production utilising fuels, fertilisers and capital equipment in which they are far from self-sufficient. But in any case, Europe of the Nine, considered as one unit, is a major net importer of food.[7] This net dependence of the Western European states on the rest of the world for food, the raw materials of the food production process, and many other raw materials essential to industrial activity has, until recently, been only an occasional problem. In the 1970s, however, the creation of the association of oil-exporting countries, OPEC, formed to control and raise the price of their product, showed how dependent the advanced societies were. The rise in the price of oil, the major energy source of industry and the basis of a vast range of synthetic materials, set off a general price rise and so an inflationary spiral which governments seemed unable to control unless they were prepared to accept a high level of unemployment. The usual instruments for the regulation of the economy were unable to cope with the challenge of this external force.

October 1973 was a watershed: it saw the collective decision of the oil producers to reduce production by 10 per cent, and price increases of approximately 70 per cent. The role of oil in advanced societies is multifold. The industry's profits are part of the financial basis for development. It is the major energy source. Even in the US, Arab oil supplies 35 per cent of needs. It is a 'commanding height' of their economies. Furthermore, it has now become a focus of struggle for emancipation and for closing the industrialisation gap between the 'Second', and some parts of the Third World. It is a weapon in Israeli–Arab conflict which compels a change in European attitudes to the struggle. It is potentially available for other political objectives of the Arab states. It is a source of vulnerability in Europe's economies of profound domestic political importance, threatening instability and reducing capacity to 'deliver the goods'. It is a new threat to the environmental lobby as Europe seeks its own resources of oil.

A second environmental factor affecting economic management is the scope of technological interdependence. Technological development has reduced the effects of distance between societies and facilitated a greater range and volume of international transactions. Communications techniques have made activities on the other side of the world, or even the moon, instant news – news which may lead to domestic pressures on governments to take action which changes or diverts the country's resources – for example, by aid programmes or trade sanctions. In this light, the development of the advanced industrial societies, particularly those with market economies which least inhibit non-governmental international contacts, has accelerated the development of interdependency between states. The advanced societies are the major producers and consumers of the product of an international advanced technology. In the fields of electronics, semi-conductors, space technology, aviation, computers and nuclear energy, countries tend to rate each other on a development status ladder which partially determines their international influence. Further, industrial development accelerates in one country rather than another partly because technological developments create a comparative cost advantage or a new or superior product in world trade. The advanced societies take the view that they cannot individually afford to fall behind technologically because the economic growth which satisfies the rising expectations of their populations depends on technological innovation, and because to fall behind could create an economic and military dependence on the countries which are technological leaders.

The United States is generally conceded to be the country at the most advanced technological level. It has the stimulus and assurance of a very large internal market and of having its own rich material resources; but its technological leads are also due to the fact that industry benefits from massive government sponsorship of research and development and from government procurement policies. The marketing base has helped to ensure an industrial structure which has a competitive advantage in other large markets and also provides a favourable environment for research activity. The United States commits more of its resources proportionately to research and development than Western Europe, and though the difference is greatest in the defence-related sphere (including atomic and space technology) it persists even when military research is excluded).[8]

In this effort government plays a large and influential role, contributing some 64 per cent of the total. In Western Europe only the French government matches this proportionate effort,[9] but in any case there is dispersal and duplication of effort among the European countries which is minimised in the United States through the overall government role in financing research, and by its procurement policies, as well as by the fact that single large companies can ensure a more integrated effort with the same funds than several smaller European companies. Thus 'In aviation the turnover of the six leading European Companies (BAC, Rolls Royce, Sud-Aviation, Dassault-Bregnet, Saab and the Airframe branch of Hawker Siddeley) is roughly $2,000m. or about the same as the annual turnover of Boeing.'[10]

The absolute costs of research and development in the new technology areas – nuclear, aerospace and electronics – and the importance of procurement policies are a major factor making for advantages in company size and requiring a governmental role. The aircraft industry is an obvious example. In the 1930s and 1940s, small design teams tightly controlled by a chief designer produced whole designs on the drawing board. About a quarter of the effort went into technical calculation on structural integrity. The main test of this was in flight. The size and speed of aircraft have since increased more than tenfold and design teams are from 500 to 5,000 people (depending on the aircraft) in the parent company of the several companies involved in the development. There are up to three times that number in the total complex of contracting companies. Total research and development costs have risen steadily and with them the actual price of aircraft. In the 1945–55 period the long-range Constellation cost £63,000. In the next two decades prices were:

1956–65
Britannia, £750,000; Douglas DC7C, £1·3m.; Super VC10, £3m.

1966–75

Boeing 707, £7m.; Concorde (approx.), £23m.; possibly £30m. to put into actual service.

Development costs of the Concorde by 1975 were £1,000m.

It has been suggested that the concern of the European states to match the technological *défi américain* through European Community projects like Euratom, and joint efforts like CERN, Concorde, the airbus and the multi-role combat aircraft, is unwarranted. Joint projects are always more costly than singly directed ones, and in any case 'there appears to be little correlation between economic growth and R and D expenditures'.[11] Technology is readily transferable, much of it without cost, through the dissemination of the scientific information on which it is based, publications, conferences, or the movement of skilled personnel, but also through manufacture under licence which is, in the long run, far less costly than independent national research and development.

Whichever view is taken, it is clear that for the Western European advanced industrial societies, the vitally important question of domestic technological promotion is significantly affected by external factors. None of the states concerned can afford to match the absolute level and scope of the United States programme of research and development, and still more markedly do they fall short of the US capacity to support the product by massive government procurement and through the large domestic market, or to exploit foreign markets with large-scale marketing organisations and various 'back-up' arrangements ranging from servicing and parts facilities to bribery. They have, therefore, a choice between two kinds of international dependency: the mutual dependence of co-operative or harmonised research, development and procurement, or the particular dependence of technological transfer from the United States.

SECURITY INTERDEPENDENCE

The other area of significant interdependence, that of security, is also governed to a considerable extent by technological evolution. The problem for the second-rank advanced industrial societies of Europe of providing for their security is dominated by the nuclear dilemma. John Erikson has put it that 'we live, sometimes dangerously, in an age jammed asymmetrically between the time of the possession of global weapons and that of the retention, not to say the reinforcement of local loyalties . . . The substance of a once familiar stability has been consumed with fiery abruptness by the onset and the cumulative, technical triumphs of the "military revolution" that centres around nuclear weaponry.'[12] This revolution has gone through a number of stages since the first atomic bomb was dropped on Hiroshima. First, came the hydrogen bomb. This was followed by tactical nuclear weapons. The combination of missile and nuclear warhead was then developed, to be followed by the evolution of warning systems. Hard sites, almost invulnerable, then nuclear submarines launching ballistic missiles were subsequent steps taken by the super-power leaders. The United States can now equip its submarines with MIRVS (multiple independently targetable re-entry vehicle systems), like Poseidon which carries ten targetable warheads. The MIRVS was actually a step beyond the MRVS (like Polaris) with its naturally falling warheads.

The importance of these successive developments is that they have kept the ultimate weapon beyond the reach of any but the super-powers and have thereby helped to maintain the dependent alliance systems of which they are the nuclear guarantors. The pace of development has proved to be beyond the individual financial resources of the European allies of the United States and it has ensured that the currently best available protective system is available only through the alliance.[13] Furthermore, because of the speed of missiles, the only effective warning system is a global system. And an effective warning system plus the use of hard sites and missile-launching submarines is regarded by strategists as the essential element in the survival of some retaliatory capacity – a capacity on which the whole theory of mutual nuclear deterrence depends.

The nuclear dilemma for the Europeans, then, has been how to cope with these factors of security dependence on the United States while maintaining a measure of political and economic independence. Their choices, the horns of the dilemma, appear to be security with dependence or independence with insecurity. The classical way, in formal logic, of rebutting a dilemma is to see whether the two 'horns' really exhaust every possible alternative and to examine the presumed connections between antecedents and consequents – in the present case, the connection between security and dependence. It is appropriate, therefore, to consider the principal policy alternative, and then to consider the conception of security which entails dependence.

The North Atlantic Treaty Organisation theoretically avoids the dilemma by formally associating the United States and the European states in an alliance of fifteen sovereign equals, taking counsel together and incurring mutual obligations. The obligations (and the object of the alliance) are to 'maintain and develop their individual and collective capacity to resist armed attack'.[14] This is an egalitarian formula. The Harmel Report on future tasks of the alliance (December 1967) says explicitly, 'As sovereign states, the allies are not obliged to subordinate their policies to collective decision.'[15] Furthermore, in practice the NATO Council takes its decisions unanimously and the presidency rotates annually between the members, as does the presidency of the various committees, including the military committee.

A regional pact, or any kind of multilateral organisation of limited membership can enhance the influence of smaller states in relation to the larger states, particularly if decisions depend on unanimity. It is preferable to bilateral arrangements, particularly if the smaller states have common interests and if the membership is sufficiently small to make individual voices count. NATO, however, cannot help but be affected by the importance of the US contribution to its total strength. The original European component depended on direct US military assistance through the BTO and indirectly on economic aid through OEEC. Apart from Germany itself, it has the largest contingent of troops actually in the German front line of the central European theatre.[16] The tactical nuclear warheads are in American custody.[17] The Supreme Allied Commander in Europe is an American. Nevertheless, for Europe, NATO has reduced the burden of the level of defence attained. It has been a forum in which to put pressure on the United States to maintain its involvement and, within it, the European states now have their own ministerial meetings prior to full Council to seek common ground in order to increase their bargaining effectiveness. As a result, American dominance is by no means absolute.

In this situation, NATO has evolved a conception of security which cannot be entirely identified with the interests of any particular member government. Thus, it is accepted that the capability of the USSR and of the Warsaw Pact in general is the prime factor to which NATO planning should attempt to respond. The NATO doctrine of strategic sufficiency requires that this capability should be matched by an equivalent defensive capability. The type of exercise conducted by NATO forces has its rationale as a response to an act of aggression by the known forces available to the Warsaw Pact. This conception is seen by NATO planners as entailing that US forces be kept at their highest possible strength in Europe and, should there be US reductions, that the European powers should make them up and generally make a greater contribution to their collective defence.

One may detect, however, underlying differences in interests and perception of interests which suggests that NATO is not an entirely egalitarian and satisfactory escape from the security dependence dilemma. It could be argued that NATO's 'forward line' strategy, which concentrates defence effort on the eastern borders of West Germany, weakens the alliance as a whole strategically by making it particularly vulnerable to surprise attack. It satisfies mainly the West German security interest and possibly that of the United States. One study suggests that, partly because of the way NATO forces have been run down and reliance placed on tactical nuclear weapons, and partly because of the build up of Warsaw Pact forces, the latter could attack with a speed and penetration which would make it impossible to use the tactical nuclear weapons and get NATO forces into the positions earmarked for them in the forward strategy.[18] The forward strategy, it is argued, is conditioned largely by West Germany's understandable reluctance to surrender its territory without a fight. This argument is officially discounted by NATO[19] partly on interpretation of the strategic position – NATO asserts that tactical nuclear weapons could be used in time, even in the event of a surprise attack – and partly on the political interpretation, with its emphasis on the peculiarly German interest. NATO insists that its strategy 'has been consistently and unanimously endorsed' by member governments.[20] However, no matter how the argument is resolved it is indicative of uncertainties within the alliance about its efficacy as a means of escape from the security dependence dilemma.

Certainly Britain, and still more openly, France, which has left NATO, have been at considerable pains to develop and maintain their own independent nuclear deterrent as a second line or homeland defence. In the French case, this effort very seriously prejudiced the Community Treaty, EURATOM, which, dependent as its programme was upon American fissionable materials, did not satisfy French needs. EURATOM, therefore, has been starved of funds largely through French reluctance to give support to the organisation.

Another uncertainty consists in the likely difference of interest between the Europeans and the real bastion of the alliance, the United States. The preference of the European powers is for relatively small conventional forces and a low nuclear threshold. The burden of heavy conventional forces is politically repugnant[21] and it can well be argued that small conventional forces make the use of tactical weapons imperative and, therefore, credible as a deterrent. The United States, on the other hand, has pressed for larger conventional forces to be subscribed by the Europeans and favours a higher nuclear threshold. Its particular interest is, evidently, to keep the battle, if it ever came, confined to the European theatre. Nuclear escalation is the most obvious threat to that interest. In these circumstances there are doubts, and they have been expressed not only by the French, that an American President would risk the bombing of American cities by promptly using the tactical weaponry in United States control in retaliation against a conventional attack on Europe. To some extent, the positioning of some 300,000 US troops of the Seventh Army in Germany, as 'hostage-evidence' of the American commitment, helps to allay the European doubts, but the demoralising effect of the Vietnam war and the dollar drain and weakening have made the withdrawal of US troops seem imminent from time to time.[22] This prospect has helped to strengthen the European resistance to US pressures to increase their own contribution to available NATO forces, since this could provide something of an excuse for the withdrawal.

The uncertainties about the NATO alliance as a security option have lent support, nevertheless, to various ideas about an independent, collective European effort in the security arena. These ideas take two main forms. First, there are the ideas expressed by Edward Heath[23] about the revival of the idea of some version of the European Defence Community, which died in 1954 when it was presented by M. Mendès-France to the French parliament for ratification and rejected. Second, there is the national alternative now being pursued by France. French planning for Armageddon is, in the context of reduced defence expenditure as a proportion of GNP from 1960[24] to the present day, to devote an increasing effort to nuclear capability development, the key elements of which are IRBM's carrying 150 kilo ton nuclear warheads, ballistic missile submarines delivering 500 kilo ton bombs, and Mirage bombers delivering 70 kilo ton bombs. (In comparison, the Hiroshima bomb was 20 kilo tons.) The independent British nuclear deterrent can be viewed from a similar *national* perspective.

The two forms, the European and the national, raise many different questions. They can be considered together, however, to the degree that they both raise the question of how far the European states, nationally or regionally, can by their own increased efforts, enhance their security and lessen their dependence on the United States, and match what has hitherto been the American contribution. This question is inextricably mixed up with hopes and fears about the development of the European Community, since defence is evidently a possible instrument of Community building.

The relevant comparisons between Europe and America and the presumed enemy, the USSR, in attempting to answer this question, are the economic, technological and political ones. How far is Europe outmatched in these categories?

The United States, with a population of 215·8 million, has an estimated GNP of 1,397·4 billion dollars, of which, in 1974, 6 per cent was spent on defence.[25] The USSR, with its slightly larger population of 253·3 million, has an estimated GNP of 468 billion roubles (one estimated dollar equivalent is slightly less than double this figure);[26] an estimated percentage of this for defence spending is 10·6 per cent.[27] The European NATO countries and France, with a population of around 300 million and a GNP of approximately 1,242·3 billion dollars, spend a much smaller percentage on defence. In 1974 only Britain, Greece and Portugal spent more than 4 per cent (5·2, 4·3 and 6·8 per cent respectively). France spent 3·4 per cent and West Germany 3·6 per cent. Luxembourg spent 0·9 per cent.[28] What this means in terms of relative sacrifice in living standards in the interest of defence spending is difficult to state precisely. The US living standards remain higher than those of the European Community as a whole and the American defence industry is stimulated by defence spending and is competitive in world markets. The European defence industry, divided between the several states, and wastefully competitive between them, is more risky, less cost-efficient and, for any one state, defence spending helps to exacerbate balance of payment problems because requirements cannot be met by domestic resources. With complete standardisation of equipment throughout Europe and a single procurement policy financed by a common defence budget, the Europeans might be in a position substantially to increase their defence expenditure without politically unacceptable sacrifice, but the prospect itself is politically remote and it would, in any case, be many years before such co-operation had very much effect on combat strength. The case for maintaining national defence industries is that to depend on imports is to become politically dependent on the supplier and also that defence is seen as a leading element in technological advance.[29]

Technological capacity, already alluded to in the context of economic interdependence, is another factor in the security/dependence calculus. The symptoms of the United States alleged technological supremacy have been expounded by a number of writers. The sale of United States advanced technology products in Europe is one suggested indicator. Seventy-five per cent of the computers sold in Europe come from American companies. One-third of all Europe's telephones are supplied by one US firm. Half the pharmaceuticals bought by the British Health Service are sold by American firms. The 'brain drain' is another suggested indicator. Europe suffers a net export of professional and technical immigrants each year, only France avoiding this problem. Further, there is a net imbalance of payments for patents and licence fees from Europe to the United States.

A different sort of indicator is spending on research and development. In this Europe and America were roughly equal in the thirties. By 1963–4, the US spent nearly four times as much as Western Europe – twice the percentage of GNP.

These 'likely' indicators do not prove US technological superiority, though they may suggest it, and, on a direct industry comparison, there are areas in which Europe arguably is more advanced. But it is in the defence-linked industries that US superiority is most apparent.[30]

The relevant political comparisons flow directly from the economic and technological. Political unity is an important factor in the achievement of the technological base on which the American defence potential rests, especially the continued weapons development. There are no problems of establishment and merger of companies in the US and, therefore, no real barriers to the creation of the great companies which can afford to spend money on research and development and then produce and market on a scale which justifies the expenditure.

Controlled massive US government assistance to research by companies and universities is probably more effective than European because it is centrally rationalised, and because development and production is sustained by government procurement. In aerospace and electronics, where government effort is concentrated because of the military applications, the gap between America and Europe is most pronounced.

Complete integration of forces, standardisation of equipment and centralised procurement are nowhere near achievement in Europe. They depend on a degree of political unity which is not even discernible on the European far horizon. It is for this reason, mainly, that possibilities of finding the necessary financial and technical resources for developing nuclear forces on a super-power scale in the UK, France, or Western Europe generally, seem to be virtually negligible, unless there are some very profound alterations in the situation, like a new and imminent threat from the East, together with a clear reduction in the US readiness to defend Western Europe.

SALT, NEGOTIATIONS ON MBFR, AND THE EUROPEAN SECURITY CONFERENCE

If it is impossible in the short term, for a combination of economic, technological and political reasons, for Europe to fill the gap which would be left by a withdrawal of the American guarantee, is it possible to increase security, without paying a price in dependency, by some other means than direct defence spending? It is in this context that SALT talks, MBFR talks, and a European security conference might be considered as another European option.

SALT talks could lessen, and to some extent they already have done so, the element of uncertainty about the strategic balance between the USSR and the USA, and its stability. They could, and to a limited degree, have, also lessened tension. They could also set limits to what the super-powers could do in arming their satellites. For example, on the 26 May 1972 the USA and USSR agreed not to transfer ABM technology to their satellites. This agreement keeps the present generation of nuclear weapons in European hands effective for longer.

The proposal for Mutual and Balanced force reductions could also affect the situation, though not necessarily favourably. One of the possible outcomes is that successful negotiations would result in a withdrawal of American forces in Europe, rather than a reduction in West European forces, so that the Alliance would be weakened in conventional forces at the same time as the psychological backing of the nuclear guarantee is eliminated. There is also the possibility that an agreement will weaken an already weak resolve in the West to provide adequate defence, since it will seem like an acknowledgement that all is well, the Cold War over, and *détente* prevails.

This is also one of the fears about moving towards a European security conference. Such a conference would have a general removal of tension as its objective, and might well result in the creation of some sort of permanent machinery for consideration of East–West issues, including Russia as a European power, but not the US. Again, the fear among European military strategists is that this could produce an illusory sense of security, thereby increasing popular antipathy towards maintaining even existing levels of defence spending.

In spite of such fears, the European states generally regard these proposals with favour. Why is this? The question raises directly the ambiguities in security and its evaluation. On the horns of our dilemma, dependence and independence are real enough, though difficult to define, but in a sense 'security' is too nebulous and 'soft' a concept altogether to be associated with anything as sharp and hard as the horn of a dilemma, either as antecedent or consequent.

One difficulty is that security must be seen in relation to possible threats and there are problems in recognising and evaluating them. The power of a state may be regarded as a threat in itself to the security of any other, but the immediacy of the threat as a security problem is determined in conjunction with posture. Power equality may of itself lead to power rivalry and some degree of hostility, but this fundamentally unmeasurable psychological factor is a very uncertain aspect of security calculation. Power, in any case, is itself a nebulous concept, definable in general terms as an ability to influence the actions of others in a desired way. Economic and military resources are measurable aspects of power, directly relevant to security, but such factors as geographical position, topography and size, or population size, age structure and skills, or the kinds of resources and productive capacity a state has, or the stability of its political system, or the resourcefulness of its elites, or the economic linkages which it has with other states which may create dependency and bargaining counters relevant to security status, or the diplomatic skills which may foster the vital perceptions by other states of the power available for deployment, or the viability of the aligned and confronting alliances of any state, are all factors of power relevant to security which are incapable of precise evaluation. A special problem in the sixties and seventies has been the two-tier security problem: the limited conventional war environment and the total nuclear war environment. Within which environment does a particular defence expenditure or posture add to security? What is the relationship between the two environments?

But analysis of the capability of other states is not the only difficulty in security appreciation. For any state there is the problem of estimating the nature of the relationship which exists between internal and external security. When does the burden of defence begin to weaken rather than strengthen a country? And to what extent does a state's effort in providing for its defence impose a policy straitjacket upon it, inhibiting movement towards *détente* with possible enemies? Does the perception of threat, or even preparation against a hypothetical threat have a self-fulfilling quality?

These are all questions which it seems appropriate to raise in the context of security and its relationship to the degree of external dependence it may involve, and the consequent restraints on government which must be recognised in all societies. Thus, if we conclude the examination by suggesting that there does not appear to be any acceptable alternative to the dominance of the super-powers in European security but that, in spite of this, the European states favour current exploratory security talks which may weaken the guarantees the USA provides, the apparent paradox may be explained by the uncertainties and the perceptual subjective elements in the notion of security itself,[31] and in the complexities of interdependence.

CORPORATIST ASPECTS OF INTERDEPENDENCE

Economics and security, the two policy areas in which interdependence is an inescapable fact of life for the advanced societies, are also ones in which interest intermediation plays a significant role. International outcomes in these areas may well be determined either *within* influential states by sectoral corporatist structures for whom the foreign policy implications of their actions are subordinated to, or rationalised by, their narrow interpretation of national interest – 'What is good for General Motors . . .' – or, in the case of those *international* sectors in which functionally specific transnational organisations (like the International Civil Aviation Association, the International Finance Corporation and the International Energy Agency) or multinational corporations are active, through a correspondingly blinkered conception of an international community interest.

The exercise of influence within states – foreign policy lobbies – does not need to be laboured here, but the degree to which it may be characterised as corporatist should be noted. One writer, who has explored the policy networks of foreign economic policy in West Germany and Japan, has concluded that 'in both countries, foreign economic policy-making appears as a showcase of corporatism [though] . . . it is a corporation without labor unions'.[32] In the case of Germany, he asserts that 'although the West German political system is frequently referred to as a "Chancellor's democracy" or "party democracy", these labels have little descriptive value with regard to the formulation and implementation of foreign economic policy. Parties and parliament find themselves on the periphery of the policy network. Their role is to ratify decisions rather than to formulate policy. The axis of the policy network is a close co-operative relationship linking the ministerial bureaucracy to interest groups in industry, trade and banking.'[33] He draws similar conclusions about the making of Japanese foreign economic policy, though there the co-ordinative role of the state is much stronger.

There are few policy problems in international relations in which interest representations at the international level by sub-national, national or international sectoral groups, in conditions approximating in many respects to the corporatist pattern of quasi-monopolistic representation, relative secrecy and, in particular, sectoral autonomy not subject to democratic controls, do not have a role.

It makes little or no difference if a policy is administered under the aegis and presumed supervision of the United Nations. In the *Capacity Study of the United Nations Development System* under Sir Robert Jackson, he stated: 'For many years, I have looked for the "brain" which guides policies and operations of the UN development system. The search has been in vain. Here and there throughout the system there are offices and units collecting the information available, but there is no group (or "Brain Trust") which is constantly monitoring the present operations . . .'[34]

Many policies are in any case worked out more or less autonomously, beyond the framework of the United Nations and its possible co-ordination and control, in commissions, councils, committees, and in *ad hoc* international conferences on specialist subjects. As this activity increases and 'as the number and activities of international organisations expand, an area grows in which major decisions are made without much democratic control by the peoples and institutions which are affected or which support these activities financially. In the field of development aid, for example, decisions by the International Bank for Reconstruction and Development (IBRD) or other multinational aid organisations determine the fate of millions, selecting the human beings to be saved from likely starvation or death through disease, choosing the country, industry, region, social group, and political regime to be supported.'[35]

Supplying information and pressing their views upon such bodies and on governments are a variety of non-governmental organisations: research institutes like Batelle and Stanford, international cartels like the freight and shipping conferences, bodies like the Business and Advisory Committee to OECD (created by industry federations of OECD member countries) or the International Centre for Industry and Environment (created to represent industry views, mainly on the United Nations Environment Programme). Many such group organisations have been stimulated and even financially supported by international functional organisations as a means of devolving part of their activity or to strengthen their supportive constituency. UNESCO goes as far as to support a Conference of INGOs approved for Consultative Arrangements with UNESCO.[36]

It is, however, the operations of the multinational company as an autonomous international actor, relatively free from any kind of popular political control of its activities in a community interest, which have excited most attention. Some writers have seen the multinational as the realisation of David Mitrany's hopes of a 'functionalist' organisational network which would be the welfare basis of a world community, national frontiers becoming virtually meaningless.[37] This view of multinationals, however, takes little account of the present realities of their operations – in particular, the extent to which, whether or not they may be of benefit in a very general sense to the world economy, they create exploitive relationships, particularly with developing countries which are not in a strong position to insist upon their share of the rewards of multinational enterprise or lack the political and governmental stability and the skills which would enable them to exploit their bargaining position. The argument ignores, too, the obvious problems of international social justice and conservation of resources which arise in the case of foreign exploitation of natural resources – particularly in the extractive industry.[38] It ignores, finally, the potential problems of imperfect competition which, in their national manifestations, have resulted in competition policies of one kind or another in all advanced industrial societies.

Robert Cox has considered the argument that trade union federations might provide a natural countervailing force which would mitigate these problems. Admitting, however, that the confrontation in 1969 of the French multinational glass company Saint Gobain in Germany, France, Italy and the United States by unions co-ordinated through the International Federation of Chemical and General Workers' Unions (ICF) could be a foretaste 'of new transnational structures through which labor could press for increased control not only over wages but also over all other corporate decisions affecting employment in the different countries in which the firm operates', he warns that 'decision-making through such transnational structures would almost certainly conflict with the attempts of the nation-states in which multinational corporations operate to plan and carry out national policies for wages and employment'.[39] And, Cox asks, 'what will be the interunion power relations and welfare consequences when unions in developed countries and less developed countries successfully co-ordinate bargaining with a single corporation?'[40] One plausible

answer, offered by the economist Stephen Hymer, is that the more or
less unrestricted development of the operations of multinational corporations would result in a world society characterised by continued
uneven wealth from one geographic region to another. 'It would tend
to centralise high-level decision-making occupations in a few key
cities in the advanced countries, surrounded by a number of regional
sub-capitals, and confine the rest of the world to lower levels of
activity and income.'[41]

Whether or not the policy autonomy and general character of con-
certative institutions in the foreign policy field *within* states, and the
operations of *transnational* functional institutions and of multinational
corporations, in an interdependent world, should be labelled 'corporatist' to indicate points of similarity with domestic corporatist tendencies is a somewhat arbitrary definitional decision. But it is possible
to conclude this examination of some of the substance of interdependence in agreement with the view that 'an increasing number of
problems in the contemporary world are seen as either generated by
non-state forces or dealt with through non-state means and . . . world
politics is becoming a series of fragmented, discretely defined issue
areas . . . determined by a congeries of forces including both nation-
states and other actors.'[42] The tendency raises the same problems of
democratic accountability, and possible constitutional solutions at the
appropriate level, as do corporatist tendencies within states.

NOTES

1 James N. Rosenau (ed.), *Linkage Politics: Essays on the Convergence
   of National and International Systems* (New York: Free Press, 1969).
2 See J. W. Burton, *World Society* (Cambridge: CUP, 1972).
3 *The Times*, 23 March 1976.
4 In Europe of the Nine, 18·3 per cent (imports) and 18·6 per cent
   (exports) in 1971: *Eurostats*, Basic Statistics of the European Community (1972).
5 For Western Europe approximately 9·5 per cent of trade and for Japan
   approximately 27 per cent: ibid., pp. 77 and 92–5.
6 See my 'New Zealand foreign policy' in R. Barston (ed.), *The Other
   Powers* (London: Allen & Unwin, 1973).
7 $1,007,078 net in 1971: see *Eurostat Supplements to the Monthly
   Bulletins* (1971–7) which show subsequent increases expressed in EUAs.
8 D. L. Spencer, *Technology Gap in Perspective* (London: Macmillan,
   1970), p. 11.
9 See C. Layton, *European Advanced Technology*, PEP (London: Allen
   & Unwin, 1969), p. 275.
10 ibid., p. 27.
11 Spencer, op. cit., p. 12.

12 John Erikson, *The Military Technical Revolution* (London: Pall Mall, 1966), p. 1.
13 For example, the US 'Safeguard' warning installation near Walhalla, North Dakota (based on two radars in phased array which detect and track the targets of the long-range anti-ballistic missile Spartan and the Sprint) cost approximately £2,326 million to install. The system has recently been reduced by Congressional action to reduce the continuing high cost of the project.
14 Article 3.
15 op. cit., para. 7.
16 Approximately 200,000 compared with West Germany's 460,000 and Britain's 56,000. In total combat troops available worldwide, the US is overwhelmingly superior to her West European allies. *Military Balance 1975–1976* (London: IISS, 1975), *passim*.
17 They number 7,000 approximately: B. Burrows and C. Irwin, *The Security of Western Europe* (London: Knight, 1972), p. 61.
18 *The Times*, 15 March 1976.
19 *The Times*, 17 March 1976.
20 ibid.
21 The size of the German armed forces has been maintained with difficulty. It has necessitated increasing the conscription period and reducing the minimum term for regular enlistment to two years. Discipline has had to be slackened and one recent report by the German Ombudsman complained of portraits of Che, Mao and Lenin adorning barrack-room lockers and the growing use of soft drugs. Idiosyncratic dress, hair styles, beards, crime, alcohol, desertion are other complaints. See *The Economist*, 27 March 1971, p. 30.
22 On this, see the well-documented assessment in University-Services Study, *European Military Institutions – A Reconnaissance*, December 1971, pp. 30–2.
23 See the Godkin lectures *Old World, New Horizons* (London: OUP, 1970).
24 See *Military Balance*, op. cit., p. 76.
25 ibid., pp. 5 and 76. On the general relationship between economics and defence see D. Greenwood, 'Economic constraints and national defence efforts', in *European Military Institutions*, op. cit., pp. 71–99.
26 See *Military Balance*, op. cit., p. 10, note b.
27 See ibid., p. 10.
28 See ibid., p. 76.
29 See, for example, *German Defence White Paper*, 1971–2. The German economy cannot afford to forgo the benefits deriving from defence projects.
30 See Roger Facer, *The Alliance and Europe: Part III, Weapons Procurement in Europe–Capabilities and Choices* (London: IISS, 1975), p. 28 and *passim*. See also Alastair Buchan, *The Implications of a European System for Defence Technology*, Defence Technology and the Western Alliance, No. 6 (London: IISS. 1967), and No. 1 in the same series, John Calmann, *European Cooperation in Defence Technology: The Political Aspect* (London: IISS, 1967).
31 See, for example, University-Services Study, op. cit., p. 190, on West German diminished perceptions of threat.
32 M. Kreile, 'Neo-corporatism in foreign economic policy: a comparative perspective', paper prepared for ECPR Workshop on Corporatism in Liberal Democracies, Grenoble, 6–12 April 1978, p. 1.
33 ibid., pp. 2–3.

34   op. cit., Vol. 1, p. 12, cited by A. Judge, 'International organisation networks', in J. Groom and P. Taylor (eds.) *International Organisation* (London: Pinter, 1978), p. 383.

35   K. Kaiser, 'Transnational relations as a threat to the democratic process', in R. D. Keohane and J. S. Nye (eds.), *Transnational Relations and World Politics* (Harvard: Harvard University Press, 1976), p. 364. Much the same point is made by Abram Chayes, a former legal adviser to the US State Department, in his *The Cuban Missile Crisis* (London: OUP, 1974), p. 71.

36   For numerous, categorised, further examples of such activity see A. Judge, 'International institutions: diversity, borderline cases . . .', in Groom and Taylor, op. cit., pp. 28–83.

37   On Mitrany and the 'functionalist' thesis see my *Europe in Question* (London: Allen & Unwin, 1974), pp. 27–41; and for this view of the rôle of multinational corporations see F. Tannenbaum, 'The survival of the fittest', *Columbia Journal of World Business*, March–April 1968, pp. 13–20.

38   See P. B. Evans, 'National autonomy and economic development: critical perspectives on multinational corporations in poor countries', in Keohane and Nye, op. cit., pp. 330–2.

39   R. W. Cox, 'Labor and transnational relations', in Keohane and Nye, op. cit., p. 206.

40   ibid.

41   S. Hymer, 'The multi-national corporation and the law of uneven development', in J. N. Bhagwati (ed.), *Economics and World Order* (New York: World Law Fund, 1970), pp. 2–3, cited in Keohane and Nye, op. cit., p. 51.

42   J. M. Rochester, 'National interest in world politics', *Review of Politics*, vol. 40 (January 1978), p. 85.

IO

The Corporatist Prospect

Our highest ideals, as efforts to realise them fail, become the source of our most profound disappointment and extreme reactions. Democracy, in the advanced societies, has departed widely in practice from the conceptions of the great liberal-democratic theorists, and then again, from the reconceptions of the apologists for these errant paths. The initial argument of this work was that the modern state, or advanced industrial democratic society, was an elusive, transient phenomenon – like any other form of human organisation, in process of adaptation to a changing environment. Secular, centralised, specialised and participatory, it has suffered the contradictory challenges of ideology, regional separatism, interdependence of functions within its enlarged competence, and apparently ineluctable oligarchical elitist tendencies within large organisations. At the same time, its real independence, in the international environment, has been reduced – particularly by technological developments.

The political culture of the advanced societies, we have argued, has not been static since 1945 but has altered in subtle but significant terms. The authority of church, family and school as socialising influence has been modified. Rapid economic growth, and with it, widespread affluence, reduced class differences, producing what was soon called the politics of consensus, and the decline in the appeal of reforming ideologies. Any complacency these developments might have induced in the 1960s was dispelled, first by the wave of protest politics, at its most dramatic in the events of May 1968 in France, and then by the severe economic difficulties of the mid-seventies. The values, attitudes and beliefs conceptualised in the notion of the political culture were opened in a very general way to question. This was ironically an exact result of the short period of consensus politics which had pushed worker, student and other forms of minority dissent into irregular channels of political expression and had, in its mood of complacency, failed to take proper notice of economic warning signs. The critique expressed in political protest invaded mass political consciousness in the seventies.

The result has been that the most long-standing and apparently secure political traditions have developed elements of insecurity. A recent British survey study revealed considerable cynicism about the representative, legislative system of parliamentary democracy – beliefs 'that "people in politics" are habitual liars who run the country incompetently on behalf of a "few big interests" (usually that of the rich and powerful) except when the interests of their own party are concerned which come before all else'. Significantly, among politically 'competent' citizens – those 'able to interpret politics in articulate, issue oriented terms' – 'cynicism is much more common than trust'.[1] And, predictably, the survey finds, 'the possibility of protest becomes imminent among the competent citizens at really quite modest levels of cynicism'.[2]

Academic cynicism is not immune to the tendency towards extreme reaction. We have examined in this work a number of theories about the nature of advanced industrial society which call into question the liberal-democratic, pluralist model. Robert Michels, who made one of the most disturbing contributions to the critique, was originally a socialist. His reading of Mosca and Pareto, and his experience of German social democracy, led him to the view, expressed in *Political Parties*, that each and every organisation, even the least favourable case – the revolutionary socialist party – was susceptible to tendencies towards elitism and oligarchy. His own critique, it has been credibly argued, was what led to his abandoning socialism, and finally led him to fascism.[3]

Our own examination of interest groups and the development of 'concertation' in advanced industrial societies does not detract from the force of Michels's analysis though it does not lead to the same conclusions. The term 'corporatism', with its derogatory implication of borderline facism,[4] is being increasingly used as an alternative to 'pluralism' as a label with a more appropriate connotation in referring to the policies of such societies. It is a term, as one writer who uses it has pointed out, which gained currency and approval in the 1930s under the influence of Pope Pius XI's encyclical of 1931, *Quadragesimo Anno*, and, in the political and economic crisis of the period, through the example of Mussolini's Italy. 'Proposals abounded for legally constituted corporations grouping all members of the same "profession" or "occupation" (including employers) recognised by the state, [and] granted public authority over their respective industries.'[5] Earlier, the conception, without the terminology, was clearly enunciated by Harold Laski and G. D. H. Cole.[6] Contemporary corporatism has been appropriately defined by Philippe Schmitter as 'a system of interest representation in which the constituent units are organised into a limited number of singular, compulsory, noncompetitive, hierarchically ordered and functionally differentiated categories, recognised or

licensed (if not created) by the state and granted a deliberate representational monopoly within their respective categories in exchange for
observing certain controls on their selection of leaders and articulation
of demands and supports'. Schmitter's definition of the pluralist
model is the exact antithesis. In it, the constituent units 'are organised
into an unspecified number of multiple, voluntary, competitive, non-
hierarchically ordered, and self-determined (as to type or scope of
interest) categories that are not specifically licensed, recognised, sub-
sidised or otherwise controlled in leadership selection or interest
articulation by the state and that do not exercise a monopoly of
representational activity within their respective categories'.[7]

Both corporatist and pluralist models are ideal types, and it is not
suggested, in this work at least, that any society perfectly corresponds
to one of them.

The categories do, however, suggest the questions worth raising
in giving an analytical account of the intermediate ground – the
real world – and they provide a basis for normative judgements in
terms of their compatibility with liberal democratic values like
participation, representativeness and accountability. They are
categories also, it must be admitted, not very amenable to precise
definition or measurement. We would, however, reject the idea that
political scientists must restrict their hypothesising to subjects suitable
for rigorous testing – that is, which are numerically verifiable.
Corporatism is a structural variable which may be observed and
described, though not, in most respects, strictly measured. It is,
however, argued here that contemporary industrial societies exhibit
a closer approximation to the corporatist model than to the pluralist,
the pattern of interest group intermediation being the critical aspect.
The increased level of 'concertation' carries with it, we have argued,
impulses towards illiberal corporatism. It does not, however, itself
constitute a direct contradiction of the assumptions of the pluralist
model and our argument, therefore, is that, though organised interests
can make a contribution to policy problem-solving and should be
consulted, if liberal-democratic ideals are valued then impulses towards
singularity and non-competitiveness, which are evident in such
practices as privileged recognition, compulsory membership (the
closed shop) and co-optation of national leaders of organisations for
governmental purposes, should be restricted.

Political parties are more efficient by reference to the same liberal-
democratic criteria and seem to achieve their balance of aggregative
and articulative functions best within a bi-polar, multi-party system
which, we have suggested, electoral rules and constitutional arrangements can encourage. Parties, however, and the parliamentary arena
in which they function are of reduced importance in corporatist
societies. Modern democracies exhibit, as Michel Crozier has argued,

'a general separation between an electoral coalition and the process of government'.[8] The phenomenon, he finds, is particularly acute in Western Europe because of, among other things, 'the barriers between different sub-systems which tend to close up and operate in isolation'.[9] Crozier's observations are part of his argument that 'we need institutional innovations to keep our systems open and democratic and to prevent them from regression', and 'we must find new regulations for a completely different social game'.[10]

This study has, in fact, stressed the importance of constitutional rules as determinants of political behaviour. In this context it is noteworthy that Mosca's reaction to elitism in democratic politics was, unlike Michels's, to remain an advocate of classical liberal principles like constitutionalism, separation of powers and representative government, and to consider the possibilities of improving the liberal polity.[11] Our analysis of the importance of rules as determinants of consensual patterns and of the way they affect the assets of competing groups within society tends to confirm the validity of this reaction.

The strengthening of consensual mechanisms in advanced industrial societies by reference to the criteria deduced in this study takes on a greater urgency in the light of the dominant place of actors in the *economic* sector in the overall pattern of interest intermediation in the advanced industrial democracies, and the relative weakness of actors in other sectors; for the economic sector is the one in which corporatist development is most marked. One writer, predicting the development of the corporatist society in the United Kingdom, has defined corporatism as 'an *economic system* in which the state directs and controls predominantly privately-owned business according to four principles: unity, order, nationalism and success'.[12]

This definition, serving to underline the importance of development in the economic sector, also, in its questionable reference to state direction and control, suggests another of the reasons why constitutional rules and the strengthening of consensual mechanisms are important concerns of critical analysis. The idea of state control, rather than ownership, of the means of production and distribution, in the interests of the community, became the goal of moderate socialists and socialist parties committed to economic growth but disillusioned with nationalisation by the 1950s. The criteria of unity, order, nationalism and success were to be found in varying degrees, though the degree of state control attempted in the United Kingdom and in other West European States was affected also by conceptions of the principles of social justice and of democratic rights. Social justice, however, because it must be sought largely in the area of welfare policy where directly concerned organised groups are relatively weak, has depended in practice on the readiness of trade unions to press for welfare legislation rather than attempt to confine the distribution of the profits of industry to the bargaining table, and upon government's being able and willing to balance the weaker interests against the pressures of the powerful.

But it is precisely the ability and will of the state in contemporary politics to direct and control the powerful sector of privately owned business that is in question. Galbraith laments what he regards as its failure. Within the advanced democratic societies leaders of great corporations, large trade unions and the government departmental bureaucracies in the same functional areas collaborate for what may perhaps be summed up as unity, order, nationalism and success within their sectors, but it is not clear that, of these collaborators, the state is persistently the decisive element, directing, controlling the others and co-ordinating between sectors. The failure of the state to assume this role has deleterious consequences for social justice and for other values which are demanded in the more participatory, less oligarchic and elitist environment of political parties, elections and parliamentary activity.

They are subordinated to the needs of what Galbraith has called the 'planning system', that major part of the economy dominated by great corporations and unions which seek, partly through the understanding they reach with specialist government bureaucracies, to make their environment more predictable and controllable. The weakness of the 'market system' (in which small firms operate) and of consumer, welfare-claimant, environmental and promotional groups leads to their relative neglect.

These are the factors which explain, too, why unity, order and success are not, in fact, marked features of the mixed economies in the seventies. Galbraith's thesis is, in effect, a rudimentary corporatist economic theory helping to explain contemporary problems like inflation with unemployment, and declining rates of growth. It is an explanation which may be interpreted summarily in terms of diffusion of decision making in the so-called planning system among large corporations in a monopolistic position in their industrial sector, working in a close relationship with specialist government bureaucracies. The absence of either purposeful central government co-ordination or of any automatic regulator like competitive market pricing helps to account for economic problems. Galbraith's thesis does not require that the planning system be successful – the very opposite. The absence of a co-ordinating mechanism means that the corporations, seeking to regulate their environment, are quite likely to be regulating their own failure.

If corporatism, then, is to be distinguished from fascism, from moderate socialism and from pluralism, as an analytical model closer to the realities and developmental tendencies of the modern state in the West, then Schmitter's categories are useful; they do not assume unified state direction and control. They can accommodate the conception of influential, specialised, more or less autonomous, governmental bureaucracies as distinct from a crude, undifferentiated perception of the state. Other categories, furthermore, can be added to augment the model without confusion. We have suggested in particular that corporatism is more than a system of interest representation; it is a collaborative but functionally segmented process of policy formulation. It is, furthermore, a process in which it is often difficult to identify a 'state' role. In the pluralist model, in any of its versions, the personification of the state or of government is an accepted analytical device. *It* is the arbiter between conflicting interests, or *it* processes them, or *it* is the object of pressures from interest groups, or *it* is itself one of a diverse number of organisations from whose competition policy emerges. In a corporatist model of society, the state as actor (or government as the agent of the state) has less clarity. It is the fictional legal source of policy but it really comprehends many public bureaucratic organisations with specialised functions and diverse client interests. Furthermore, 'public' and 'private' are not easily distinguishable, since the state (in its legal fictional sense) holds shares in private industry, and government bureaucrats have their place on boards, while reciprocally, private organisations have their representatives on what are legally 'governmental' bodies with legislative, judicial and administrative functions.

The terms 'state corporatism' or 'corporate state', therefore, with their tendency to imply an identifiable corporate purpose, i.e. the state as a corporation, must be distinguished from the corporatist model.[13] In the real-world twentieth-century politics from which it is an analytical abstraction, corporatism comes about as a development and perversion of the consensual society[14] – the society in which government policy decisions are more or less confined to the area of a prevailing consensus. It is a product of government's need to avoid acting in an authoritative manner and it is a diffusion of state power and purposes rather than a unity of control.

Some writers regard the development of corporatism, in this sense, as little more than a necessary and unalarming development of structural differentiation and functional specialisation in advanced democratic industrial societies. It has been powerfully argued, for example by Lehmbruch, that it is brought about by 'certain requirements of consensus-building specific to economic policy making'.[15] Parties are not regarded as efficient consensual mechanisms in this area and they also tend, it is suggested, to make the kind of decision which accommodates conflict rather than that which is rational – geared to stimulating economic performance. The argument concedes that there may be an extension of the range of corporatist decision making beyond wages and prices policy to other aspects of economic policy making, but suggests that, beyond this, its influence will be limited and parties and the parliamentary systems will hold their own. The corporate state will not evolve.

This is a hopeful and persuasive argument. However, though the corporate state (or state corporatism or fascism) has, historically, been a product of crisis, imposed by forces which have seized state power, there is no clear reason why a piecemeal evolution of sectoral corporatist control should not come very close to 'state' corporatism, and even make the subtle transformation. The management of the economy is generally perceived to be the prime responsibility of modern government and to yield that to corporatist control is already a great deal. The inherent contradiction between the parliamentary and corporatist pattern, and the surrender of so much of importance to corporatist decision making, leads to cynicism about the parliamentary system, which reduces either to apathy or protest politics. As Crozier observes, 'a general drift toward alienation, irresponsibility, and break-down of consensus seems to prevail everywhere'.[16] Furthermore, somewhat paradoxically, corporatism does not really strengthen the consensual authority of trade unions, employers' organisations and other groups involved in concertation, for it leads to alienation and further weakening of their already weak mass base, particularly in times of economic difficulty.

The situation could well strengthen the appeal of extremist authoritarian parties. Again the potential for constitutional action may be noted. A chamber, or a council, for public debate and consultation with the major organisations presently involved in interest intermediation sectorally, *with representation based on the existing most participative structures* (e.g. the shop floor), has much to commend it. Even with their imperfect representative base, such organs in France, Holland and the European Community play a useful part. The French Social and Economic Council comments in considerable detail on the Plan, the Dutch Council (rather too small to attract much publicity) has a leading role in working out the incomes policy and makes, subject to Cabinet veto, regulations for industry. The Economic and Social Committee of the EEC has an influential consultative role. Elsewhere, for example in Luxemburg, the United Kingdom and Italy, such bodies have achieved only limited roles. However, size, powers and, above all, representative base are key variables, and in the UK, for example, as we pointed out, the National Economic Development Council was deficient on all three counts, though its improvement has been frequently urged. The most recent proposal, at the time of writing, deserves to be cited at some length, both for its vigorous expression and the experience and authority of its author, Peter Parker, Chairman of British Rail:

The future of Neddy ought to be thought about much more clearly as a planning instrument . . . the way to handle the threat of corporatism is to get the corporate bodies, which are both unions and industry, into one chamber, with an independent president and a constitutional position to invite down your Prime Minister and your Chancellor perhaps twice a year. Give it prior rights in looking at legislation in the fields of social and industrial policy and they would then have public debates which would be covered, à la Hansard. Politicians who had stumbled about in this morass of industrial relations would have had the advantage of a thorough debate in this chamber.

It would be a consultative chamber, exposing corporate power, incidentally forcing it to establish its legitimacy – the legitimacy of the CBI, the legitimacy of the unions. Then leave Neddy to do the job of expressing the planning that Government needs in the three sectors. You cannot run a country through tripartism, separation of powers. Government must govern and it's through a body like Neddy on a tripartite basis that they can expose their plans and have them talked about.[17]

The participatory and representative character of the organisations involved in such a council would be important to its success and the reform would not therefore provide an absolute guarantee against the alienating effects of corporatist decision making. It is not entirely implausible to suppose that continuing problems of unofficial action, or action by minority unions, might provoke repressive legislation, reducing the scope of freedom of association, weakening the position of unrecognised minority unions, strengthening the control of existing leaders participant in the concertation process. We would not, however, argue that there is anything immutable about movement towards corporatism along the continuum of which the ideal types – pluralism and corporatism – are the polar extremes. Corporatist elements appear to be liable to ebb and flow in the politics of advanced societies, and, in some respects, the present work offers explanations of why the ebb and flow takes place – the rudiments of an explanatory theory of process.

The positive development of corporatism may be associated, first, with technological developments of increased cost and risk favouring large-scale organisation and environmental control – structural factors. With the technological developments great increases in material prosperity have followed in which all classes of the population have shared, though unequally. An extension of the state's role and functions is to some extent related to the efforts of Labour and Social Democratic parties to ensure that material prosperity was evenly distributed, and also to conceptions by the same parties of the need for planning according to Keynesian principles of macro-economic demand management. The increased burden of government for such purposes is some explanation of the resort to sectoral self-government through departmental and interest group bureaucracies in collusion. But paradoxically the democratic ideal of participation and involvement has also played a part – an ideal of healthy pluralism, of decisions based on consensus rather than enforced. It is a dangerous paradox. A facile perception of the elements in common and a failure to distinguish the critical differences between pluralism and corporatism could become the basis for a significant politico-cultural support for corporatism: a legitimising ideology.

Economic growth after the Second World was favourable to the unquestioning development of these structures and conceptions and it was conducive also to the relative failure of democratic parliamentary institutions. With their initial goals achieved, left-wing parties drifted towards a moderate 'centre' position, not wishing to disturb the pattern of economic progress any more than the parties of the right, which drifted in the same direction. Parties, therefore, failed to articulate any profound differences or radical responses to such economic problems as did manifest themselves, especially the increasing pressure of inflation. In the circumstances, for the ordinary citizen and the party worker, elections and party activity seemed less important. Much the same attitude pervaded other specialised consensual mechanisms including the trade union. There were tendencies to specialisation within the trade union movement, leaving a confederal apparatus in being at the apex of the structure with an area of operation far from the traditional concerns of trade unions and the current concerns of their members. Parliaments, without organisational reform which might have increased their efficiency and without expert assistance, seemed to have only an inconsequential role. Parliaments were ill-fitted to cope with the complexity of economic management or to criticise the performance of the government. Government itself, in any case, preferred to depoliticise economic management by devolution to corporate structures.

An ebb in the tide of corporatism evidently depends on the reversal of some of these positive factors. Thus the slowing down of economic growth and higher levels of unemployment are conducive to increased dissatisfaction among trade union members. Communicating itself to leaders, this tends to result in more responsive attitudes on their part and a more jaundiced view of co-operation within corporate structures. Parties also may, recent experience suggests, yield collectively to increasing pressure from their militants for adherence to the doctrines which previously distinguished them. Contemporary moves towards regional devolution and international regional integration could possibly relieve some of the burden of central government and, with the creation of new levels, enhance participation.

None of these factors, however, may be considered as constituting an absolute imperative towards or away from corporatist development eliminating the possibility of deliberate political choice. They are factors conducive to change, but neither necessary nor sufficient, except possibly in the virtual absence of political will and the intelligence to promote it.

NOTES

1   Alan Marsh, *Protest and Political Consciousness* (Beverly Hills: Sage, 1977), pp. 222–3.
2   ibid.
3   See David Beetham, 'From socialism to fascism: the relation between theory and practice in the work of Robert Michels', *Political Studies*, vol. 25, no. 1 (March 1977), and vol. 25, no. 2 (June 1977).
4   It has been called 'fascism with a human face': see R. Pahl and J. T. Winkler, 'The coming corporatism', *New Society*, 10 October 1974.
5   Leo Panitch, 'Corporatism in Canada', Paper presented to the ECPR *Workshop on Corporatism in Liberal Democracies* (Grenoble, April 1978), p. 14.
6   See F. M. Barnard and R. A. Vernon, 'Socialist pluralism and pluralist socialism', *Political Studies*, vol. 25, no. 4 (December 1977), pp. 474–90.
7   Philippe C. Schmitter, 'Still the century of corporatism?', *The Review of Politics*, vol. 36, no. 1 (January 1974), pp. 85–131.
8   Michel Crozier, *The Governability of West European Societies* (pamphlet), The Noel Buxton Lecture, University of Essex, 1977, p. 11.
9   ibid., p. 4.
10 ibid., p. 9.
11 See Beetham, op. cit., p. 163.
12 J. T. Winkler, 'Corporatism', *European Journal of Sociology*, vol. 1 (1976), pp. 100–36 (my italics).
13 Schmitter distinguishes between societal corporatism and state corporatism. State corporatism (the corporate state) is only minimally distinguishable from fascism by virtue of its much more limited concern with mass mobilisation: op. cit.
14 See A. Etzioni, *The Active Society* (New York: Free Press, 1968).
15 G. Lehmbruch, 'Liberal corporatism and party government', *Comparative Political Studies*, April 1977, p. 99.
16 Crozier, op. cit., p. 12.
17 Cited by Brian Connell, 'In a nationalised piranha bowl', *The Times*, 15 May 1978.

Index